Praise for *Slaying the Giants in Your Life*

"David Jeremiah's new book will inspire you to take a new look at your life. Through his excellent Bible teaching and inspirational illustrations, fresh faith will arise in your heart to face and conquer the spiritual giants who oppose you."

JIM CYMBALA
Pastor, The Brooklyn Tabernacle

"Because there are still some giants to be slain in my life, I was anxious to read this book. I was hooked halfway through the chapter on *Fighting Your Fear*. Dr David Jeremiah skips the small talk and quickly brings you face to face with the giants. This gifted communicator has written a book of hope and victory. Any honest person wishing to live a more fulfilling and productive life should not be without it."

KEN DAVIS
Author, Speaker, Entertainer

"As one who has faced a few giants of my own, I am deeply moved at reading the triumphs of those who have gone before us. David Jeremiah offers not only inspiration, but motivation for us to stand and face our personal Goliaths."

DAVE DRAVECKY
Former Major League Pitcher and President, Outreach of Hope

"Are you wondering how to rise above the negative emotions and experiences that are holding you down? Then read *Slaying the Giants in Your Life* by Dr. David Jeremiah. It conveys the wise and seasoned counsel of a man who has faced and overcome his own giants—and helped thousands of others to do so as well—through the Word of God. The principles he sets forth work. Don't spend one more minute in frustration and defeat. Get into this compelling book and get on with living!"

FRANKLIN GRAHAM
President, Samaritan's Purse

"The stories in this book are full of 'meat and potatoes' with no fluffy stuff . . . it is captivating and each story has a special dimension which seems to penetrate my heart and life. Hope and healing are the strong projections and we surely can appreciate what they can do to change a life. This book will be a tool in changing lives, attitudes, and perspectives . . . I am delighted to give my full enthusiasm and endorsement to it and know that it will bless the readers as it has encouraged me."

BARBARA JOHNSON
Author of *Stick a Geranium in Your Hat and Be Happy*

"Pastor David Jeremiah has an uncommon knack at diagnosing the major problems people face every day and then provides them with solid Bible based solutions that can change their lives. This interesting book will bless thousands of readers. I heartily endorse it!"

TIM LAHAYE
Author of the Left Behind fiction series

SLAYING THE GIANTS IN YOUR LIFE

DAVID JEREMIAH

W Publishing Group

www.wpublishinggroup.com

A Division of Thomas Nelson, Inc.
www.ThomasNelson.com

SLAYING THE GIANTS IN YOUR LIFE
© 2001 by David Jeremiah.

Published by W Publishing Group. P.O. Box 141000, Nashville, Tennessee 37214.

Unless otherwise indicated, Scripture quotations used in this book are from The New King James Version, copyright © 1979, 1980, 1982, Thomas Nelson, Inc., Publishers.

Scripture quotations identified AMP are from The Amplified Bible: Old Testament. Copyright © 1962, 1964 by Zondervan Publishing House (used by permission); and from The Amplified New Testament. Copyright © 1958 by the Lockman Foundation (used by permission) (www.Lockman.org).

Scripture quotations identified MSG are from The Message, copyright © 1993. Used by permission of NavPress Publishing Group.

Jeremiah, David.
    Slaying the giants in your life / David Jeremiah.
        p. cm.
    ISBN 0-8499-1689-5
    1. Consolation. 2. Christian life. I. Title.

BV4905.3 .J47 2001
248.8'6 — dc21

2001026966

Printed in the United States of America

01 02 03 04 05 BVG 6 5 4 3 2 1

To Glenda Parker,
who retires this year after twenty faithful years of ministry
as my secretary and administrative assistant.

Contents

SLAYING THE
GIANTS
IN YOUR
LIFE

GIANTS IN THE LAND

Listen . . . Can you hear them coming? You can run, but you cannot hide. You might as well come out and fight.

Yes, the giants are abroad. We've encountered them in the Scriptures, where they're known primarily as the *Anakim*. From the very first pages of Genesis, they've been there, snarling and threatening: "giants on the earth . . . mighty men" (Genesis 6:4).

They cast their long shadow over everything we aspire to do, every new land we seek to inhabit, every dream we hope to pursue. Today we'd call them bullies, but they're the same old giants, and they have us intimidated in the same old way. After years of cowering in fear, we begin to measure ourselves against them: "Who can stand before the descendants of Anak?" (Deuteronomy 9:2). Who will come out to fight Goliath? Who will climb into the ring with the champion? Who will go for us?

The people of God paid a great price to reach the land of their dreams, but what did they find when they arrived? *Giants!* Naturally *they* would be in the land of milk and honey; the giants always get there first, and they take what they want. Our first impulse is to listen to the delegation that brings back a recommendation to surrender. It's a big world; why not find some other land? Maybe milk and honey are too rich a diet, anyway. Perhaps water and stale bread will be enough. We can learn to settle for less.

But God won't have us accept that recommendation. He expects a bit more:

"Hear, O Israel: You *are* to cross over the Jordan today, and go in to dispossess nations greater and mightier than yourself, cities great and fortified up to heaven, a people great and tall, the descendants of the Anakim, whom you know, and *of whom* you heard *it said,* 'Who can stand before the descendants of Anak?' Therefore understand today that the LORD your God *is* He who goes over before you *as* a consuming fire. He will destroy them and bring them down before you; so you shall drive them out and destroy them quickly, as the LORD has said to you." (Deuteronomy 9:1–3)

Of course, the Anakim aren't found in our telephone directories. The giants we face have different names: *Fear. Discouragement. Loneliness. Worry. Guilt. Temptation. Anger. Resentment. Doubt. Procrastination. Failure. Jealousy.* Call them what you will; they're only giants, after all, like Goliath. He was a shade over nine feet tall, but it only added up to a bigger dent in the pavement once he fell. The bigger they come, the harder they fall.

Which giant is giving you grief? Perhaps Fear has your number. Maybe Loneliness has locked you out. Whatever giant may be bullying you, the message of this book is that God is the greatest Giant of all. He goes before you like a consuming fire. It's clear from the Scriptures that we serve a God who *sends*. He is constantly sending His children into new and wonderful lands—lands of marriage enrichment, lands of career fulfillment, lands of rich spiritual abundance. You probably know exactly what kind of land He has led you to; and now you stand on its outskirts, yearning to place a tentative toe over the borderline—except for the shadows of those giants. But can't you feel it? The hand of God Himself is on your shoulder. He whispers to you, as to the Israelites, *Go in to dispossess nations greater and mightier than yourself, cities great and fortified up to heaven.*

I don't know about you, but those marching orders send my heart racing. They send a chill up my spine and leave me restless, eager to move. I want to see the wonders God has laid out for me. I want milk and honey and not another scrap of stale bread. And you know what else? I want to see those giants get what's coming to them. *He will destroy them and bring them down before you; so you shall drive them out and destroy them quickly, as the LORD has said to you.* What a great day that will be.

Isn't it about time we stand tall and face the giants in our lives? This book is our training manual, but don't forget we'll need the heavier artillery for the battlefield: the sword of the Spirit, which is the Word of God; the helmet of salvation; the shield of faith. Above all, we go with God Himself, who always makes two promises before sending us out to grapple with giants:

1. He will be with us.

2. He will empower us.

That means you'll never walk alone, and you'll never walk in weakness. God has the strength to bring you victory over any oppressor. You could ask Joshua about that. Or Moses, for that matter. Or Abraham, Daniel, Isaiah, David, or any of the apostles. Giant-killers all, and in the end they became giants themselves.

Perhaps that will happen to you. Read on, and prepare to do battle in the land of the giants.

1

FIGHTING YOUR FEAR

YOU CAN WIN THE BATTLE AND LIVE VICTORIOUSLY

Aaron Swavely was at a softball tournament when the news came. A gorgeous April day, the simple joys of softball—and here was the blackest nightmare he could imagine.

Aaron learned that his little family was spread among three different hospitals. His beloved wife, his nine-year-old son, and his seven-year-old daughter had been pulled from the wreckage of a head-on collision. Standing in the infield of the baseball diamond, he seemed incapable of moving or of doing anything other than thinking that he couldn't remember kissing his wife good-bye that morning.

A thought and a cry began to take form inside him; the thought, that he might lose his whole family; the cry, for God to wipe away the last terrible five minutes.

Diana Teters was asleep, dreaming about grandchildren. Her daughter, due to deliver any day now, was visiting for the weekend with her other children. A sharp blow to her head brought her awake sharply, then there was the sound of her daughter calling for help: "I'm bleeding—and I can't get out of bed!"

But a strange voice warned Diana not to move, saying she could go to her daughter in a minute. But the minute turned into six hours. The intruder—the man who had awakened Diana with a blow to the skull— forced her to tape her husband's eyes. Two little granddaughters, five and three-and-a-half years old, stood quietly in the room. They huddled face to

1

the wall, uncertain what was occurring. Diana was taped up. Her son arrived home, but the intruder intercepted him at gunpoint.

Meanwhile, Diana could think only of her pregnant daughter, helpless and bleeding. And she felt very afraid. All she knew to do was to pray silently, over and over: "Keep him calm, Lord—keep the man calm so he won't hurt us any more . . ."

Ivory Wilderman knew the truth when she saw her doctor's eyes and heard his solemn greeting: "Did you come alone?" The message on his face was a poor biopsy for Ivory. Minutes later, it was confirmed: the doctors had found breast cancer.

Only minutes ago, Ivory's life had never held more promise. At forty-six, she felt the best things in life lining up for her. There was a new job, a new apartment, a new car and—best of all—a new relationship that could lead to marriage. Life was good; God was blessing. "I wanted to press the pause button and just enjoy the moment I was in," she says today, looking back.

But life has no pause button. Suddenly Ivory's world began to race out of control in fast-forward. The specialists gave her no more than a 20 percent chance to survive. For the first time, she began to wonder what the experience of death might bring. As she lay awake at night, her fear felt like suffocation. "It was as if a great plastic bag were being fastened around my head," she explains.

"There was nothing to do," she says, "but to call out the name of Jesus."

THE ULTIMATE ENEMY

There's no feeling quite like the icy grip of fear. And it comes in so many varieties.

I've been there; so have you. You've just sampled three stories from friends of our ministry. They were good enough to write us and share their crisis points (and don't worry: if you'll be patient until the end of the chapter, I'll tell you how each of them came out).

The letters came after I preached a series on *A Bend in the Road*, inspired by my own fight with cancer. Our offices at Turning Point were showered with amazing accounts of turning points and defining moments.

We expected to hear from perhaps eighty of our listeners; I think the final count was eight hundred. And letter after letter spoke of that most deadly of all enemies—*fear*.

That's the terrible thing about the road's bend, isn't it? It's the place where we cannot see what lurks around the corner. Ann Landers, the syndicated advice columnist, was at one time receiving ten thousand letters a month from people with all kinds of problems. Someone asked her if there was one common denominator among all her correspondents. She said that the great overriding theme of all the letters she read was *fear*—fear of nearly everything imaginable until the problem became, for countless readers, a fear of life itself.

Yet fear is simply a part of the fabric of living. God equipped us with it so we would be wise enough to protect ourselves from the unexpected. Fear provides us with sudden bursts of strength and speed just when we need it. It's a basic survival instinct, a good thing—as long as it remains rational. But there's also that brand of fear known as *phobia*. A phobia is what results when fear and reason don't keep in touch. A woman named Marjorie Goff, for instance, shut her apartment door in 1949. Then, over the next thirty years, she emerged only three times: once for an operation, once to visit her family, and once to buy ice cream for a dying friend. Marjorie suffered from agoraphobia, the fear of open spaces, and the most terrible thing she could imagine was something that might bring pleasure to you or me: an outdoor walk.

I've also read about a young truck driver whose route takes him across the Chesapeake Bay Bridge every day. The thought entered his mind that he just might feel compelled to stop the truck, climb out, and leap from the bridge to his death. There was no rational reason to hold such a belief, but that very fear took complete hold of him. He finally asked his wife to handcuff him to the steering wheel so he could be fully assured that his deepest fear wouldn't come true.[1]

That's exactly what fear does when it builds its power over us; it shackles our hands and keeps us from doing the routine things in life—working, playing, living, and serving God. We give in to the slavery of terror.

One in ten of those reading this book will suffer from a specific phobia of some type. The other nine will be more like me: they won't be controlled by some irrational fear, but they'll still wrestle with the garden variety of terror—those awful moments when life seems to come undone. Any pastor can tell you stories like the ones at the beginning of this chapter. We sit in hospitals with terrified family members. We hold the trembling hands of those who face uncertain futures. We're often present in the waiting room when the doctor brings the message that dashes hopes, or when the police lieutenant tells us there's no trace of the runaway child. And what about life after the unexpected divorce? The death of a spouse? The loss of a livelihood?

I've had my own moments of overpowering fear. I've stood before huge crowds, afraid to speak. I've sat in football stadiums and watched two of my sons take vicious blows near the neck, then lie motionless on the turf for minutes that seemed like hours. I've sat in the hospital with my daughter Jennifer after she suffered a severe concussion in a soccer game. I doubt any fears are more terrible than those with our children at the center. I've also known the fear of my own impending death, when the doctor brought news of serious disease.

Fear has been described as a small trickle of doubt that flows through the mind until it wears such a great channel that all your thoughts drain into it. Tiny fears, almost unperceived, can build up day by day until we find ourselves paralyzed and unable to function. And there are so many varieties. Craig Massey details six general categories that most of us face: poverty, criticism, loss of love, illness, old age, and death.[2]

WHERE FAITH AND FEAR MEET

But what about Christians? One would think fear to be excess baggage for those who live in the presence of an almighty God. It *should* be—but it usually doesn't work out that way.

The Bible, as a matter of fact, doesn't paint a picture of the fear-free life. Judging from the Scripture, God's people seem to be tormented by the same fears as everyone else. The disciples, who had Jesus beside them, seemed constantly fearful—of storms, of crowds, of poverty, of armies, of the loss of their leader. We think immediately of the day Jesus told them to cross over to the other side of the Sea of Galilee. The night closed in like a blanket, a storm came from nowhere, and the disciples found themselves in a fight for their lives as the ship was tossed on the waves. Even when they saw Jesus approaching on the water, they were terrified: They thought He was a ghost! (See Matthew 14:22–33.) They let fear get the better of them.

The proud Israelite army lived in fear of one man. Of course, the tape measure on that man read nine feet, six inches. Goliath played mercilessly on their fear, taunting them with challenges he knew they wouldn't dare accept. King Saul was ruled by fear—of the giant, then of the boy who slew the giant. David himself wasn't free of fear before the big battle. But he took his slingshot and his five stones and stood tall anyway. As Mark Twain once said, courage isn't the absence of fear, but the *mastery* of it; it's the place where fear and faith meet. In David we have a story of the power of courage.

But we also have stories of the power of fear. Perhaps most notable of all is the one about the delegation of spies who were sent into Canaan. They were commissioned to go on a fact-finding expedition into the unknown territory that lay ahead. This was the Promised Land—home at last, after generations of slavery in Egypt. It was the land of Abraham, the homeland of their dreams. But they had been away for generations. The land held as much mystery as promise. No doubt about it, Canaan was the bend in the road of the Exodus, and the Israelites couldn't see what loomed around that bend. So they assembled in Kadesh Barnea and decided to send out the scouts.

The experience of these men had an impact on Israel that lasted forty years. It cost them years of heartbreak and tragedy. Should they have rushed right in, without the tentative act of sending the spies? We can't say that, for God allowed and encouraged the reconnaissance mission. We can say the men should have come to a different decision. The majority failed to see the lay of the land with the perspective God wanted them to have. He didn't ordain the spirit of fear that drove the committee's recommendation.

As we study this narrative carefully, we find key principles about the tyranny of fear and the freedom of faith.

1. Fear Disregards God's Plan

"So we departed from Horeb, and went through all that great and terrible wilderness which you saw on the way to the mountains of the Amorites, as the LORD our God had commanded us. Then we came to Kadesh Barnea. And I said to you, 'You have come to the mountains of the Amorites, which the LORD our God is giving us. Look, the LORD your God has set the land before you; go up *and* possess *it*, as the LORD God of your fathers has spoken to you; do not fear or be discouraged.'" (Deuteronomy 1:19–21)

God's mandate was clear: *Here is your land. Here is My gift to you. Now go grab it!*

With their greatest hopes and dreams laid out before them like beautifully wrapped presents beneath a Christmas tree, they should have surged forward with joy. They should have claimed all the abundance and fulfillment God wanted them to have. Yet having come so far, having made it through the wilderness with its dusty despair, its hunger and thirst—they couldn't cross the finish line. They had prevailed over Pharaoh's army, over the high tide of the Red Sea, over the challenge of the journey, but they couldn't take a stand against this final obstacle: *fear.*

You may stand at the threshold of God's greatest promise for you, but you'll never claim His blessings if you let fear dominate your life. He wants so much richness for you in His perfect plan, and only your shortsighted fear can withhold it from you. Listen carefully to the words of Paul on this subject: "God has not given us a spirit of fear, but of power and of love and of a sound mind" (2 Timothy 1:7). Power doesn't shrink back in uncertainty; love isn't conquered; a sound mind doesn't deal in irrational speculation. God has a rich territory, a promised land with your name on it, and He wants you to charge toward it with a cry of victory, not a wail of fear.

The Bible even tells you what that cry of victory should sound like: "You did not receive the spirit of bondage again to fear, but you received the Spirit of adoption by whom we cry out, 'Abba, Father'" (Romans 8:15). Call out His name. This verse assures us we can claim the intimacy with Him of a small child calling out to Daddy. He has adopted us as His own, and we have all the rights of the children of the King. We don't have to face anything alone.

The truth is that He has a plan and that we can claim it with joyful assurance. Fear disregards that plan. Have you ever seen a timid, cowering prince? Stop living as a helpless street orphan when you bear the credentials of the royal palace.

2. Fear Distorts God's Purposes

Fear does one very predictable thing: It distorts our view. Fear robs us of our perspective. Listen to Moses as he summarizes the attitudes of his people:

> "And you murmured in your tents, and said, 'Because the LORD hates us, He has brought us out of the land of Egypt to deliver us into the hand of the Amorites, to destroy us. Where can we go up? Our brethren have discouraged our hearts, saying, "The people *are* greater and taller than we; the cities *are* great and fortified up to heaven; moreover we have seen the sons of the Anakim there."'" (Deuteronomy 1:27–28)

Fear brings out our worst. It ushers in complaining, distrust, finger-pointing, and despair. You can see them all in these verses. God had provided victory over the Egyptian oppressors. He had given deliverance through the wilderness. He had offered a new plan for living through the commandments on Mount Sinai. And now He was offering real estate—the gift of a new land for building a nation. But in fear, the people were cowering in their tents to gripe about God's intentions. "God brought us all this way just to deliver us to the Amorites."

Fear does that to us, doesn't it? When you talk to a terrified friend or family member, you find yourself wanting to say, "But that's silly!" For it's easy for us to see the irrationality and absence of perspective of other people ruled by fear. The spies brought back a distorted picture, and they infected the whole nation with it. "There are giants in the land! *Anakim!*" That word held terror for the Israelites. It was synonymous with monstrous, marauding giants. But of course, while they did see a giant or two, the only formidable one was the giant inside their heads—and that giant's name was *Fear*.

It's worth reading the parallel account in Numbers 13:32–33, where we find the fears of the spies painted in even darker tones. The land "devours its inhabitants," they said. "We were like grasshoppers in our own sight, and so we were in their sight."

Fear is an army of giants, for it multiplies one into many. At the same time it does that, it also makes us grasshoppers in our own eyes. We lose sight of the promise that we can do all things through Him who strengthens us. We lose the ability to see anything in its true perspective. Fear, not the *object* of the fear, devours its inhabitants.

In the imaginations of the spies there were massive, fortified cities teeming with giants. So great was their distorted perspective that they even made an evil giant out of God. "Why, He brought us all this way to make us food for the heathen," they said. I defy anyone to find any logic at all behind their conclusion. But haven't we all said such a thing? "God is out to get me! He's brought me all this way to make me miserable!" The greater the fear, the weaker our reasoning.

Fear distorts our perception of God's purposes. It shows life through a fun-house mirror—without the fun.

3. Fear Discourages God's People

The third effect of fear is that it reaches its tendrils out to everyone around us. Discouragement is contagious. When you give in to your fears, you make the world around you an environment of discouragement. That word, *discourage*, means to take away courage. Fear causes us to drain away the vitality of people we care for.

This is a devastating principle, isn't it? Fear is catching; eventually it breeds hysteria. Ten men out of twelve came back with what the Bible calls a "bad report," and those ten infected an entire nation—not just for a week or a month, but for a generation. The golden hopes and dreams of the Israelites— for land, for security, for a new beginning—were ruined for forty years because of the fear of ten men. When the spies returned from their journey, they brought a giant back with them—one much more terrible than the mere men they had seen. This giant of fear prowled through their camp and devoured the faith and courage of a nation.

If you don't think fear is contagious, stand in the hallway at work and call out one word: "Fire!" You'll be successful in changing the moods and plans of hundreds of people in an instant. You'll also endanger everyone around you. Fear is more infectious than any disease you can name. It roams the landscape and discourages God's people.

4. Fear Disbelieves God's Promises

"Then I said to you, 'Do not be terrified, or afraid of them. The LORD your God, who goes before you, He will fight for you, according to all He did for you in Egypt before your eyes, and in the wilderness where you saw how the LORD your God carried you, as a man carries his son, in all the way that you went until you came to this place.' Yet, for all that, you did not believe the LORD your God, who went in the way before you to search out a place for you to pitch your tents, to show you the way you should go, in the fire by night and in the cloud by day." (Deuteronomy 1:29–33)

The challenge before the Israelites wasn't something that came out of nowhere and demanded that they trust some mysterious, untested providence. This was the invitation of the God who had gone with them throughout their journey. This was the loving Father who had remained so steadfast by their sides, and who had provided every need. This was One worthy of the same trust a tiny child would place in his loving parents—and so much more worthy.

Indeed, God called them the *children* of Israel, and the Bible tells us that He carried them along as you would carry an infant. He had watched over them as you would guard your newborn baby. He had led their steps, provided their food, seen to their protection, and done everything possible to nurture a loving and fully trusting relationship. The point of the wilderness experience was for the people to bond with their Father. After generations of slavery under their tyrannical masters in Egypt, God wanted His children to learn something of the wonderful journey that transpires when we follow Him.

But learning always involves testing. And that's what happened when the spies were appointed—the people were given a test to reveal whether they really trusted God or not.

The children of Israel had everything they needed to pass this test. But I believe they experienced a principle that seems more true and clear to me with every passing day. It seems to me that every defining moment of faith is just like starting over. Yes, we have the past to build on; just like the Israelites, we *should* be able to look back and say, "God has brought us this far; He will bring us home." Memory and experience should empower us. But we struggle to do that very thing; the moment's crisis seems to magnify itself. The rearview mirror should give us perspective, but we don't look at the mirror at all—our eyes are frozen by what's in the headlights.

The Israelites certainly are a testimony to that. There were giants in their headlights. And those giants seemed so fantastically massive that they blocked out what God had done in the past, what He was doing in the present, and His Word on the future.

Fear disbelieves God's promises.

5. Fear Disobeys God's Principles

Deuteronomy 1:26 says, "'Nevertheless you would not go up, but rebelled against the command of the LORD your God.'" It's a harsh truth but an insistent one: Fear is disobedience, plain and simple. How can fear be anything other than disobedience to God, when He has given us everything we need to walk in faith?

There's a little phrase in the Bible—such a simple phrase, and one that God sees fit to repeat so often, all throughout the Scriptures. It goes like this: *Fear not.* That phrase, if you'll notice, is stated in the *imperative* tense— which simply means it is a command. How many times must God command us not to fear? "Therefore, to him who knows to do good and does not do *it,* to him it is sin" (James 4:17). The next time you find yourself overcome by fear, remember—along with all of God's other promises and assurances—to dwell in fear is to live in sin.

But doesn't that seem a bit strict and inflexible? Your first response might be, "But I can't help it! I don't want to be fearful, but it's out of my control." And if that's how you feel, you've forgotten that God has given us everything we need to deal with fear. He has provided us with principles of faith that help us live courageously.

And when all is said and done, any alternative to His way boils down to simple disobedience—something that is always costly. For the nation of Israel, it meant a lost generation. The adult group of that time was forbidden from finding their journey's end for forty years. They were sentenced to a restless, nomadic life of wandering homeless in the desert, waiting for the last of that forsaken group to finally die. Only two of them were permitted entry into Canaan: Joshua and Caleb, who had stood firm in their faith. Courage earned them their home, yet they, too, wandered beyond the borders during those forty years, attending the funerals of their friends.

When the last body was laid to rest, the nation could finally claim its true home.

FACING THE GIANT OF FEAR

God longs for you and me to simply accept the gifts from His hand. He has a more wonderful and fulfilling home for someone, a life partner for someone else, a thrilling new opportunity for ministry, or career direction for still someone else. But fear cuts us off from accepting these prizes. I often counsel friends who are feeling God's tug at their hearts. He has something special for them to do, and they can look forward to blessings in abundance if they'll only be obedient and trusting.

They want to accept the call—but fear holds them back, always some new fear. *What if I'm making the wrong decision? What if this isn't the right partner for me? What if my business venture fails? What if I get homesick on the mission field? What if, what if?* Somehow they can't hold to a simple assurance of God's trustworthy and loving nature. It doesn't seem to register that He never calls His children only to desert them. (*Would He lead us this far only to deliver us into the hands of the Amorites?*)

And I've seen where this failure of trust leads—right to the doorstep of heartbreak. Those who shrink back from accepting God's gift condemn themselves to lives of fitful, restless wandering through the wildernesses of their jobs and their communities and their broken dreams. Fields of milk and honey stood in wait, but they settled for less.

My question to you is: Isn't that kind of disappointment in life far more to be feared than the risk of taking God at His word? Of course it is. The question, then, is what to do about it. How can we face our fears?

1. Confront Your Fear Honestly

You may long for your fear to simply vanish or wear off, but it isn't going anywhere—not on its own. If you want to defeat it, you must be like David: Gather up your stones and advance boldly!

First, understand what is at the root of your fears. Often people have come to me and said, "I don't know what I'm afraid of; I just have a spirit of fear." Is that your experience? Look a little deeper and get a specific reading on what is causing your feelings. Ask God to search your heart for you. He knows where the problem lies, but you need to let Him show you. Otherwise, you're going to simply run away—and like Jonah, you'll find that you can run, but you can't hide.

I read the remarkable story of a family from Canada. These people were convinced a world war was looming, and they were terrified. They decided to run away, hoping to find some corner of the planet where they would be free and clear from the fighting. In the spring of 1992, they relocated to a quiet little spot known as the Falkland Islands, an obscure piece of British real estate. The family relaxed and enjoyed five days of tranquillity before the Argentinians invaded their backyard and began the famous Falkland War.[3]

There's nowhere to run. Better to take a stand and face the truth of the fear. What is it that really concerns you? Why?

2. Confess Your Fear As Sin

We've already seen that fear boils down to disobedience. God says, "Fear not." But we fear; we're therefore in sin. The only thing to do is to come to God for honest confession.

Again, some may feel this stance is harsh or unrealistic. After all, we can't help what we feel, can we? Up to a point, that's very true. Emotions come to us on their own. But it's also true that we have the power to *act on* our feelings. We can choose by will to obey God's voice. We can make it our daily, serious intention to fill our lives and thoughts and plans with His Word and His truth. "I sought the LORD, and He heard me, and delivered me from all my fears" (Psalm 34:4). To walk with God is to walk fearlessly.

So we identify the fear, then we confess it. As we bring our fear before God and own up to it, we do one other thing. We repent. That means to disavow the sin completely, to turn and walk the other way. Then we can look toward the steps that lead us to victory over our fears.

3. Claim God's Promises of Protection

The next step is all about taking advantage of wonderful, untapped resources. Most people simply don't realize the treasure that lies at their fingertips. The Bible is filled with practical promises. Any one of them, if we choose to take hold of it, leads to liberation from some tough problem of life.

If I were a person with a fearful spirit, I'd go to the store and buy a package of three-by-five index cards. Then I would turn to certain verses in my Bible and copy them onto the cards. I'd place one on the visor of my car. I'd tape one to the wall of my rest room. One would be slid under the glass of my desk. Another would find a home in my wallet, and I might even tape one to the television remote! I'd type the text in colorful letters on my computer screen so that I'd see it there whenever I walk through the room. I would then be well prepared for the first tingle of oppression from a spirit of fear. I could reach for that Bible verse, read it out loud, repeat it again, and ask God to demonstrate its truth in the battlefield of my heart and spirit.

Are you interested in tapping into that wealth of promises? I'll give you several, and I suggest you read them out loud and reflect on their vital significance for you.

- *Deuteronomy 31:6.* "'Be strong and of good courage, do not fear nor be afraid of them; for the LORD your God, He *is* the One who goes with you. He will not leave you nor forsake you.'"
- *Psalm 27:1.* "The LORD *is* my light and my salvation; whom shall I fear? The LORD *is* the strength of my life; of whom shall I be afraid?"
- *Psalm 118:6.* "The LORD *is* on my side; I will not fear. What can man do to me?"
- *Proverbs 3:25–26.* "Do not be afraid of sudden terror, nor of trouble from the wicked when it comes; for the LORD will be your confidence, and will keep your foot from being caught."
- *Proverbs 29:25.* "The fear of man brings a snare, but whoever trusts in the LORD shall be safe."

The next one is a personal favorite. I suggest you put a big star beside it.

- ★ Isaiah 41:10. "Fear not, for I *am* with you; be not dismayed, for I *am* your God. I will strengthen you, yes, I will help you, I will uphold you with My righteous right hand."

Those verses are the best fear insurance you can invest in. Memorize them. Write them out, or print them on cards, and place them in locations where you might be attacked. Let the Word of God fortify your spirit.

And of course, those verses are only the beginning. Read through God's Word, and you'll find so many more assurances for times of fear. The inspired writers knew what it was like to be afraid in the ancient world; they had fears we can't even imagine. Peter and Paul had to face fear. Jesus prayed in Gethsemane, knowing exactly what lay ahead for Him in the hours to come. All of these found their strength in God, and you can benefit richly from their spiritual wisdom. Look up *fear* in your Bible's concordance, and then look up *afraid*.

Take in all these passages, soak in their power, and the next time the devil comes to get a response out of you, you'll be ready. Pull five verses from the living water just like five smooth stones in David's pouch, and let them fly! Don't worry about that fearsome giant; the bigger they come, the harder they fall.

The next step may sound so simple, so basic, that you may shrug it aside. I hope you won't do that!

4. Cultivate a Closer Relationship with God

Yes, you can confront your fears by drawing near to God. Think back to those spies who entered Canaan.

Up to now, we haven't mentioned that there were two dissenters in the group. They went on the same trip, saw the same walled cities and the same giants, and they brought back a minority opinion. Joshua and Caleb listened patiently to all the worst-case scenarios and calmly said, "We can do this."

As I've read this narrative over the years, I've always felt the difference between the ten and the two was that they used different yardsticks. The negative group measured the giants by their own stature, while Joshua and Caleb measured them by God's stature. These two were the only ones who finally measured up to the privilege of entering the Promised Land. The others fell short.

What made the difference for Joshua and Caleb? The Scriptures state it clearly.

In Numbers 32:12 we read: "For they have wholly followed the LORD."

You'll find the same message in Deuteronomy 1:36 and Joshua 14:9. Joshua and Caleb were simply different creatures from the rest. The Bible makes it clear that they were absolutely filled with the Spirit of God, and they walked with Him in every way. It caused them to think differently, act differently, decide differently. And when the time of crisis came—the time when we find out what people are made of—Joshua and Caleb were living proof of what it means to have godly courage. These two looked at a land that "devoured its inhabitants" and said, "This is God's will for us. Let's do it!"

Your fear level is ultimately a referendum on the closeness of your friendship with God. It's a spiritual yardstick. Do you see things in human dimensions or godly ones? After you spend time with your Creator, you're simply incapable of shrinking in fear at the appearance of every human anxiety. You've seen His power. You've seen His love and faithfulness. You've seen that His purposes are the best for us. If you have "the fear of God," as we used to say, you won't fear the things of this world. If you don't have the fear of God, then everything else is to be feared.

There's one other verse that in my judgment is the essential New Testament verse on this subject. Think about it carefully; I'd suggest memorizing it: "There is no fear in love; but perfect love casts out fear, because fear involves torment. But he who fears has not been made perfect in love" (1 John 4:18).

The opposite of fear, you see, is not courage. It's not trust. The opposite of fear is *love*. This verse captures that beautiful and powerful truth. As we've already seen near the beginning of this chapter, "God has not given us a spirit of fear, but of power and of love and of a sound mind" (2 Timothy 1:7). There it is again—fear versus love. I think parents understand this principle, for they know that little children often wake up in the dark of night. And they're afraid of the darkness. I've experienced it again in recent times with our grandchild, little David Todd, who comes for a visit. When he's in our home, he'll wake up in that unfamiliar bedroom in the middle of the night, and he'll begin to cry. It's not just any kind of crying, but an "I'm afraid" kind of crying. You parents know what I mean.

So what do we do? I doubt any of us would rush into the room and say, "Come on, David—be courageous!" No, you and I are much more tender than that. We lift the little boy in our arms, nestle him tightly to us, and speak softly with assurance. We tell him we love him, and that everything is all right. We help him realize he's in a safe place, and that we're very near as he sleeps, even if it's dark; we will always protect him. And we pour in all the love we can until the fear is cast out, and our little child sleeps in peace. That's what God does for us when we call on Him.

Harry Ironside, a great preacher from years ago, told the story of playing a game called Bears with his young son. The grownup would be the bear, and he'd chase the boy all over the house. But one day the game got a bit too intense. The boy was cornered by the "bear," and he suddenly became truly frightened—it wasn't a game anymore. He hid his face, trembling, and then turned around quickly and threw himself into his father's arms with the words, "I'm not afraid of you! You're my daddy!"

Our Father wants us to leap into His arms that way when we're afraid. He wants us to realize who He really is, and that we need never fear. And the key to that assurance is love, the opposite of fear. To experience in full the love of God is to feel the deepest security in heart, soul, mind, and strength. It is to understand, down to the depth of our being, that God loves us so much He will always fold us in His arms; that He'll always be near, even when it's dark; that He is our "Daddy" and that we need not be afraid. And we realize all of this as His incomprehensible love washes through us and cleanses us from fear and anger and selfishness. Then and only then do we find ourselves capable of returning love—for remember, "We love Him because He first loved us" (1 John 4:19).

And that's when it happens: Love begins to dispel fear. Yes, we'll be visited by fears again, because they're part of living. But they'll never have the same hold on us. They'll be the reasonable fears of touching the hot stove or crossing the busy street. The irrational, controlling fears will not be allowed to dominate the heart, for the heart is home to the Holy Spirit now. He will not allow it. As a matter of fact, we won't have time to nurture some deep fear and build it up to become a giant, because the Spirit will see that our hands are active in ministry. It's an amazing principle: The more you reach out to other people with needs, the smaller your fears become. Again, this is love casting out fear.

It's one more good reason to become active in ministry. Be an encourager. Be an ambassador of the love of God. I know of no better prescription for misery of any kind. As you can see, there's nothing trite about my advising you to cultivate a closer relationship with God. That's the ultimate fear strategy. Children who are afraid call on their parents. It's no different for adults who are afraid, but the Parent whose name we call is so much more powerful, so much more loving, so much more responsive. If your life is filled with anxiety and irrational fears, draw near to God, starting today. Increase your time in His Word. Devote more time to prayer, and keep a prayer journal of how He comforts you in times of fear.

My final point calls on you to be certain you're able to draw near to Him.

5. Commit Your Life to Jesus Christ

There is one ultimate fear every human being must face—one fear that stands taller than all the others. The ultimate giant is Death itself.

The fear of death causes people to do strange things. I once knew a man who kept a canister of oxygen in every room in his home. His cars had those little tanks. The bathrooms, the bedrooms, the kitchen, garage—everywhere there were oxygen canisters. One day, as I visited with him, I asked him the meaning of this obsession. He explained, "Well, I have a little bit of a heart problem. I'm afraid that one of these days I might have a heart attack, and I won't be able to get the oxygen I need—then I'll die."

He concluded, "I'll do everything in my power to hedge my bet." And so, to smother his life in security, he made it into a life that was all about oxygen canisters.

Caution is a good thing; phobias are unhealthy. When the appointed day arrives when God has called you home, all the oxygen canisters in the world will not buy you another second of life. The real question is, are you desperate for another second, another hour, another day? If so, why does death hold so much terror for you? Are you so eager to avoid the beautiful gates of heaven and the open arms of God?

I know now that I'm not afraid of death. I can say this because I've been right out to the edge of mortality, looked death in the face, and discovered that I'm not afraid. I'm willing to move on to my next destination—though I'm not eager to get a head start. I happen to love life. I'm devoted to my ministry and my family, and I have no desire to die. But it's a wonderful thing to come to a sense of peace about the finality of this life. It's good to be able to say, "I'm not afraid to die."

Paul understood that it's a win-win situation for God's people. He wrote, "For to me, to live *is* Christ, and to die *is* gain" (Philippians 1:21). We can stay on earth and experience the joy of Christ, or we can move on to the next life and occupy those mansions He's gone to prepare. Either way, we've got it made. Why fear for things in this life? Why fear the doorway that leads to the next one?

Yet you and I both know people who move through this life wearing the shackles of a lifelong fear of death. The chains hold them back from any enjoyment or fulfillment in life. But there's an interesting passage in Hebrews that tells us how we ought to think about death:

> Inasmuch then as the children have partaken of flesh and blood, He Himself likewise shared in the same, that through death He might destroy him who had the power of death, that is, the devil, and release those who through fear of death were all their lifetime subject to bondage. (2:14–15)

There it is in a nutshell—the most important truth of history. Death had dominion over this world. All people had to live in its tyranny, and life was dominated by death. Then God came into the world in the guise of human flesh, in order to share everything we experience. He stretched out His arms on that great wooden cross, and He gave Himself up. As the sky darkened and the earth shook and history turned upside down, Jesus hung between heaven and earth, bridging the ultimate gulf that could not be closed in any other way.

That changed everything. He brought eternity back to you and me, and He brought us home again to God. The power of death was totally broken. Death has no power at all outside of the lies and distortions of the deceiver. The devil wants you to believe that death is still a giant. He wants you to believe your sins still give death the final word, and that you must therefore live in terror. But the truth is that Jesus paid the debt. Your sins will not be held against you now if you'll accept the gift that Jesus purchased with His life.

We can rest in that assurance and find liberation from fear. We can trust

God, as Aaron Swavely did. He was at a softball game, you may remember, when he heard his wife and children had been in a serious automobile accident. His daughter, Alisha, was in the gravest danger; she was in a coma. The doctors offered little hope that she would ever come out of it. Aaron simply turned her over to Jesus. He tried in his heart to be like Abraham, to trust God with his precious child.

Alisha, seven years old, did enter heaven. The family grieved deeply, and worked through their pain. But they had done one thing—they had allowed Alisha to be an organ donor. And when they think of her today, they know that a sixteen-year-old boy is alive because of her liver. Two others have sight. Life is most difficult of all when the unthinkable happens and we lose a child. But Aaron and his family got to know God even more deeply through the crisis. They learned that He uses everything and everyone. They can face nearly anything after God's help through that time.

Diana Teters lived through a miracle. When the intruder entered their house and attacked them, he intended to kill them all. But something stopped him; perhaps the prayers of Diana on the spot. Her husband worked for the bank, and that's why the man had broken in. After taking her husband and granddaughters there and getting money, he left everyone unharmed—except for stitches and bandages. Everyone came out all right, and the show *Inside Edition* told the Teters's story. The police considered it a miracle that no one was killed; Diana wasn't surprised at all. Today she is praying about going to visit the intruder in prison. God wants her to reach out.

As for Ivory Wilderman, she endured surgery, chemotherapy, and radiation. No matter what happened, she told herself, God would be there. Through the long nights of uncertainty she called out God's name, sought Him through the Scriptures, and clung to her faith with desperation. God drew near. "The victory came," she said, "as I took my thoughts captive, prayed, read the Bible, recalled verses I'd memorized, and sang potent praise songs. With each conquest, the fearful thoughts grew weaker." Today she is married, a mother (miraculously after the treatments), and the founder of a successful support group for cancer victims. "God is victorious!" she says with joy.

Yes, God is victorious. So are we, when we take the counsel of these wise, wise friends. Fear not! There are giants in the land, but next to our Lord they're little more than grasshoppers.

2

Destroying Your Discouragement

YOU CAN WIN THE BATTLE AND
LIVE VICTORIOUSLY

*H*ANDS. WHAT SIMPLE, AMAZING GIFTS THEY ARE—and how thoroughly we take them for granted.

Carolyn knew what it meant to sit before a piano and allow her fingers to fly up and down the keyboard. She'd fill the house with soaring gospel music. Carolyn could also type eighty-five words per minute. Needlework, cooking, even something as simple as tying the ribbon on a package; all these things flowed through her hands, and she had taken them for granted—she knew that now.

But her hands were only the beginning of what Carolyn lost. When she suffered a stroke in 1991, it was a miracle she even lived; the doctors didn't believe she would make it to morning. Though she did survive, Carolyn had to make a new start on nearly everything. She had to learn how to read, to write, even to speak, as if she were a small child. How could so many simple things disappear so quickly?

The stroke had come like a thief in the night and robbed Carolyn of nearly every ability except the ability to cry. And she did that more than ever before.

It was clear to Doretha that her husband drank too much. But what could she do about it? Whenever she confronted him about his problem, he flew into a rage—which only made the drinking worse. Since there didn't seem to be any viable options, Doretha simply tried to ignore the problem and concentrate on raising their son. She focused everything on motherhood.

Soon, that wouldn't be an option either.

One autumn evening in 1995, Doretha's husband was foolishly handling his gun while he was under the influence of alcohol. His hands slipped, the gun went off, and a bullet took the life of their son.

With her husband in jail, Doretha was left to the silence and despair of an empty house. She no longer had any real desire to live, but she was also afraid to die. A lifetime ago, at age thirteen, she had joined a church; but issues of life and death and eternity were all equal mysteries to her now.

Doretha remembers climbing into her car late at night and driving for hours in the hope that maybe she'd drift off to sleep and quickly be delivered from her waking nightmare. But something protected her every time. In the daylight, she began visiting churches. It was good medicine at the time, but the effects wore off when she left the sanctuary and reentered the roaring silence of her home.

What exactly are the limits to human tolerance? What are the units of measurement for pain and discouragement, and how does your discouragement threshold differ from mine?

I'm not sure about the answer to those questions, but the human spirit can be an amazing thing. Take the case of Lawrence Hanratty, who was named the "Unluckiest Man in New York City." This poor fellow, profiled in the *Los Angeles Times*, was nearly electrocuted to death in a construction site accident in 1984. For weeks he lay in a coma, with his lawyers fighting for his liability claim—until one of them was disbarred and two of them died. Hanratty's wife ran off with her lawyer.

Hanratty lost his car in a terrible crash. After the police had left the scene of the accident, criminals came along and robbed him. Then, an insurance company fought to cut off his workers' compensation benefits; his landlord tried to evict him. He suffered from depression and agoraphobia. He required a canister of oxygen for breathing and took forty-two pills per day for his heart and liver ailments.

But a city councilman took up his cause. Neighbors began to rally around him. Incredibly, Lawrence Hanratty summed up his life this way: "There's always hope."[1]

LOSING HEART

Would you be able to talk about hope after a string of unthinkable calamities? Have you accentuated the positive and eliminated the negative during the low points of your life?

We know the words are true—*there's always hope*—but sometimes it's hard to believe them. All of us suffer through bouts of discouragement. The dictionary defines *discourage* as "to deprive of courage, to deter, to dishearten, to hinder." All those *D* words—and you can throw in doom, depression, defeat, despair. The mind dwells on them when life has us pinned down.

The New Testament uses three Greek words to carry the idea of being disheartened, dispirited, or discouraged. We always translate them as "to faint" or "to grow weary." For example, Paul warns us to take special care not to become the source of discouragement for our children: "Fathers, do not provoke your children, lest they become *discouraged*" (Colossians 3:21). Then in 2 Corinthians 4:1, he speaks to those who may become disheartened in ministry: "Therefore, since we have this ministry, as we have received mercy, we do not lose heart." And later in that chapter, he encourages us not to become discouraged as the "outward man" deteriorates, because what's inside us is being renewed daily (v. 16).

And we shouldn't be discouraged by the plight of our loved ones, for in Ephesians 3:13, Paul writes, "Do not lose heart at my tribulations for you."

Jesus brings up the subject in the context of prayer. "He spoke a parable to them," Luke 18:1 tells us, "that men always ought to pray and not lose heart." There's so much truth in that verse. We must live and breathe and take up residence in prayer, or we're sure to faint, to grow weary, to lose heart. It takes diligent faith to live above discouragement.

And lest you think this is purely a personal issue, remember that entire nations can run out of hope. It happened during the darkest days of Israel and Judah, when the invaders rolled in. The Babylonians destroyed the holy city of Jerusalem, looting its glories and carrying away its people to enslavement in a distant land. It seemed that God's chosen people had lost it all—their land, their pride, their very identity as a nation set apart for a special destiny, for now God's children were dispersed across the nations.

These were the darkest times, days of lamentation and weeping and silence.

But as Lawrence Hanratty said, there's always hope. A ruler named Cyrus the Persian came to power, and he gave permission for Jewish exiles to begin the homeward journey. In the time of the first return and the rebuilding of the Temple, we think of two biblical heroes: a priest named Ezra and an administrator named Nehemiah. Each has a book of his own in our Bible, but there was a time when their two accounts were combined in one longer book.

Ezra was the priest to broken hearts, and Nehemiah was the rebuilder of broken dreams. The second one has a liberating lesson for us about the renovation of hope from the rubble of discouragement.

BUILDING BLOCKS

The fourth chapter of Nehemiah's book puts us in the middle of exciting times. Nehemiah, the gifted organizer, has arrived in a chaotic situation, but he has galvanized a community and jump-started the rebuilding operation. With the walls lying in ruins, the people of Israel haven't had the luxury of peaceful sleep. Raiders from the outlying provinces have been able to attack by night and keep the Israelite settlers discouraged and fearful. This has been done very deliberately. The threat of a Hebrew revival is an unwelcome one to the neighbors; all this talk of rebuilding must be snuffed out.

Therefore the Israelites have been under constant attack from every side—Sanballat and the Samaritans from the North, Tobiah and the Ammonites from the East, Geshem and the Arabs from the South, and the Ashdodites from the West. Nehemiah 4:8 tells us they've formed a kind of dark alliance to bring pressure on the construction workers. And the greatest weapons in their arsenal are fear and discouragement.

But God has different ideas. He has empowered his visionary servant Nehemiah in a mighty way, and, day by day, the work goes on. Brick by brick the walls are rising again. Here in the fourth chapter of Nehemiah, as we join the story, the work is halfway complete. The people can smell victory. And yet the wisdom of experience tells us that the midpoint is a precarious place to be. A bit less than half, or a bit more than half, isn't so bad; but it's dangerous to be exactly in the middle. Johnny Mercer's old song "Accentuate the Positive," says, "Watch out for Mister In-Between." That's actually rather profound.

The Bible tells us that right in between, at the halfway point, a fresh wave of discouragement breaks out through rumors of marauders and mayhem. Nehemiah realizes that he must deal with the lagging spirits of his people. I think you'll recognize that the principles he used haven't changed. Nehemiah had to deal with discouragement in the same ways we do. As we review these principles, you're likely to say, "Oh, yes—I've been there; I've done that."

Let's discover how Nehemiah handled the problem.

1. Recognizing Discouragement

Factor One: Fatigue. Vince Lombardi observed that "fatigue makes cowards of us all." The wall-builders found that to be true. "The strength of the laborers is failing," said Judah (Nehemiah 4:10).

The construction project required fifty-two days of backbreaking labor. Halfway finished, the workers had been going at it for a month. Fatigue was catching up with them, and when energy runs short, so does courage. Haven't you found this to be true? You're working twelve-hour days, finishing the annual report. You're working on weekends. Or you're cleaning the house all day, then helping the kids with algebra homework at night. For a while you'll rock along, doing what you feel you must. But sooner or later your personal limits will catch up with you. Every human body is governed by its own mathematical formula involving time, pressure, and exertion. If you exceed the limits of that equation, the cracks start to appear. You begin to be tense, irritable, and gloomy. Those are the times when your enemy, the devil, circles your name on his agenda.

As I've become older, I hope I've grown wiser. And one little bit of wisdom I've grasped is that I can no longer push myself as hard as I used to. I'm an odd one to be lecturing to you on this topic, for I've always been a Type A personality. I doubt that will change. But these days I see the importance of pacing myself. I need to build in a little more margin in my life, and I need to protect those margins; otherwise, if I push too hard for too long, I'm going to see diminishing returns on the investment of my time and talents—and then the deluge of discouragement.

That certainly happened in Jerusalem. The people were weary, discouraged, and one other thing—they were frustrated.

Factor Number Two: Frustration. We've just seen Judah's complaint in the first part of verse 10, when he observes that the workers' strength is failing. He continues, *"There is* so much rubbish that we are not able to build the wall."

Have you ever worked for days and weeks on mundane details, then stepped back and wondered if your efforts had any significance? Tired as they were, the Israelites no longer saw the proud, gleaming walls of their dreams. Visions of glory seemed like a mirage in the desert. There was nothing but broken bricks, mud, and debris. The tenth verse records that they were suddenly frustrated with the ever-present rubbish and rubble of heavy construction. Have you ever noticed how ugly a building site can be? There will be a sign with a beautiful painting of a glass tower, sparkling in the sunshine—and behind the sign is an ugly hole in the mud. At Jerusalem, the old walls had been torched. Now there were great piles of worthless debris everywhere.

The frustration of those endless mountains of rubble was weighing on Nehemiah's people. They would nearly collapse in weariness as the sun went down, then, arriving for work the next morning, it would appear to them as if nothing had been accomplished. It seemed as if the debris had a life of its own and was multiplying. They were *burned out.*

That's a buzzword of our times: *burnout.* We all use it. In past generations, a man might work his entire adult life at one trade for one employer, then retire after fifty years with the gold watch; if he ever felt "burned out" along the way, there wasn't the word to articulate it. Today, we're always shifting careers and pointing to burnout. I've heard it said there are three ways to live: You can *live out,* you can *wear out,* or you can *burn out.* I'm hoping to live out, and I'm sure you'll agree that's the best alternative.

But we need to define this concept of burnout with care. I hear people use the word to mean *working too hard.* That's not a definition of burnout. Many of my friends work hard and energetically without ever burning out, because they work with focus and perspective. They have something called vision, and they move forward toward attainable goals.

25

The true nature of burnout is working too hard at the wrong thing. It's striving for a goal you can't accomplish—perhaps a goal no one can accomplish. Burnout is pulling the whole weight uphill all by yourself, reaching the summit and realizing you're only going to topple to the bottom to start all over again. It's a feeling of despondency, and Nehemiah's workers were suffering from rubbish burnout. They couldn't see the picture of the shining city, only the debris. In a word, they were frustrated.

Factor Three: Failure. Nehemiah 4:10 tells us so much. "The strength of the laborers is failing [fatigue], and *there is* so much rubbish [frustration] that we are not able to build the wall [failure]."

The Israelites throw up their hands here and pronounce their failure. Fatigue and frustration are a good recipe for failure. "We're tired," they say. "We're fed up. We can't do this. It was a great idea, but we've been at it for a month and we can't take any more." Negative talk is infectious, spreading like a virus to infect a community. Nehemiah's people hadn't failed at all, but it appeared that way to them. Failure is one of life's giants, and we'll give the subject a chapter of its own later in this book. But for now, let's look at it as a force for discouragement.

Failure is universal. Every human being who has ever lived—with one exception, two thousand years ago—has succumbed to failure. What makes the difference is how we handle our failure. The great danger is in letting our negative thoughts and impressions be compounded by the adversity we suffer. When things go wrong we're more willing to give an ear to the enemy, the world's greatest *de*-motivational speaker, and we slowly but surely begin to buy into his lies and distortions.

"I haven't accomplished anything at all," we murmur. "I'm a failure."

Factor Four: Fear. Read the words of Nehemiah 4:11–12: "And our adversaries said, 'They will neither know nor see anything, till we come into their midst and kill them and cause the work to cease.' So it was, when the Jews who dwelt near them came, that they told us ten times, 'From whatever place you turn, *they will be* upon us.'"

We explored this topic of fear in the first chapter, but fear has something to do with discouragement, too. Imagine the weary workers, building their walls in the midst of all the ugly rubble. The job was grueling enough, but there was also the matter of these neighbors stopping by to put a word in their ear. These visitors were saying, "We've got a few surprises in store for you. You won't know when, you won't know how, but just when you least expect it, we'll slip in and kill you. And we'll take you out by increments, one by one, until the walls stand half-built with no one left to complete them."

Nothing derails the work of God's people like a negative word. Everyone who tries to serve the Lord knows the truth of this. I receive my fair share of critical letters. Someone hears me on the radio, or someone sees something we've published, and they attack by U.S. mail. It goes with the territory of having a large ministry. But it's interesting to me how the enemy always knows just when to put one of those letters on my desk. They come in times of struggle. They come at the In-Between Moment, when we're just about to regain our focus and move forward for God's kingdom again.

That's when the venomous words always materialize from some quarter. We're tempted to say, "So that's how people feel. Well, maybe I ought to just turn in my Bible and quit."

Criticism is toxic. Perhaps you're coping with it right now. Perhaps the bitter words of others are eroding your spirit in the workplace or even your home. Perhaps there are people who play on your fears until you become very discouraged.

Now that we've recognized all the factors that lead to discouragement, how can we respond?

2. Responding to Discouragement

First Response: Cry out to God. "Hear, O our God, for we are despised; turn their reproach on their own heads, and give them as plunder to a land of captivity! Do not cover their iniquity, and do not let their sin be blotted out from before You; for they have provoked *You* to anger before the builders . . . Nevertheless we made our prayer to our God . . ." (Nehemiah 4:4–5, 9).

I'm going to make a radical suggestion to you. Next time you encounter some major setback in your life, reverse your usual procedure—that is, cry out to God *first* instead of *last*. Most of us wait until we've exhausted all other alternatives before appealing to God as a last resort. I don't know about you, but I grit my teeth when I hear someone say, "We've tried everything; now all we can do is pray."

Don't wait until last to look up. When discouragement comes, start at the top! Go to the Lord and ask Him to help you sort through all the issues. May I tell you what works for me in times of discouragement? I sit down with my computer and my journal and I begin to talk to God. I say, "Lord, I need to talk with You right now. Some things are going on in my life that I can't understand, and I'm having a hard time with it. I need to tell You about it."

For me, it helps to begin setting the issues down in writing as I verbalize my feelings to God. As I do this, something begins to change in my spirit.

First of all, I bring everything out of that dark "anxiety closet" into the light. Writing it down and reading it out loud brings clarity. I discover that things weren't quite the way I thought when they were smoldering within me. I've imposed order on them, examined them in the light.

Second, I've done as Nehemiah did—I've cried out to God. This is the most important thing. Sometimes we just need to let go, be a child, and cry out to Daddy. That brings the innocence and dependence that are the beginning of wisdom. It cuts through our discouragement. If you don't think this is a very spiritual approach, read through the psalms. When David was beset by worries (and he was beset by a multitude of them), he did exactly what I've prescribed above. He wrote them down and cried them out. He was brutally honest about his discouragement, and you can be, too.

Second Response: Continue the Work God Has Given You to Do. "So we built the wall, and the entire wall was joined together up to half its *height*, for the people had a mind to work" (Nehemiah 4:6).

Why is it that our immediate reaction to adversity is to quit? Like the angry little boy on the playground, we take our ball and go home. People leave churches; they quit jobs; they walk away from marriages—all because they've encountered the predictable season of discouragement. And of course, that's the worst thing we can do. We always come to regret our emotional walkouts. Satan knows that if he can play on our emotions and get us to quit, he can keep the problem from being resolved. He can keep God's work from moving forward. But take a look at Nehemiah. He felt all the discouragement of his people, but he never set down the trowel, never missed a beat in laying the next brick. He knew he had to keep on keeping on. Yes, there were problems to deal with—but he wasn't going to set aside the mandate God had given him. "The people had a mind to work," the

Scriptures tell us. Nehemiah helped them see that productive labor is just what the doctor ordered sometimes. It's healthy and therapeutic to work off our frustration.

Needless to say, it's also a great way to bring a little discouragement to the enemy. Later on, Sanballat and Geshem tried one more stunt to make Nehemiah slow down on his work. They invited him to a conference. Anyone in the business world will tell you that conferences and committees are great ways to slow down productivity! And I've always loved Nehemiah's comeback. "So I sent messengers to them, saying, 'I *am* doing a great work, so that I cannot come down. Why should the work cease while I leave it and go down to you?'" (Nehemiah 6:3).

Modern translation: "Please accept my regrets, but God's agenda outweighs yours right now." The main thing is to keep the main thing as the main thing. We need to have a firm grasp on what God called us to do, put on the blinders, and keep plugging away. As we've seen, clear goals are the best preventive maintenance for burnout.

No matter how devastated you may feel, no matter how down in the dumps your spirit may be, keep up the good work. Experience leads me to believe that the times we *least* feel like working are the times we most certainly *should*. Emotions are treacherous advisers. We need to be disciplined and stay on task. Nehemiah knew his people didn't need to bail; they needed to build. They didn't need to walk; they needed to work. And our discouragement will have a way of sorting itself out.

Third Response: Concentrate on the Big Picture.

Therefore I positioned *men* behind the lower parts of the wall, at the openings; and I set the people according to their families, with their swords, their spears, and their bows. And I looked, and arose and said to the nobles, to the leaders, and to the rest of the people, "Do not be afraid of them. Remember the Lord, great and awesome, and fight for your brethren, your sons, your daughters, your wives, and your houses." (Nehemiah 4:13–14)

Nehemiah's men were fanned out across the perimeter, working on little sections of the wall—and that was part of the problem. They were so separated that they couldn't communicate and encourage each other. They could only see their own little hole in the wall, their own little pile of rubbish. It was very difficult to maintain any perspective.

We, too, tend to reduce the world to the cubicles we work in. "A desk is a dangerous place from which to view the world," said John le Carré. Your cubicle may not have a window, but you can always keep one wide open in your spirit. Open it to God. Open it to others. Hold on to the Big Picture. Nehemiah's workers were down and out. The muddy bricks and old debris made a discouraging picture, but only a few steps back and a little imagination upward revealed a portrait of the New Jerusalem. You may see nothing but drudgery in your life; you need to see what He is doing in you, with you, and for you. You need to hold on to that hope. It will help you prevail in the darkest of times.

Nehemiah 4 shows how Nehemiah handled the problem. He positioned the people along the wall in rows. Suddenly they could see the unity of their work force, the proud line standing firm along the walls. Can you see a mental picture of that? Now the workers could see that every man meant one more section of the wall under repair. Add it all up, and the total is a new city.

Once I saw a cartoon filled with a crowd of hundreds of little characters packed together, all looking perplexed, all with identical thought bubbles above their heads, countless thought bubbles, all reading, "What can one man do?" From our side of the cartoon panel we can see how ludicrous that is. Each little man is in his own private torment, and yet they're not only an "each," they're an army, if only they could see it. Don't let the enemy isolate you.

Erma Bombeck is sorely missed. For thirty years she wrote a popular syndicated newspaper column, published fifteen books, received numerous awards, appeared regularly on *Good Morning America*, and gave a great voice to millions of little people. I miss that voice, for it brought laughter and hope to all of us. But few of her admirers were aware of the sufferings she experienced. She had breast cancer, a mastectomy, and kidney failure. She worked through her trials, one by one, and maintained her grasp of the Big Picture. She once wrote,

> I speak at college commencements, and I tell everyone I'm up there and
> they're down there—not because of my successes but my failures. Then I

proceed to spin all of them off—a comedy record album that sold two copies in Beirut . . . a sitcom that lasted about as long as a doughnut in our house . . . a Broadway play that never saw Broadway . . . book signings where I attracted two people: one who wanted directions to the restroom and the other who wanted to buy the desk. What you have to tell yourself is this: "I'm not a failure. I failed at doing something." There's a big difference . . . Personally and career-wise, it's been a corduroy road. I've buried babies, lost parents, had cancer and worried over kids. The trick is to put it all in perspective . . . and that's what I do for a living.[2]

She did it very well; that's why we loved her so deeply. She made us laugh at ourselves and think about life in perspective. She made us look up for a moment from the little holes in the walls that define our piece of geography. She helped us remember we're all a part of something bigger.

Pastor and futurist Leith Anderson, a good friend of mine, writes the following in his book *Leadership That Works*:

In the heat of a tough leadership battle it is easy to lose hope, become pessimistic, and convince ourselves of defeat . . . But as Christians we must open our eyes to see the view from where Jesus sits . . . When I am discouraged and my hope runs thin, I remember that I am part of something much bigger than I am, and much more important than the local church of which I am a part. I belong to the church of Jesus Christ, and the gates of Hell will not overcome it (Matthew 16:18). Seeing the worldwide kingdom of God, not just my little corner of it, is enormously encouraging to me. It builds my faith and strengthens my hope.[3]

From there, Anderson details example after example of good things coming to pass in the world because of Christ and His church. He takes us on a quick journey across the globe, and we see the many countries where souls are coming to salvation at phenomenal rates. Then Anderson brings us home again. There are now 102 million people attending church each week, he tells us. To make that number meaningful, we look at that other weekend pursuit, professional sports. It turns out that baseball, basketball, and football games in the United States drew a combined ninety-four million fans during the same year. In other words, more people attend church in *one week* than professional baseball, basketball, and football games in *one year*. In fact, when all the numbers are crunched, attendance at sporting events works out to about 2 percent of church attendance. So the next time somebody says, "Oh, if only people were as passionate about their church as they are about their teams," you need to remind them that pews are fifty times more popular than stadium seats, week after week. It's all a matter of perspective.

I also like what Anderson tells us about our young people. For every 100 worshipers in their seventies on a typical weekend, there are 160 to 200 who are in their twenties! Does that surprise you? Most of us have bought into the myth that young people are staying away from our churches in droves. It's simply not true on a statistical basis, looking at the Big Picture.[4]

The world is filled with voices of discouragement, but there is one place where we can always go to be uplifted.

Fourth Response: Claim the Encouragement of God's Promises. "'Do not be afraid of them. Remember the Lord, great and awesome, and fight for your brethren, your sons, your daughters, your wives, and your houses'" (Nehemiah 4:14).

In times of discouragement, run—don't walk—to the Word of God. You may hear yourself say something like, "I'm too low for Bible-reading today. My heart wouldn't be in it." My friend, that's the point! When your heart is ailing, it needs a transfusion of hope and power. I tell people to learn the principle of force-feeding: Get the book out, open it up, sit yourself down, tune your mind in, and read the Word aloud. These are practical things you can *do*; don't wait for your feelings, for you can act your way into feeling easier than you can "feel" your way into acting.

I know how hard it can be. I have those mornings when my spirits are at low ebb as I approach my appointment with God. I speak to Him very frankly: "Lord, I need something special from You today. I'm going through a rough place here. I want more than words on a page; more than ideas and spiritual concepts. I need *You*. I need Your voice. And so I'm asking You to meet me in Your Word today, Lord."

There are also times when I've said, "I refuse to put this Book down until I hear from You, Lord." Don't you think He's pleased by our yearning to know Him? He's going to answer you if you approach with a determined heart. He's going to help you see just what you need to see in His Word, and He's going to give you the grace that will help you prevail through the bumps in the rocky road of life. This is no ordinary book. God's Spirit dwells in its pages, and He yearns for you to find Him in passages like this one:

> God *is* our refuge and strength,
> A very present help in trouble.
> Therefore we will not fear,
> Though the earth be removed,
> And though the mountains be carried into the midst of the sea;
> *Though* its waters roar *and* be troubled,
> *Though* the mountains shake with its swelling. (Psalm 46:1–3)

We can run to the New Testament, too. In 2 Thessalonians 3:13, we discover that it's possible to become discouraged even while doing all the right things: "But *as for* you, brethren, do not grow weary *in* doing good." Those words *grow weary* carry the meaning of discouragement. This is a remarkable idea and one I find very helpful. You may be out visiting the sick, engaging in prison ministry, teaching Sunday school, working with needy people, or any other good deed. You may be serving Christ with all your heart and still become discouraged. The Bible says don't grow weary in your service.

And why? Look to Galatians 6:9 for the answer. "And let us not grow weary while doing good," that verse repeats, then adds, "for in due season we shall reap if we do not *lose heart*," that is, *become discouraged*. You see, we find ourselves feeling low because we've lost perspective about Whom we're serving, why we're doing it, and how God plans to reward us. We need to remember the reaping.

Don't lose sight of those things. Run to God's Word, keep your nose in the Book, and draw the strength you need to keep your spirit strong.

Fifth Response: Carry Someone Else's Burden. Let's come back to Nehemiah and his massive renovation project. If we read a bit farther into the fourth chapter, we'll find something very moving. We'll find a pattern of people helping one another.

Nehemiah's band of stragglers, the remnant of fallen Israel, had bonded together to become a team. They were unified in commitment. Some were carrying, some were guarding, some were building, and all of them were wearing swords. The final word of this passage is that they stayed up all night; they were too caught up in their work to go home for the evening. Nehemiah tells us they didn't even change clothes except for washing. United we stand. They understood that if they were to prevail, they'd need to watch one another's backs. They'd need to help the weaker ones carry, and help the shorter ones reach. They'd need to fill in for those who were older and more weary. They carried one another's burdens.

Discouragement tends to cut us off from doing this. It sends us inward, where pity parties are common and perspective is rare. How often I've forgotten my own little worries when I've been busy calling on someone who was sick, or making my rounds at the hospital. Going in, I've told God that I had nothing to give these people; coming out, I've felt abundantly blessed. Our own burdens become lighter when we've been carrying the burdens of others. That's the way God planned things. He doesn't want you to bear your own load. He wants you to join a burden-bearing community. He wants you to be entrenched in a network of encouragement.

Do you need encouragement right now? My best advice to you is to go encourage someone else. Are you caught up in your own needs? Go fill the needs of others. You'll reap what you sow, and the love you give will return to you.

But some people have actually told me, "I don't know anyone who needs encouragement." Would you like to know the very best place to find them? In your church. Fred Smith, a businessman, asked a church usher about his responsibilities. The man said, "Nothing more than being there, shaking hands, finding my place in the aisle, taking the offering, and showing up for an occasional ushers meeting." Smith thought this didn't sound very biblical, but he observed in the conversation that this man had a passion about the ministry of hospitality. So many people come to church filled with cares and anxiety, the usher had noticed, and they need a warm handshake, a listening ear, perhaps a hug. The man had found his place to serve God quietly but profoundly.[5] This weekend, make it a project to go to church as a pure encourager. Ask God to direct your steps to someone who needs a dose of love.

Look for burdens to bear. You'll find your heart lifted. Pull your eyes away from the discouragement you feel, and place them on the courage others have shown—others like Carolyn, whose story opened this chapter. She had once played the piano, typed expertly, and enjoyed so many gifts. But a terrible stroke devastated her. Still, she set her mind and heart on learning to speak, read, and write all over again. "God didn't want me to give up," she told me. She believed in Him, and she knew He believed in her. She also had a godly husband and a loving son. Their love got her through the dark night of despair and the long road to recovery. She now plays the piano and types on the keyboard with one hand, and she's grateful for it. She's grateful just to be alive.

And I draw strength from Doretha, whose husband shot her son in a drunken accident. There were many black months before she came to the end of her despair. One evening at midnight it all came crashing in on her. She fell to her knees in her bedroom and called out, "Lord, help me! I'm tired of living this miserable life." It seemed as if the weight of the world had been on her shoulders. But having called out to God, she felt a certain dizziness. There was something different inside her; she knew she could sleep, and that's what she did—deeply, restfully. She began the next day as a new creature. She felt so much lighter that she actually looked in the mirror to see if she'd lost weight. Her shape was the same as always; it was the face that was new. It *glowed*.

Doretha couldn't comprehend the newness of things. She wanted to understand the change that had come across her, but she was a bit embarrassed to ask. In a little secondhand bookshop she found a book entitled *Here's Hope: Jesus Cares for You—The New Testament*. That word *hope* seemed to leap out at her. That's what was different about today. She took the book home with her and began to read hungrily. It wasn't long before she came across these words: "'Come to Me, all *you* who labor and are heavy laden, and I will give you rest'" (Matthew 11:28).

"God changed my whole life," Doretha told me, "mended my broken heart, saved my husband in jail, brought me and my husband closer together, showed us how to love and be loved—and not to take life for granted. Jesus is the hope of the world. God still answers prayer."

God brought Doretha and her husband into blessed light from the deepest of holes, and I have no doubt He can do the same for you. The depth of the hole can never compare to the depth of His love, the reach of His arms, and the height of His glory.

Let's come into those arms, all of us who are heavy laden, and feel the lightness of casting our burdens down, until our faces shine with the brightness of Doretha's.

3

LIBERATION FROM LONELINESS

YOU CAN WIN THE BATTLE AND LIVE VICTORIOUSLY

FOR LINDA, LIFE HAS TOO OFTEN been another word for *good-bye*.

Linda was raised in a farmhouse during hard times, Great Depression years. Poverty, polio, dust storms, tornadoes, and crop failures were the backdrop of her childhood. A German battlefield took her brother; cancer took her mother. Early on, Linda learned all there was to know about good-bye.

The prospect of marriage, however, brought the hope of fresh beginnings. Linda and Richard, the boy she met in a white-frame country church, began a new life together. But that, too, was interrupted when the Korean Conflict hit the headlines. Linda said good-bye as her new husband left for service, and the loneliness returned. Then she said good-bye to her father and father-in-law who died, and a brother and sister-in-law who were tragically murdered.

Richard came home; maybe life would finally be filled with joy—and a family. Instead, what followed were years of frustration trying to conceive children. The couple found the vacant nest to be a lonely place. That period, too, came to an end; there were eventually children. At first, she found contentment. But Linda discovered that the simple presence of off-spring brought no guarantee of happiness. As they grew, the kids made poor decisions that broke their parents' hearts—decisions leading to unwed pregnancies, divorces, custody battles, alcoholism, and imprison-ment. She missed the little children she had once nestled close. She felt lonelier than ever as the years advanced. She and Richard held one another close.

Then Richard began to weaken. He was diagnosed with Lou Gehrig's disease.

Did Linda have the strength for this, the most painful good-bye of all?

Beth had always been in a hurry. She had bustled down the aisle of her church at the age of nine, embracing her new faith with the same eager impatience she gave to everything else. Today she reflects that she would have sought God's will if she hadn't had to wait around for it. There were places to go, people to meet.

Beth's impulsiveness brought results she never anticipated: alcoholism, two failed marriages, and single motherhood with six children. Quick decisions had brought her to a place with few options, and she realized she could never manage her household without some new man in her life. Given her situation, it appeared that she couldn't afford to be selective.

Beth's life became an endless series of soap opera reruns, weighed down by one disastrous relationship after another. The men came, used her, and departed again. Beth saw the pattern, but where could she turn? She thought wistfully of God; hadn't she given her life to Him so many years ago, and hadn't He promised to care for her? She believed in Him still. She even believed He might forgive her, but her own grace was neither as wide nor as deep. She couldn't forgive herself. Only from the deepest pit did she call His name: from the depths of drunkenness, in the times when some man abused her, as well as during those worst times of all—when she watched her growing children repeat her mistakes.

That's when the miracle happened. God answered her prayers, and those of the mother and loving sisters who patiently interceded for her before Almighty God. He became very real to Beth, and He began to show her the ugliness of her life and the hope of a better one. But "happily ever after" was delayed. First, Beth was going to have to learn the hard truths of obedience.

God began removing from her life the people—the emotional crutches—who kept her from depending fully on God. Her drinking buddy patched up a broken marriage and moved from the state. That was her best friend. But her sisters, too, married and moved away. She had leaned on their support many times. Beth was facing a turning point in her life, and she was facing it alone. Her drinking became worse, until even the men stayed away from her. She lived only for her children, though she knew how deeply she was failing as a mother.

Soon, something would have to give.

Philip Zimbardo, writing in *Psychology Today*, has said, "There is no more destructive influence on physical and mental health than the isolation of you from me and of us from them." He points to studies that show loneliness as a central agent of depression, paranoia, schizophrenia, rape, suicide, mass murder, and a wide variety of diseases. We've all seen the polls that point to shorter life spans for lonely people.[1] And when surveys are taken to discover the central concerns of society, loneliness nearly always tops the list. We were created for fellowship, and deprival of it is deadly.

Max Lucado writes about walking through a cemetery and coming across the tombstone of one Grace Llewellen Smith. No date of birth or death is listed; no facts about her life or work or interests, other than the names of her two husbands. But there is this epitaph:

> *Sleeps but rests not.*
> *Loved, but was loved not.*
> *Tried to please, but pleased not.*
> *Died as she lived—alone.*

Lucado found himself wondering, *Mrs. Smith, what broke your heart?* He was haunted by those words: *Died as she lived—alone.*[2] The chilling realization is that if epitaphs were always so honest, there would be cemeteries filled with Grace Llewellen Smiths. We all know her, hundreds of times over. And we know it in ourselves, for as Morris West has written,

> It comes to all of us sooner or later. Friends die, family dies, lovers and husbands, too. We get old; we get sick . . . In a society where people live in impersonal cities or suburbs, where electronic entertainment often replaces one-to-one conversation, where people move from job to job, and state to state, and marriage to marriage, loneliness has become an epidemic.[3]

What is this thing called loneliness? It is a sick feeling in the stomach that seltzer water won't cure. It's an anxiety that doesn't come or go, but remains with you at all times and smothers you in the still of night. It's a sharp pang that jolts through you when you hear a certain old song or revive an old memory. It's a subtle stress that quietly wears you down until you feel devoid of energy or enthusiasm. Above all, loneliness is a longing for completeness.

And how do we handle these unwanted cravings? We seek to fill them with every other thing, from food to drink to drugs to work. We strain the relationships we have by placing obsessive demands on them. We flee into fantasy worlds or to new cities, businesses, churches, relationships.

Some handle loneliness by taking their own lives. Teenagers, who experience it deeply and desperately, have brought an upsurge in suicide attempts. The recent rash of school shootings, bringing anguish to my own neighborhood twice, have often been linked to the confusion of loneliness.

And yet it's a crisis we all face. I was preaching on this topic the day after I performed the wedding for my youngest son. He had flown from the nest, and I was already missing him.

THE EXPERIENCE OF LONELINESS

We can't discuss a problem as widespread as loneliness without exploring some of the many ways it manifests itself. For everyone it tastes a bit different. The diversity of it is expressed so well in the Beatles song about Eleanor Rigby, who picks up rice from the sanctuary floor after people's weddings, and "lives in a dream." Nearby, Father McKenzie wipes the dust from his hands after a funeral, feeling the emptiness of life. These two lost souls have gone about their lives almost elbow to elbow, inhabiting the same world without connecting—until one buries the other.

Life need not be so painful.

Let's study a few portraits in loneliness.

The Lonely Single

I live in the San Diego area, and our city has one of the highest populations of single adults in the country. I've met so many of them in our church, and they've painted a picture for me of returning to an empty home, cooking dinner for one, and watching TV shows with no one to discuss them with. Listen to how Ann Kiemel expressed it upon the occasion of a lonely New Year's Eve when she was single:

> God,
> it's new year's eve
> and i took a hot bath
> and poured powder and lotion
> and perfume recklessly,
> and donned
> my newest
> long, dainty
> nightgown.
> i guess i was hoping
> all that would erase
> the agony
> of being
> alone
> in such a gallant,
> celebrating,
> profound moment
> when everyone so likes
> to be with someone
> to watch
> a new year in.
>
> it hasn't helped
> too much.
> i've tried to sleep
> hoping that would beat
> away the endless hours, but
> after all afternoon and two hours
> tonight, i'm worn out from sleep.

41

i've stumbled from one room
to the next,
wanting to cry . . .

o God,
the walls are so silent . . .
and there is no one around
to laugh and
change the subject . . .
i so wish for a friend's lap,
to bury my head
and let my tears spill
unabashedly and freely . . .[4]

Some would say, "Oh, stop the pity party! Why indulge in self-pity?"

But there are many more who would say, "I recognize those feelings. There was a time when I could have written that poem myself"—about New Year's Eve, about a solitary Christmas season, about a Fourth of July with no fireworks, or about any of the long months that stretch between them.

The Lonely Spouse

Many single people have been shocked to discover that marriage is no surefire panacea for loneliness. Among the loneliest souls in this world are married people, though God Himself created the glorious institution of matrimony. He put husbands and wives together to provide perfect oneness and intimacy—the miracle of two souls becoming one flesh. Yet we squander the gift.

This point was brought home to me in a week when I had just preached on the subject. A woman wrote to tell me I'd hit a sensitive spot. "Tragic but true," she said. "I try not to dwell on the loneliness of marriage, but the truth is *I am lonely.* My husband and I are both Christians. He is a good man who works hard and provides for me. But all that work keeps him from being there to meet my emotional needs. We're like two ships who pass in the bathroom. I don't want to nag. I simply try not to think about the hurt and the emptiness. But in the end, I'm still lonely."

The Lonely Survivor

It's also possible to have a full, abundant marriage and lose the one on whom you've come to depend. It's a bittersweet gift to be the survivor of a marriage ended in death. I've counseled those who have told me that words can't express the emptiness of losing a soul mate. Life has been constructed of shared experiences, shared feelings, shared preferences in restaurants and furniture and music—so many thousands of little things linking two spirits. Your spouse has truly become a part of you, and now that part is gone. There is no complete healing for such a wound.

There's also the experience of divorce, more manifest in our times than any other. If you haven't been through that valley of shadow, you know those who have. Again, the lonely survivor must bring a new life out of the chaos of loss. And in this case, there are feelings of failure, recrimination, rejection, unfinished business, parental guilt—so many dark by-products of the divorce phenomenon. For the divorced, loneliness can be tinged with bitterness.

The Lonely Senior Citizen

Every day the percentages increase. The assisted-living centers grow more crowded. More gray hairs sprout on your head and mine. Every one of us is growing older, and there's nothing new in that. I know many people who are caring for their children and their aging parents simultaneously, and they know that retired people have acute attention needs that are a challenge to meet. Senior citizens feel the hurt of giving their lives to children who now simply don't have time for them—or don't have as much time as their parents would like.

They've discovered how wonderful a gift it is to be needed, and how difficult we find it on that day when no one needs us anymore. They can remember great accomplishments, the respect of the community, a house filled with friends and family. They've seen their friends and their spouses pass from this life. It seems no one is left who remembers, no one who understands.

The golden years weren't supposed to be like this. They were supposed to have luster. The Bible speaks of gray hair as a crown to be honored by the community, not a mark of obsolescence to be scorned. Some lonely seniors find themselves wondering why they're still lingering in this life.

The Lonely Sufferer

I'll never forget the letter I once read in a book called *Loneliness Is Not Forever*. A man was attempting to describe the pain that had become his reality. He wrote,

> It was when the lights went out and the room was suddenly plunged into darkness that the awful awareness came. The traffic of the hospital went on like an uncontrolled fever outside my door. But inside that room it became still, so still that you could sense, even believe, that the walls were moving and the room was becoming smaller. I was never a lonely person up until then . . . But now I knew what it was. My family had gone home together to that familiar, safe place. But I was here alone, isolated, facing the uncertainties of what hospitals mean.[5]

Physical problems have emotional symptoms because pain isolates us. Misery loves company, but it deepens in solitude. We feel all alone; we feel no one understands our pain. And we feel very lonely.

The Lonely Servant of God

In this world are a few courageous souls who are willing to lay everything before God—their time, their work, even their homes. They serve all across the world in the mission field, quietly and often forgotten. They've left behind family and friends and everything familiar. You and I, too, often go about our lives without stopping to give them a thought or a prayer of blessing. This man or woman serves God in an alien culture, struggling with language and customs—and loneliness.

I'd love to show you my letters from missionary friends who describe the experience of being *disconnected*. They're connected to higher purposes, of course, and God has special rewards for them. But in the here and now, it can be a lonely life.

The lonely servant of God may be isolated by leadership, too. In Numbers 11:14, Moses spoke of the heavy burden of trying to carry the destiny of so many people. That's a burden that weighs us down. We say that it's "lonely at the top," and that's true—but the leader is not at the top; he's beneath the heavy burdens of those in his charge. And if those at the top are really at the bottom, here's another paradox to ponder: The one who walks out front must turn his back on those who walk behind him. It's true. Leadership, too, isolates. Leaders of great churches and large ministries can be very lonely people; it simply comes with the territory.

These are all pictures of loneliness. I hope we can agree that it's no sin to be lonely; it's a symptom of being human—of being created in the image of the God who first made us because He delighted in fellowship.

EXAMPLES OF LONELINESS IN THE BIBLE

David the King

So many of the psalms present the most eloquent evocations of loneliness in the history of literature. David understood the subject deeply. He knew what it was like to hide in the coolness of caves as the soldiers hunted him down. Yet he also knew what it was like to sit upon the throne. Whether he was despised or exalted, there was loneliness to contend with. Here are only two of countless examples:

> For my days are consumed like smoke, and my bones are burned like a hearth . . . I am like a pelican of the wilderness; I am like an owl of the desert. I lie awake, and am like a sparrow alone on the housetop. (Psalm 102:3, 6–7)

> Look on my right hand and see, for *there is* no one who acknowledges me; refuge has failed me; no one cares for my soul. (Psalm 142:4)

Whenever I feel lonely, it helps me to know that a man as great as King David—a man after God's own heart—could feel just as I do. I commend you to the psalms when the solitude overcomes you; there you'll find a lively and fully human friend who shares your feeling.

Jeremiah the Prophet

This Jeremiah—the author—points you to *that* one—the prophet. His story is one of the most heartrending you're ever likely to read. The book of

Lamentations is a kind of "spin-off" of Jeremiah's own book, for the two were originally one large book. We don't read Lamentations very often today, because most people aren't attracted to funeral poetry. That's what these verses are. Jeremiah wrote them down as he watched his beloved city of Jerusalem go up in flames before his eyes. He watched his people fall apart and their culture and heritage swept away.

The prophet preached against all this, of course. And he knew no one would listen to his words. Today we remember Jeremiah as "the weeping prophet" because of the tears he shed over fallen Jerusalem. It's difficult to preach a message everyone ignores, and the life of Jeremiah stands as a testimony to that fact. His deep loneliness is an agonizing thing to read and study.

"Oh, that I had in the wilderness a lodging place for wayfaring men," he wrote, "that I might leave my people, and go from them! For they *are* all adulterers, an assembly of treacherous men" (Jeremiah 9:2). He was sick of the whole spectacle. He was saying, "If I could just find a cheap motel out in the desert, I'd check in and never check out." That's an expression of the alienation he felt. Being a prophet is a lonely experience.

Paul the Apostle

Even the New Testament, bursting with its good news of redemption for all humanity, has its share of loneliness. Consider the case of great New Testament evangelist and teacher, Paul the Apostle.

He was the human author of much of the New Testament; the founder of countless missionary churches; and the mind behind the book of Romans, the greatest treatise on theology ever conceived. Paul went everywhere, spoke multiple languages, knew everyone. And he experienced deep loneliness. The last of his letters is 2 Timothy, for he was writing to that younger man who was his closest friend. Here is Paul at the end of a life crowned by staggering achievements, and he describes the grief of his solitude. Listen to his heart:

> Be diligent to come to me quickly; for Demas has forsaken me, having loved this present world, and has departed for Thessalonica—Crescens for Galatia, Titus for Dalmatia. Only Luke is with me . . . At my first defense no one stood with me, but all forsook me. May it not be charged against them. (2 Timothy 4:9–11, 16)

46

Do you feel the pain that flows through those verses? Such a great man who has poured out his life for these very churches, and he stands alone. At this point in his life he qualifies for many of the categories we've already described: He is a lonely servant of God, a lonely sufferer with his "thorn in the flesh," a lonely senior, even a lonely single adult. He may be the incomparable Apostle Paul, but he feels *your* pain. It's possible to accomplish so much, bless so many, change the world so explosively, and still experience the icy chill of solitude. In *this*, at least you're not alone.

Feeling lonely is not a sin, but we sin when we begin to indulge it. We sin when we begin ignoring the biblical prescription for confronting it. We sin when we let it possess us and ruin our lives.

But we need not fall into that sin. The Bible offers us an escape.

LIBERATION FROM LONELINESS

Acknowledge the Reality of Your Loneliness

The first thing you need to do is to be honest about your feelings, and the *last* thing you need to do is resort to pious platitudes. Loneliness is real and it is painful. It is in no way a reflection of weakness as a Christian or a member of society.

We as Christians love the pious platitudes, however. A. W. Tozer has some instructive words for us about the layers of superficial gloss with which we coat real problems:

> Some say brightly, "Oh, I am never lonely. Christ said, 'I will never leave you nor forsake you,' and, 'Lo, I am with you always,' so how can I ever be lonely when Jesus is with me?" Now I do not want to reflect on the sincerity of any Christian soul, but this stock testimony is too neat to be real. It is obviously what the speaker thinks should be true rather than what he has proved to be true by the test of experience.[6]

I know you've run into this kind of thing before. You try to tell a friend about your feelings, and before you can even finish, your friend flashes a spiritually smug smile and issues Pious Platitude #437. Such stock replies leave us cold, because they deny the reality of human experience and struggle. These sentiments are technically true, of course, but they're also insensitive and unrealistic about the fallen world we live in. We need encouragement, not sermonizing, and we need clear-eyed acknowledgment of the situation, not a sanctified gloss that pushes us toward saying, "I see I must not admit my pain because, after all, I'm a Christian. I'll just have to cover it up. Jesus is with me, so I suppose I have no right to feel lonely even for a moment."

Let me assure you there's nothing Christian at all about such a perspective. We are to face our struggles, whatever they may be, clearly—with no denial. Loneliness doesn't necessarily come because of something you did, or something someone else did, or because of something you lack. It comes because you are a human being, and it's given to each of us to be lonely for a season. Accept it as part of the human experience. Then you'll be able to move on to God's way of dealing with it.

Accept God's Provision for Your Loneliness

We need to remember that only God can ultimately solve our problems, including this one. When something is broken we consult the original manufacturer, and for human beings God is the Original Manufacturer. He created us with certain attributes, and one of them is that we have an emptiness only He can fill. People can't cover it, though He gave us a separate need for them. Neither money nor things can fill the void. Nothing in this world will ultimately satisfy us short of knowing the One who made us. So the most basic loneliness of humanity is the loneliness of estrangement from God. It has no remedy but one.

For more than three decades I've been a people-watcher. I can tell if you are a believer or not simply by observing how you handle your problems. If you lack the inner strength of a godly man or woman, you'll finally buckle under the stress, the strife, and the struggles. You will lack the most basic resource for dealing with the most basic problem. But if you know Him, here's what happens: You're connected to Someone who came into the world, hung on a cross, and experienced *ultimate* loneliness so you would never have to do so.

How is that so? Hear the cry of Jesus in Matthew 27:46: "My God, My God, why have You forsaken Me?" At that moment He carried the sin of you and everyone else on His bruised and bleeding shoulders. In any other case you would have been ostracized from God's presence forever because of your sin and rebellion—while He would have enjoyed perfect fellowship because of His perfection. Instead, He forfeited that perfect fellowship for you and for me. He took the punishment we had in store, which meant the black loneliness of God, His Father, turning His back on Him. Perfect light can have no fellowship with darkness.

Now you and I walk in the light. We can know God intimately as His beloved children. It's possible to know liberation from loneliness in the warmth of His love. It happens as we embrace His lordship over us and He takes residence within us. He fills that void, and we begin to know peace and fulfillment and abundance. The Spirit of God is glowing from our hearts, just where He is supposed to be, just as God planned for us. There may be moments of disconnection and loneliness, but the ultimate kind is no longer a threat to us.

It's important to acknowledge this point. If you don't know Jesus, there's nothing else that can be done; there are no other options. If you do know Jesus, then every hope and joy is possible for you. Miracles can happen. The storehouse of heaven is open to you. The fellowship of the saints is available to fulfill your longings for companionship. Above all, the Spirit of God in your heart can identify with everything you experience. He will be there not to poke at you and accuse you, but to gently encourage you, comfort you, and point you to a better way.

Why would anyone refuse this awesome gift? Have you accepted it?

Allow God's Word to Fill Your Mind and Heart

Now, having acknowledged your feelings and embraced your faith, you can immerse yourself in God's Word. Let it overflow from your mind and your heart.

The voice of God will speak with clarity to the lonely. You need only open the pages of the ancient Book, as millions have done across the centuries. It has comforted them, regardless of their time, their place, or their peculiar struggles. No pious platitude here, just the truth! The Word of God will soothe and encourage you.

Oh, there are so many wonderful passages for you in your time of loneliness! It's a challenge to know where to begin, but try these two for starters:

When my father and my mother forsake me, then the LORD will take care of me. (Psalm 27:10)

For He Himself has said, *"I will never leave you nor forsake you."* So we may boldly say: *"The LORD is my helper; I will not fear. What can man do to me?"* (Hebrews 13:5–6)

Any list of verses would go on for many pages, but these two alone are packed with enough power to recharge your batteries when you're running on empty. Go first to God's Word—*run*, don't walk.

Activate Your Network of Christian Friends

You should also run to the fellowship of other believers. There is always this promise: "If we walk in the light as He is in the light, we have fellowship with one another" (1 John 1:7).

This next statement may seem rather blunt, but it's true: *Loneliness is a choice*—not the isolated moments we all experience, but lingering, pervasive loneliness. God has provided you with everything you need, and if you choose to dwell in the lifestyle of loneliness, that's a choice you've made. He has given us His Son. He has given us His Word. Then He has given us the precious gift of our brothers and sisters in faith. Simon and Garfunkel once sang, "I am a rock; I am an island," but the Bible's song is that Jesus is the Rock so that you need never be an island.

That's why God made the provision of the church. Most of the books of the New Testament are written to whole congregations. And every time the word *saint* appears, it's always in the plural because the concept of "Christian individualism" is an oxymoron; it's foreign to biblical Christianity. We are incomplete without the unity of believers serving one another through their particular gifts.

You don't know anyone? Well, he who would have a friend must show himself friendly (Proverbs 18:24).

You don't like to take the initiative? How will anyone know about you if you don't make yourself known?

You feel no one really cares? It's hard to care about a face in the crowd. No one knows your needs if you linger in the background.

Loneliness is a choice. A good church in your area offers a wide array of opportunities for you to connect. Join the choir. If you don't like to sing, join a Bible study group. If you can't get there, join a Sunday school class. There are organizations, meals, programs, presentations—all of which have been established to help you connect and use the spiritual gifts you're assured of having by virtue of being a Christian. Let me particularly suggest that you volunteer for service. Great relationships are forged in colaboring for good causes.

Here's a passage I love that extols the virtues of simple companionship:

> Two *are* better than one,
> Because they have a good reward for their labor.
> For if they fall, one will lift up his companion.
> But woe to him *who is* alone when he falls,
> For *he has* no one to help him up.
> Again, if two lie down together, they will keep warm;
> But how can one be warm *alone?*
> Though one may be overpowered by another, two can withstand him.
> And a threefold cord is not quickly broken. (Ecclesiastes 4:9–12)

My church once built a ministry upon that last verse. We called it the Triple Cord Prayer Ministry. Take a piece of string and you can snap it with little effort; but entwine it with two other cords and it will withstand all your efforts to break it. Together, we're greater than the sum of our parts.

This is a godly principle at the very center of how God works in the world—He works through people intertwined together, even with all the messy knots and entanglements of our being involved together. Alone, we are so limited; together, we can forge movements that change world history. Our gifts multiply and multiply again. My gifts for ministry are in my tongue that preaches, my mouth that projects it, my fingers that turn the pages and reach out to serve others. But what would any of these parts be without the others? That's Paul's point—body parts are only so much biological tissue, but when they come together, they live and breathe and have life. God wants you to be so much more than biological tissue. He wants you to be part of something alive and dynamic and greater than yourself.

SEARCHING FOR STRAYS

God also wants you to reach out to make the cord stronger. Yes, I've charged the lonely with taking the initiative. But I think each of us also has the responsibility to look out for the stray sheep. Just as Jesus spoke of leaving the ninety-nine to seek out the lone lamb, you and I have a special ministry in pulling in those who are estranged and alienated. We should rise on Sunday morning, have our time with God, and ask Him to send us to the one who needs us the most. It's easy for us to gravitate to the great herd of sheep where we're comfortable and loved. That's a good thing, but let's also go where we're needed. The ministry of acceptance and encouragement is our distinguishing mark in this world.

Many today know the name of Anne Frank whose family was imprisoned in its own home during the Second World War. We read about the family's troubles in the diary that Anne kept all through the experience. Millions have read it or seen the movie based upon it. This family lived every day with the fear of discovery. And yet along with the claustrophobia and daily fear, Anne nurtured other feelings in her heart—including joy. Anne spoke of climbing the ladder to the loft and looking out at the blue sky. She said, "'As long as this exists,' I thought, 'this sunshine and this cloudless sky, and as long as I can enjoy it, how can I be sad?'" She reminds us that we can lose everything external—people, things, even prestige—"But the happiness in your own heart can only be dimmed."[7]

You and I can have that kind of overcoming hope as we look to the heavens, but our hope is not in clouds or sun or sky. We have Jesus Christ, the Lord of the universe, living in us. The ground beneath us may crumble, and the skies may pour torrential rain or the chaos of the whirlwind. But those things are not eternal as He is. The light of day lasts a few hours, and the light of a lifetime burns for perhaps eighty years. But the Light of the Savior shines now and forever. That's why my circumstances don't define me, don't limit me, don't even thrill me. My hope is in Him, and He will never fail. He will never depart. He will always be greater than our needs—just as my friend Linda discovered.

Remember Linda, the "good-bye girl"? Life for her had been all about separation, and the hardest of all was the death of her husband. Before he succumbed to Lou Gehrig's disease, there was a lengthy period of illness—a long good-bye. But during that time, something changed in Linda. She saw the grace and peace written across his face and in the little notes and gestures after he lost his ability to speak. Linda knew that God was the source of his courage and joy in the face of death itself. "Today, I walk in deep sorrow and loneliness," Linda admits. "However, I don't journey alone. My Savior walks with me, surrounding me with eternal love. Soon my life's road will make a final bend—homeward. And I'll see my husband and my Lord face to face. Praise God!"

And how about Beth? What happens when your life is in chaos, you meet God, and things become even bleaker? God seemed to be subtracting friends and emotional crutches from her life. She felt so lonely, and even intensified her drinking. The voice of the deceiver was whispering in her ear, "You're no good. It's too late for you, and soon your children will be mine!"

Every day, as she returned home from work, Beth listened to Christian radio. There was a sermon series on the power of prayer, and Beth began to try the principles she was hearing. Her sense of worthlessness began to drain away, replaced by an incredible feeling of her supreme value to God. She looked into church activities, and soon she actually found herself counseling others. Imagine such a thing! Satan had said she was worthless, but God was telling her that the depth of her pain could be useful to others.

Most amazing of all, God began to move through the lives of Beth's children like a sudden gust of heavenly wind. Seeing the change in their mother made a difference. In time, as she learned to depend on Him, God opened channels for her to spend time with her children. She was able to move to a new home, closer to them. Today she has a thriving ministry to women in her church through Bible study, and she's living proof that loneliness and things even worse can be overcome in God's mighty power.

Beth thinks about the past quite often. She says, "Those were the worst and best days of my life. God met me when I needed Him most. But most important, He prepared me for the changes I had to undergo."

Can you find God in the maze of lonely and confused feelings? Can you grasp that He may be preparing you for a fresh life and a fresh hope? He will never leave you nor forsake you. Reach out, take His hand, and discover what it means to slay the giant of loneliness.

4

WINNING AGAINST WORRY

YOU CAN WIN THE BATTLE AND LIVE VICTORIOUSLY

Your local YMCA is crowded with people who have come to relax. They take refreshing swims or work up a healthy sweat in the weightroom. It's a place where you go for recreation—unless you happen to be the man in charge. George McCauslin directed a YMCA facility in the Pittsburgh area, and things weren't going well for him. The job was eating him up inside.

George was struggling with his work. The club's membership was on a downward spiral. It was operating in the red with high debt, and George had to contend with critical staff problems. People came here to work off their tension; where could the director go with his own?

He went nowhere at all, of course. George worked obsessively, feeling that if he simply put in a little more time, he could somehow put together all the pieces. It wasn't long before he was behind his desk 85 hours per week. And somehow, when he finally came home, he was too tired to sleep; he was already thinking about an early start for the next day. Vacations were few and when he was away, the YMCA and its problems weighed even more heavily on his slumping shoulders. A therapist told him that something had better give, because a nervous breakdown was well on its way.

That's when George began to think about God. Where did He fit into this unhappy, chaotic picture?

Daniel was a promising college student. At age nineteen he had committed his life to serving Christ, and his sights were set on entering the ministry. All around him were fun-loving students—just kids, really—who were soaking

54

up all the good things about the college life and its atmosphere. But not Daniel; he was struggling to simply keep a meal down. His stomach was tied in knots, and it had been months since he'd enjoyed dinner without the fear of terrible stomach pain. The doctor did some tests and told Daniel he had the beginnings of a serious ulcer.

An ulcer—at age nineteen? Weren't those for fast-lane executives and Wall Street traders?

No, said the doctor. Ulcers are for chronic worriers. And Daniel knew he was speaking the truth. It seemed as if the mildest thing could cause him to snap—a car that wouldn't start, a textbook he couldn't find. He was as tight as a bowstring. And he was dwelling in the world of the worst-case scenario. *What if* this, *what if* that? What's the worst that can happen?

Daniel knew that his health had been compromised, but, just as damaging, so had his joy. Wasn't he supposed to be living the abundant life? Hadn't Jesus said His yoke was easy and His burden light? Surely this anxiety couldn't be a pleasing thing for God to look upon; surely the Lord must have had better plans for His child.

We can all agree that when it comes to membership in the human race, worry is part of the package. We also know that it's a useless and unhealthy vice. Corrie ten Boom used to recite a little couplet: "Worry is an old man with bended head, carrying a load of feathers which he thinks are lead." She understood that anxiety is ultimately foolish because it concerns that which *isn't*. It lives in a future that can't be foreseen. It deals in what-ifs and could-bes, speculation and possibility. And as long as we dwell on the worst-case scenario, we guarantee our own misery, for an extensive catalog of calamity is always within reach of the imagination.

The Bible chooses its worry language carefully. The basic biblical word has the meaning of "to take thought" or "to be careful." Those are good things, at first glance. But the Greek gives us the word picture of a divided mind. The worrier has a mind torn between the real and the possible, the immediate and the potential. He's trying to fight the battle of life on two fronts, and he's bound to lose the war.

The worrier attempts to live in the future, and that presents him with two problems: The future isn't here, and the future isn't his. Nothing can be done, and no amount of worrying affects the issue one iota. The future is unknown, uncontrollable, and therefore irrelevant in terms of our peace of mind.

When Jesus preached the greatest sermon of all history (found in Matthew 5–7), He was very clear on this issue of anxiety. In a nine-verse passage in Matthew 6, He uses the expression "Don't worry" three times. So if you'd like to have the teachings of Jesus on the subject of anxiety, we can state them in full in two words: *Don't worry.* And the next time you do give in to worry, you can ask yourself which section of that teaching you don't understand.

Before we take a close look at the passage in which Jesus discusses worrying, may I offer two simple disclaimers?

1. *Don't worry* does not mean *don't plan.* It's true that in Matthew 6:34 Jesus says, "Do not worry about tomorrow." The King James Version had it as, "Take therefore no thought for the morrow," and many people seized on that as a prohibition against career ambition, financial planning, life insurance, or any number of things. But no one who takes the time to read the Gospels would say that Jesus has a problem with planning—He planned for His ministry after His death, resurrection, and ascension. He spent plenty of time preparing His disciples for Jerusalem and beyond. He also taught that we shouldn't break ground on that new high-rise until we've done the paperwork (Luke 14:28). To live without planning isn't pure spirituality; it's pure insanity.

2. *Don't worry* does not mean *don't be concerned.* There are those who quote Philippians 4:6 ("Be anxious for nothing") as an excuse for a careless lifestyle. "Don't worry, be happy." But that's not what we're talking about at all. If you don't worry about your children playing near traffic, you're a terrible parent. If you're not concerned about walking off the roof of a skyscraper, you'll learn the meaning of that old poster that said, "Gravity: It's not just a good idea. It's the law." There are things you need to be concerned about. There's a difference between carefree and careless.

But realistic concern and restless anxiety are separate matters. So where is the difference? In short, concern focuses on the present; worry is attached to the future. The present is before us, and there are actions we can take. The future is out of our hands.

What Jesus is teaching about is the captivity of worry, and in Matthew 6 we'll discover what worry is all about and how we can face it.

FACING THE GIANT OF WORRY: MATTHEW 6:25-32

We're going to explore one of the most encouraging and comforting of all Jesus' teachings. It's part of the Sermon on the Mount, and it's actually divided into two sections—verses 25–32, then verses 33–34. Let's find out what is revealed in the first of those.

Worry Is Inconsistent

> "Therefore I say to you, do not worry about your life, what you will eat or what you will drink; nor about your body, what you will put on. Is not life more than food and the body more than clothing?" (Matthew 6:25)

Worry is simply inconsistent. Jesus is asking, "Who gave you the body you live inside? Who established its requirements—for food, for clothing, for shelter? Do you think He has gone anywhere? Don't you think that same Provider will see to your needs?"

In essence, this is an argument from the greater to the lesser. Consider the God who has created us a little lower than the angels, ordaining and establishing the miracle of human life in all the beautiful complexity of the human organism. Then He has fashioned with His powerful hands the heat of the sun, the revolving world, and the four seasons. He took an awful lot of trouble, didn't He? Why, then, would He be careless about these little things—a crust of bread, a patch of clothing, a dry haven from the storm? A God so tall could never overlook something so small, according to Jesus. "Is not life more . . . ?" Those are His words.

If you buy into a Creator God, you must buy into a Sustainer God—or you're simply inconsistent. The evidence of His loving and timely care is all around us. Use your mind and you'll find comfort for your soul.

Worry Is Irrational

> "Look at the birds of the air, for they neither sow nor reap nor gather into barns; yet your heavenly Father feeds them. Are you not of more value than they?" (Matthew 6:26)

Jesus' first argument is irrefutable. He who gave us life can surely sustain that life. But Jesus has anticipated the follow-up question: God *can* provide, but *will* He provide?

Jesus attacks this second question from the opposite direction. Now He moves from the lesser to the greater—in this case, from birds to human beings. He says, "Look into the trees and you'll see the little sparrows. A plain copper coin will buy you two of them. Few things are sold so cheaply. Does your Father value you less than a copper coin? His hand is behind every bird that falls to the ground; if He's got the whole world in His hands, doesn't that include you?" (see Matthew 10:29).

Sometimes we make fascinating discoveries when we bring two separate Scripture passages together. Consider this matter of the value of sparrows. Take a side trip over to Luke 12:6, and you'll find another market value: *five* sparrows for *two* copper coins. Put Matthew and Luke together and it's two for a penny and "buy four/get one free."

A copper coin was worth one-sixteenth of a denarius; a denarius was one day's wages. So what Jesus is saying is this: "A copper coin gets you two sparrows; two coins get you five. Not even the free sparrow, who has no market value, can fall to the ground without your Father knowing about it. He follows every movement, whether it's bird or beggar or baron."

As a matter of fact, says Jesus, if He knows every sparrow that falls to the ground, He knows when one of your hairs does likewise. Somewhere He has a database that tracks the very hairs on your head. And if He is so meticulous with the smallest, most incidental inventory items, won't He also tend to your deeper concerns?

Once again, Jesus gives us an argument we can't refute, this time from the lesser to the greater. We must conclude that worry is inconsistent and irrational. But there's another problem with it.

Worry Is Ineffective

"Which of you by worrying can add one cubit to his stature?" (Matthew 6:27)

Have you noticed all the units of measure in this passage? It's fascinating how Jesus deals with the concept of anxiety by calling on various lengths and weights and values. It's because when we deal with worry, we're dealing with matters of perspective and true worth. So we have coin and cubit, hair and sparrow.

A cubit, as Noah knew, comes to about eighteen inches—the length of your forearm, since rulers and yardsticks were rare. There are two possible interpretations of Jesus' point here. One is, "Who can sit back in his chair and worry himself a few extra inches in height?" If that were possible, the implications for basketball would be profound. But it's not possible, and I say that with some regret. When I was growing up, I watched the great players of the NBA and wanted to add a cubit—well, at least a few inches—to my height. I was six-foot-one, and I wanted badly to be six-five. But no amount of dreaming, no amount of yearning could add an inch to my height. Wilt Chamberlain's and Bill Russell's jobs were safe.

That interpretation of the verse seems clear, but perhaps Jesus was going a bit deeper. What if we're talking about days instead of inches—futures instead of forearms? "Which of you by worrying," He might be saying, "can add a day to your life?" The answer, of course, is that we can't add a day, an hour, or a flickering moment. Worry divides the mind and multiplies misery. It subtracts from our happiness. But it never adds.

What if we took a walk through the cemetery in your community and discovered that each tombstone included a gauge indicating the years of life that person lost through worrying? We might be amazed. Could it be that some of us take five, ten, or fifteen years off our longevity by the force of gravity weighing us down with needless anxiety? I've known a few of these. I've counseled people who have worried themselves out of this world early, simply because they couldn't leave things in God's hands.

Worry is the most ineffective use of your time. A friend of mine told me about visiting his brother, who kept a little white mouse in a cage. The mouse could climb onto the inside of a big wheel, and as he ran the wheel spun 'round and 'round. My friend's brother said, "It's fun to watch this little guy. It's as if he wakes up and says, 'Must get on the wheel! Must keep running!'" The average pet mouse, we're told, will run nine thousand miles on such a wheel in his lifetime, and he's *still inside the cage*.

That's the way it is with worry—a lifetime of frantic running with no destination. After a while you run out of the strength God gave you, and you're still in the cage. "Worrying doesn't rob tomorrow of its sorrow," someone said. "It robs today of its strength."

Worry Is Illogical

"So why do you worry about clothing? Consider the lilies of the field, how they grow: they neither toil nor spin; and yet I say to you that even Solomon in all his glory was not arrayed like one of these. Now if God so clothes the grass of the field, which today is, and tomorrow is thrown into the oven, *will He* not much more *clothe* you, O you of little faith?" (Matthew 6:28–30)

We can agree that worry is an unattractive thing, shabby and gloomy and careworn. But what does lightheartedness look like? Jesus gives us a clue in these verses. Have you walked through a beautiful garden in the springtime? It's very difficult to be weighed down by the cares of the world when you're surrounded by the majesty of God's beautiful art. Solomon was a glorious king, Jesus tells us, with the wealth of several kingdoms at his disposal. But all of his sparkling finery pales in comparison to the simplest lily that God placed beside your feet.

And how many office hours have those lilies put in? How many dues have they paid? Have you ever seen a lily suffering through an anxiety attack? They neither toil nor spin. They simply sway in the breeze, reaching heavenward toward the source of their water and sunshine and sustenance. They do neither more nor less than they were designed to do, and what they were designed to do is to glorify God. Would that you and I could glorify God with the simple eloquence of that little flower.

Yet the greater point is that God values you so much more than a lily. The lily is merely something He created for your pleasure, for *you're* the one that bears His image. And if He cares for each petal or stem that blooms and fades within a season, how much more does He care for you? How much more does He take to heart the things that cause your anxiety?

He took the answer to that question and displayed it on a cross two thousand years ago. He'd never suffer and die for the same children He planned to neglect. That's why worry is illogical.

Worry Is Irreligious

"Therefore do not worry, saying, 'What shall we eat?' or 'What shall we drink?' or 'What shall we wear?' For after all these things the Gentiles seek. For your heavenly Father knows that you need all these things." (Matthew 6:31–32)

Inconsistent, ineffective, illogical, and *irrational* are concepts we can quickly latch onto. The next one requires a bit more contemplation for modern thinking, but it comes from the Word of God and we must mold our minds to it. Jesus shows us that worry is irreligious.

What does *irreligious* mean? Isn't it true that the word *religion* is out of fashion among evangelicals today? Jesus' point is that to worry is to be just like everyone else—and "everyone else," to the Jew of that time, meant the Gentiles. There were two kinds of people: the Jews and everyone else. And through a special relationship with His special people, God had spent thousands of years demonstrating—through covenant and conquest, through wilderness and wandering, through kingdom and calamity—that He would be their God and they would be His people. Gentiles had no reason to believe such a thing, and it was natural for them to spend their lives in anxiety over food and shelter and clothing. But God's people should know better; it was written in bold letters across their law, proclaimed in their tabernacles, and should have been emblazoned in their hearts.

The goodness of God was the essence of their religion, and worry was a total denial of it. Worry denies your Father in heaven and your family on earth. It reduces us to the ways of the pagans who worship blind, deaf, and powerless idols, who live as if the desperation of a sacrifice at the altar will bring another few drops of rain. In the old days that might have been expressed in Baal worship, but it's just as alive today. We've simply removed the stone gods and replaced them with shiny new ones such as career, materialism, pleasure, and power—all the attainments we worry about in our denial that God will care for every need.

Do I ever worry? Of course I do; I've raised four children to adulthood, and that qualifies me as an expert on the subject. But for me, worry is a small town I pass through, not a place to hang my hat. It's a momentary phase, not a lifestyle. For many people, worry becomes so ingrained in their personalities that, once the old worries are gone, they search for new ones. They've become dependent on worry as a lens through which to view life, and they've forgotten any other way to live. Do you want to become that kind of person? I know I don't.

Jesus is talking about our unbelief, and yet notice the tenderness of His words: "For your heavenly Father knows that you need all these things." He is saying, "Rest, take comfort. Every need you have is on God's agenda. Have you forgotten He is taking care of everything? Let your runaway mind come home and find rest."

FIGHTING THE GIANT OF WORRY

We find so many inconsistent, irrational, illogical, ineffective, and irreligious factors when we take a close look at worry. We have as much reason to avoid it as we do some deadly narcotic—for that's exactly what it is. But perhaps you've already become dependent upon that drug. Perhaps you need to become free from its tyranny. How can you do it?

1. You Need a System of Priorities

"But seek first the kingdom of God and His righteousness, and all these things shall be added to you." (Matthew 6:33)

We've seen that the biblical prognosis of worry is a division of the heart. It's a mistake to try dealing with the issues of today while dwelling on the questions of tomorrow. We need all our energy and concentration for the here and now.

And where do we find Jesus' words on worry? They're right in the center of His teaching on personal possessions. I don't think that's a coincidence. The great overriding issue, after all, is priorities. What is most important to your heart? Those who base their lives on the acquisition of things tend to be the ones saddled with anxiety. But Jesus has a simple prescription: Get your priorities in order. Seek the things of God first; live the righteous life He would have you live. Focus right there, putting aside every distraction. Then, let the chips fall where they may. As you do so, everything you need will materialize ("all these things shall be added to you").

Can it truly be that simple? Could such a formula really work?

If not, then you might as well put your Bible away, for nothing else in it will stand up. This teaching goes to the very heart of the central message of Scripture. But if these words *are* true—as you and I confirm in our hearts—then life can be embraced with joy and exuberance. It's something to enjoy, not to worry about, and the "what ifs" no longer have any power over us.

Most of us know this verse; actually living it is another matter. When I worry, I know I'm guilty of violating the ringing declaration of Matthew 6:33. I know I'm failing to live out my beliefs. Maybe it's that way in your life. Maybe the cycle of worry has become so powerful that you can't seem to break it. If so, then you need to step back from the complex tangle of your life and ask yourself how you've ordered it. What are your priorities? Do you really trust the Father who loves you, or is it all simply lip service? Can you live out your belief that God is sovereign?

Rebuild your system of priorities, with God at the center of the structure. If you build from that brand of brick, you'll be sheltered from the storms of worry and stress.

2. You Need a Strategic Program

"Therefore do not worry about tomorrow, for tomorrow will worry about its own things. Sufficient for the day is its own trouble." (Matthew 6:34)

What we have here may be the most important ammunition of all—a systematic strategy to weed out your worry. Jesus is saying something quite interesting: You won't sink under the burden of today's crises, but tomorrow's agenda puts you over the weight limit. Have you ever tried to carry too many bags of groceries at the same time? After cleaning the eggs from your driveway, you'll know better—and you'll make two trips instead of one. Jesus tells us to carry today's bag today and make a fresh trip tomorrow.

Living in the present tense is an art. Do you know someone who's "not all there," for his or her eyes are focused on some invisible horizon? This person is preoccupied with absent problems. But have you ever known someone who lives completely in the present? Such people seem lively, full of energy and charisma and getting their money's worth out of every new thing that comes along, and you won't catch them worrying. That's how Jesus wants us to live—a day at a time. There's a reason God placed us within the moment, bracketed away from both the past and the future. They're both off-limits to us, and we need to post "No Trespassing" signs. The past is closed for good, and the future is still under construction. But today has everything you need. Come here and make your home.

Many years ago the *Chicago Daily News* carried an article by a prominent physician by the name of Osler who made some wise observations about worry. Throughout his career he had observed the physical effects of worry upon the lives of his patients. And he used an analogy about the careful design of an ocean liner. If the hull of the ship is pierced by means of some collision, the steel doors of the hold can be lowered so that only a portion of the ship is flooded. And then Dr. Osler went on to make this important application. He wrote that we should design our lives just as carefully. We all have our unforeseen collisions, and we must learn how to lower the forward hold doors against dangerous tomorrows; we must lower rear hold doors against the past; and we must learn to live safe and dry in the compartment of today.

> *All the water in the world*
> *However hard it tried,*
> *Could never sink a ship*
> *Unless it got inside.*
> *All the hardships of this world*
> *Might wear you pretty thin,*
> *But they won't hurt you one least bit*
> *Unless you let them in.*
>
> —Anonymous

Don't dwell on tomorrow's stress. Jesus has told us that tomorrow will take care of itself. Take note also of this powerful word:

As your days, *so shall* your strength be. (Deuteronomy 33:25)

As your days go, so goes your strength. What does that mean?

I've walked with the people of my church through bankruptcy, disease, divorce, legal problems, and every variety of trial. People tell me, "I don't know how I can face it." And I'm never insensitive to their anguish; in no way do I minimize their crises. But I do share with them the rich practical wisdom of the Bible: *Leave tomorrow alone.* When that day dawns, God will give you the grace and the strength you need for it. At the present time, you have the grace and the strength He has given you for today. Your calendar gives each day its own number. Live them in that order, just as God arranged them. Stay in one square at a time.

A friend of mine takes his family on long automobile trips across the country. He has two small children, and each day they look forward to the day's "treat." The treat consists of a little bag for each child with an inexpensive surprise—and a Scripture passage. As they undergo each daylong ride, they have a little surprise to look forward to in the form of a simple gift and an eternal truth from God's Word that the family will discuss together as they drive. Life's road trip holds the same for you and me. Each new day will bring a new little package from God, with a little grace-gift to refresh us and the always-present truth of God's Word. But you have to wait for each day to have that package in your hands.

We don't totally ignore the future. We plan and prepare. But calm preparation and obsessed anxiety are two different things. Lower the door in the forward compartment. Shut off the waters of tomorrow that always drain today of its strength.

Mark Twain once said, "I'm an old man and I've known a great many troubles, but most of them never happened." Future-based anxiety is empty.

Don't dwell on yesterday's mess. One thing is always true about yesterday—it's gone. It's complete. It's out of reach, and there's nothing we can do about it. My son was a quarterback in college football, and I can watch videotapes of his wins and losses. Instant replay is a cruel thing when our team doesn't come out on top. No matter how many times I run the tape, our defense misses the tackle or drops the pass or stumbles just short of the goal line. Every time I play it back, something in me thinks that this time the play may come out differently. But once the whistle has blown, the play is over, and we have to let it go.

That's difficult to do sometimes, isn't it? I know believers who have come to Christ from very troubled, perhaps sordid backgrounds. Occasionally the past creeps up on them and the enemy whispers, "Don't forget who you *were* and what you *did*—you haven't really changed." Guilt is powerful. I remind these people of the infinite forgiveness of God. He has placed our past sins as far from us as the east is from the west. God has forgiven.

But still, people insist that they can't forgive themselves. At that point I observe, "That's amazing—you have a standard higher than God's!"

If He can cut away the past, we must be able to do likewise. If you've confessed it, it's been forgiven. Put it away forever and move on; imagine it's been buried in the bottomless ocean of God's grace, and it has no more power over you. You might as well worry about something that happened several hundred thousand years ago, for it has that much relevance.

Don't dwell on yesterday's success. It's possible to feel anxiety about positive things, too. What if there were a time when everything seemed right in your life? What if you received that great award, or had a wonderful experience in your youth, or had a happier period in your family? An aging athlete can think back to the time when he had that little bit of extra speed or endurance that made him an all-star. And we dwell on these things, lamenting the good old days and how they've passed away.

Paul the Apostle, one of the most successful men who ever lived, made an interesting declaration at the close of his life and career. He said that he hadn't achieved his great goal yet, but that he kept his focus on one thing— forgetting what was behind him and pushing forward to the one wonderful thing still before him: the high calling of Christ. Paul could have sat in that prison and lingered in the scrapbook of his memories—the miracles, the young churches, the glorious spread of the gospel at his hands. But he put even those wonderful memories behind him because the future sparkled even brighter.

That's what you and I must do. We must dwell on the miracle of what lies before us today, this moment, this second. All else is dim by comparison.

Don't dwell on yesterday's distress. This could be the hardest thing to do—letting go of our heartbreak.

Everyone is served their cup of sorrow in season. There's no avoiding that in this world. And a considerable portion of my work of ministry is holding the hands of people and walking with them through the valley of the shadow. But I hope I can help them walk finally back into the light, for that valley is no place to build a home. Grief and mourning are clean, biblical emotions, but they're not permanent ones. Every extra day of dwelling in those shadows is a day of joy lost—a day of not seeing the wonderful things God wants us to see.

The important thing is to keep on walking. Don't look over your shoulder to yesterday's happiness or sadness; don't crane your neck to see what may lie beyond the bend in the road. You need to put one foot in front of the other and take one step at a time. Live in the present tense, and make every day a beautiful gift to God, unmarred by the lines and wrinkles of worry. The Lord says to us, in the verse of an anonymous poet,

My name is I AM.

If you live in the past,
It will be very hard,
for I am not there.
My name is not I WAS.

And if you live in the future,
It will be very hard,
For my name is not I WILL BE.
But if you live in the present,
It is not hard,
For my name is I AM.

I saw a sign not too long ago that said, "Free Gas Tomorrow." What a deal! But when I returned the next day, the sign still said the same thing—and tomorrow was still a day away. It's always just beyond our reach. We might as well be fueled by the grace and strength God has made available to us just for this day.

J. Arthur Rank had a system for doing that. He was one of the early pioneers of the film industry in Great Britain, and he also happened to be a devout Christian. Rank found he couldn't push his worries out of his mind completely; they were always slipping back in. So he finally made a pact with God to limit his worrying to Wednesday. He even made himself a little Wednesday Worry Box and he placed it on his desk. Whenever a worry cropped up, Rank wrote it out and dropped it into the Wednesday Worry Box. Would you like to know his amazing discovery? When Wednesday rolled around, he would open that box to find that only a third of the items he had written down were still worth worrying about. The rest had managed to resolve themselves.[1] I challenge you to make a worry box. Take some kind of action against worry.

George McCauslin knew he had to do something. The YMCA director's anxiety problem was a threat to his emotional health. He scheduled an afternoon off from work. With the hours he was putting in, that took a great deal of determination. George drove to the western Pennsylvania woods, a place he associated with peace and tranquillity. He took a long walk, trying to empty his mind and concentrate on the fresh air and the pleasant aromas of nature. It was a good idea. His tight neck was relaxing, and he could feel the slightest few ounces of tension draining away. As he sat beneath a tree and pulled out his notebook, he breathed a long sigh. This was the first time in months he'd felt anything close to relaxation.

George felt as if he and God had grown far apart, so he decided to write his Creator a letter. "Dear God," he began. "Today I hereby resign as general manager of the universe." He read it back to himself and signed it, "Love, George."

George laughs as he tells the story. "And you know what happened? God accepted my resignation."[2]

Daniel, the college student beset by an anxiety-riddled stomach, did much the same thing. He packed up his little car and headed into the mountains for a two-day retreat with nothing but a sleeping bag, a canteen, and a Bible. He asked God to break through his torment during the retreat, and that's what happened. As he read the Gospels, he came to the verse we've already discussed: Matthew 6:33. For the first time, he really understood the vital significance of seeking first the kingdom. And from that moment, he's had a battle plan for challenging his anxiety.

"As we become people who can praise the Lord in spite of our needs," he writes, "He has promised that we will become a people who will find their needs met."[3]

FOUR VERSES, SIX WORDS

I'd like to leave you with some weapons you can use—four verses to help you when your mind is prone to anxiety, and six words to rally around. Copy the following verses down and keep them handy. Better yet, commit them to memory.

- "Call upon Me in the day of trouble; I will deliver you, and you shall glorify Me" (Psalm 50:15).
- "Cast your burden on the LORD, and He shall sustain you; He shall never permit the righteous to be moved" (Psalm 55:22).
- "Casting all your care upon Him, for He cares for you" (1 Peter 5:7).

And here is the pinnacle passage concerning worry:

Be anxious for nothing, but in everything by prayer and supplication, with thanksgiving, let your requests be made known to God; and the peace of God, which surpasses all understanding, will guard your hearts and minds through Christ Jesus. (Philippians 4:6–7)

And what are the Six Words of Wisdom for Worriers?

Worry about nothing—pray about everything!

Make those words your battle cry as you take on the giant of worry.

5

GUARDING AGAINST GUILT

YOU CAN WIN THE BATTLE AND
LIVE VICTORIOUSLY

ROBERT GARTH WAS RUNNING THE RACE, and he felt ready to break away from the pack.

Not that he hadn't been slow off the starting blocks. Robert had been born into a poor family in Detroit. His house was small and his clothes were shabby and shameful to him. But at age fifteen, Robert had found the key to help him escape his limitations. His young body was built for speed; he could run like the wind. And that gift had bought him a ticket to the Junior Olympic tryouts. If he ran well, then his dreams might come true—for him and for all his brothers and sisters. All the fastest sprinters in the region would be at these trials. But he thought of his stained shirt and torn jeans. Now, at his defining moment, how could he walk in rags among the best and the brightest?

It was the night before leaving for the Junior Olympic Trials. Robert sat brooding before the television set, thinking about his gray life. Somehow his thoughts began to drift toward the warehouse where he did a few odd jobs for cash. He began to think about Joseph Moceri, the man who paid him. Mr. Moceri always pulled a thick wad of bills from his back pocket when the job was done. He counted them out carefully as he peeled them off, one by one. It was always cash—and the man was always alone. Those facts suggested certain possibilities, unpleasant possibilities that Robert couldn't stop thinking about.

A picture began to form in Robert's mind—a picture of Mr. Moceri coming into work the next morning, a picture of a shadowy figure lurking

70

behind the door with a blunt object, of the figure knocking Mr. Moceri unconscious and sprinting out the door with the money—sprinting away with the remarkable speed of a track star.

It was an ugly picture, but there was another one that pulled at him. This was a picture of himself at the trials wearing bright, stylish clothing fresh from the best store in the neighborhood.

The next morning at five o'clock, Robert was on his way to the warehouse. He eased behind the door and waited. That's when events began to quickly play out. But they didn't play out in a way that was consistent with the pictures he'd seen in his mind. They didn't play out as they did on TV thrillers. They played out, instead, to disaster.

Mr. Moceri strolled through the warehouse with a coffeepot in his hands. He was moving more slowly and cautiously because of his burden. Robert crept toward him from behind. At the last possible moment, his foot brushed some object on the floor and made a noise—just enough noise to destroy Robert's life. Mr. Moceri quickly whirled around to see a young friend he knew well, one raising a blunt instrument above his head. Sadly, Mr. Moceri said, "Please. I'll give you whatever you want."

Robert hadn't prepared himself for a face-to-face confrontation. This was all wrong, and he panicked. He swung the club furiously at Mr. Moceri's head, knocking him to the floor. Then he knelt and thrust his hand into the unconscious man's pockets, pulled out $67, and hurried away.

That afternoon, Robert was on his way to the Junior Olympics. He knew nothing of the ambulance that rushed Mr. Moceri to the hospital, nor did he know Mr. Moceri would die that night. The next day, he learned it all. That was the beginning of the nightmare.

Robert Garth's performance was less than exceptional at the trials. He came in fourth in the 200-meter sprint, a race he'd been certain he could win. And just like that, the trials were over. It was time to go home.

Back in Detroit, Robert tried to pick up his life where he'd left off. He'd always been pretty popular at school. But it was no good now; nothing felt the same. There was always the secret that isolated him. He had to face it— he was an unrecognized murderer.

His focus on the track was gone. His formerly good grades plummeted. From the awful chaos in his mind there was no escape, with one exception;

there was alcohol. Robert hadn't been much of a drinker in the past, but now he drank as often and as heavily as he could, seeking the blessed oblivion that blocked out his memories, if only temporarily.

Somehow he made it through high school; maybe he could turn the corner. The awful incident was behind him, wasn't it? The important thing was to keep running, to put some miles between himself and the terrible event. In time, perhaps he could forget. Marriage would help. Robert and his high school sweetheart announced their engagement and planned the wedding.

The marriage lasted three years, producing a daughter and nothing else good. The union never had a chance at success, really. The young bride couldn't understand her husband's bleak, morbid moods. What had happened to the old Robert she had loved? Finally, Robert's wife filed divorce papers, packed up her belongings, took their daughter, and moved away.

Robert had few options. He moved back home briefly, but it was only another dead end. He and his father couldn't get along. So he climbed even deeper into the bottle.

He tried other things—moving to another city, moving home again, new jobs, new starts. The track star was running, always running, but there didn't seem to be a finish line and certainly no trophies; just a dark, endless track and a cup of sorrow. The bleak face that greeted him in the mirror had thirty years on it now. There was no trace left of the athletic fifteen-year-old. He often found himself wandering through the city streets like a crazy man, mumbling bitter words to himself. The murder, all those years ago, was still on the books, unsolved. No one suspected the identity of the assailant. Everyone had forgotten.

Everyone except himself. And one night, walking among the alleys, it occurred to him that he was tired of the knowledge—or at least, of knowing it alone. Perhaps he should end it all. Then there would be peace. There would be no more *knowing*.

But he couldn't do it. Deep inside, something directed him toward the other option—the one even more frightening than suicide. Instead of letting *nobody* know, it only seemed right to let *everyone* know. And just like that, Robert found that his feet had changed direction. They were leading him now, he realized, toward police headquarters. Those feet, once so quick, took him slowly through the door and up to the desk.

There, before the clerk, Robert cleared his throat and stated that he'd like to confess to a fifteen-year-old murder.

THE INVISIBLE GIANT

Guilt is a giant with interesting powers. This giant is the most invisible, but the heaviest one of all. There are people all around us who are being slowly crushed, slowly suffocated by the giant of guilt. It kills slowly but with excruciating pain. Think of Judas, hanging from a tree; Shakespeare's Lady Macbeth, with blood on her hands that would never wash away; the expectant woman who aborts her child and lives with remorse for the rest of her life. There are so many stories I could tell, and you could add to the list. But I believe the most powerful one of all is found in the Bible. It plays out in the books of history and then moves through pain and resolution between two psalms. It's the psychodrama concerning a man named David.

David had it all—every good thing life has to offer—and he knew it. For starters, he ruled the greatest nation in the world. He was not only God's anointed, but also the people's choice. Once he had been an obscure young shepherd; now he was the most important man alive.

He could sing beautifully and play musical instruments. He could dance artistically. He was a military hero and a conqueror of armies and antagonists of titanic stature. David had the heart of an artist, the soul of a priest, the mind of a philosopher, and the body of a warrior. Perhaps it was an embarrassment of riches, too much for any one man to be given. In any case, David had finally found an enemy he feared: midlife. He'd grown up in the fields where lions dwelt. He had come of age fleeing for his life, hiding in caves from a jealous king. Whole armies had pursued him. Now he'd made it to the top, but he was bored and restless. He needed a new giant to conquer. Sadly, he found one that got the best of him.

David found himself restless on the battle lines, where he was spending time with the troops. At home, he found he couldn't sleep and he took a stroll on the palace roof. It was there that a sight in the courtyard below caught his eye. There was a woman, a strikingly beautiful one, bathing in the twilight. David couldn't take his eyes away; afterward, he couldn't take his thoughts away. Instead, he sought her out. It all led, of course, to an act of adultery that quickly gave way, as always, to remorse. He sent the woman home and tried to move on. But the whole incident escalated into a nightmare when word came that Bathsheba was pregnant. Everyone knew that her husband was away at battle. They also knew who was home from that battle. David realized his moral authority as a godly king would quickly erode if the truth came out. What could he do?

David settled on a solution that made a transgression into a tragedy. He sent for the husband of Bathsheba, a man named Uriah. David invited him to his quarters for dinner and wine, then sent him down to spend time with his wife. No matter what happened between the couple, this would create a window of opportunity that would erase any suspicion that Bathsheba's child was illegitimate.

But David hadn't allowed for one contingency: the innocence and goodness of the husband. Uriah said, "King David, I wouldn't feel right about spending time with my wife tonight. After all, the other soldiers in my unit are in the trenches right now. Here I am eating at a fine table, drinking palace wine — it's not right for me to enjoy all these luxuries." And so he slept that night on the steps of the palace.

David's plan had gone awry. He couldn't think of what else to do. Finally he gave Uriah a note to carry to the general. The note decreed that Uriah should be sent to the very front lines, the bloodiest ground, then deserted by the troops and left to die. This would produce a pregnant widow who could be quickly married.

After all the wine and the feast, David was sending Bathsheba's husband back to war carrying his own death warrant. Murder and intrigue had been added to adultery. David knew the gravity of his bloody deeds, and he was sentenced to the penalty of living with himself over the next year. In the meantime, we have two records of what transpired in his soul: Psalm 32 and Psalm 51. They should be read in reverse order; 51 shows the excruciating pain of his guilt, and 32 shows his resolution and renewal.

Both psalms give us an intriguing window into David's spiritual journey. And they reveal to us a legacy of silence, sorrow, and secrecy — the telltale marks of the guilty.

THE AGONY OF GUILT: PSALM 32

Silence

When the damage has been done and the guilt sets in, our first impulse is silence. Listen to this somewhat awful description:

> When I kept silent, my bones grew old through my groaning all the day long. (Psalm 32:3)

What else is there in times of guilt, but silence? We can't talk to people, even those closest to us. We can't talk to God. Psalm 66:18 tells us that "if I regard iniquity in my heart, the Lord will not hear." This was no small thing for David, a man who kept counsel with God constantly on every subject. Now a gulf of silence stretched between them. The man after God's own heart found himself exiled from it.

Sometimes the silence can be deafening, can't it? The only sound was David's groaning, and he tells us that his very bones became old through this period. His soul was suffering, and his health began to follow suit—something you can always count on happening.

Sorrow

No one is more eloquent than David on the dimensions of suffering. He writes:

> For day and night Your hand was heavy upon me; my vitality was turned into the drought of summer. (Psalm 32:4)

A great army stood at his beck and call. A palace and a kingdom obeyed his every whim. But his conscience could not be ruled.

David was trapped inside his own guilt. Sorrow overcame him, sapping his life of all its considerable vitality. There was no reason to dance. There were no words to sing. The only poetry he had was the poetry of grief.

Secrecy

As we've seen, guilt is a force of isolation. He couldn't talk to friends. He couldn't talk to God. He was worse than an adulterer—he was someone who would murder to avoid negative publicity. Only Bathsheba and Joab, his trusted adviser, knew the truth. The king spent a year living with an intolerable secret, in psychological exile from God and from people. David, by constitution an open and transparent man, had to face agonies he had never before encountered.

Finally God reached into David's world to offer a way out. He provided something profoundly loving and terribly painful. He sent an accuser.

THE ACCUSATION OF GUILT: 2 SAMUEL 12:1–7

The whole story is laid out for us in the book of 2 Samuel. It tells us that the voice of God came to a man named Nathan who, for all intents and purposes, was David's pastor. He served as the palace prophet. And now Nathan was sent by God to confront sin and corruption at the highest political level. It was a frightening assignment, but it came with the territory.

Nathan was bold, being a prophet, but this was a daunting task all the same. How does one confront a king? Nathan achieved his goal in a very clever way. He told David his own story by way of misdirection, changing the terms and settings. He related current events in the comfortable distance of a parable.

Two men lived in a city, he said, one rich and one poor. One had the finest flock in the kingdom, the other only one little ewe that was something of a family pet. The little lamb was a part of the family, eating from their hands and drinking from their cups. No more than a little lamb, but a beloved one in the life of a poor family.

Meanwhile, the rich man was entertaining a visitor. Dinnertime came around, and the host didn't want to make a withdrawal from the wealth of his own herd. Instead, he thought of the poor man, out there living in that little hut—the man with the single scrawny lamb. He took the man's pet by force, and served it as dinner for his visitor.

David the king sat back and listened with absorption, caught up in the story—for to him, it was no more than a story. He never anticipated the twist in the punch line. He never equated wool with women, or misers with monarchs. All David saw was an outrage to civility. He blurted out to Nathan, "As the LORD lives, the man who has done this shall surely die!" (2 Samuel 12:5).

Nathan, of course, knew that this was a compelling ruling from the king, who was sentencing himself to death.

"David," said Nathan, no doubt pointing a bony finger at the very face of the ruler, "*You* are the man."

What a moment it must have been, as the truth came home to roost. It must have been a stake through the heart. It must have been a public humiliation. And it must have been, in some sense, a relief. Now the thing was out on the table. At least the furtiveness, the secrecy, was over. The solitude of the secret was the worst part. Now there would be public repercussions, but David had come to a place where he could accept that. It was high time to set his house in order.

THE ADMISSION OF GUILT: PSALM 51

Psalm 51 is already one of the most absorbing passages in all of God's Word, but perhaps one of the most intriguing portions is the superscription, that little introduction that often accompanies a psalm. This particular one reads: "A Psalm of David when Nathan the prophet went to him, after he had gone in to Bathsheba."

In other words, we have here the aftermath of Nathan's confrontation. David has been humiliated and confronted with the full gravity of his wickedness. What does a man say to God at such a moment? How does he handle the awful state in which he finds his soul?

He Accepts Full Responsibility for His Sin

It all begins with owning up. Many of us are masters of shifting the blame. It's a natural human impulse, and scapegoats come cheap.

But not David. If you browse through Psalm 51, you're going to find personal pronouns again and again: *I. Me. Mine.* In the passage below, which encompasses the first three verses of the psalm, I've indicated those words with italics:

> Have mercy upon *me*, O God . . .
> Blot out *my* transgressions.
> Wash *me* thoroughly from *my* iniquity,

And cleanse *me* from *my* sin.
For *I* acknowledge *my* transgressions,
And *my* sin is ever before *me*. (Psalm 51:1–3)

There's no mistaking who takes the rap, is there? It's refreshing to see. Today, it's easier to blame our subordinates, or the board of trustees, or the media, or stress, or society, or an unhappy childhood. Most of us don't herd sheep anymore, but we keep plenty of scapegoats on hand.

Don't overlook the importance of this starting point. The journey of recovery starts here or nowhere. You've got to own up to what you've done. President Truman kept that famous plaque on his desk that said, "The buck stops here." David, a commander in chief himself, knew the significance of that philosophy. To push away guilt is to ensure, ironically enough, that it goes nowhere. You must embrace it to distance yourself from it.

He Acknowledges the Sinfulness of Sin

Another pet coping device we often use is to minimize the transgression. "Oh, it was no big deal," we say. Think of the rationalizations David might have used: *I was dealing with stress. I simply made a poor decision, but it was an isolated incident. It was a learning opportunity, really. The man was bound to die in battle anyway—I'm his commander, after all. The woman was beautiful, and the king is entitled to beautiful wives. A king must be a little ruthless to be successful in today's tribal environment.*

Most people would carefully choose words that mitigated the damage and toned down the rhetoric. David's vocabulary, however, isn't like that at all. He chooses four significant words to take in the scope of his actions.

- The first is *transgressions* (vv. 1, 3). The word is one of moral gravity; it means a revolt against the law. "Lord," David is saying, "I've rebelled against Your laws."

- The second is *iniquity*, a word capturing the perversity of man's nature.

- The third is *sin*, a word needing no introduction. It means "to miss the mark."

- The fourth is *evil,* which sums up the whole sordid mess—a vile thing worthy only of condemnation.

Transgressions. Iniquity. Sin. Evil.

When you've failed to live by God's standards, listen carefully to your language. Ask your spouse or your best friend to listen for you. Do you use words with the gravity of these four, or do you use words like *stress* and *circumstances* and *unavoidable* and *this is how God made me?*

The concept of confession comes into play. Confession is all about naked honesty before God or before fellow Christians. It means describing our actions with the same words God uses, and no dissembling or distortion. Confession will not allow us to foolishly hide, as Adam and Eve did in the Garden; it will force us to change from the inside out. "The sacrifices of God *are* a broken spirit, a broken and a contrite heart—these, O God, You will not despise" (Psalm 51:17). David knew what it meant for his actions to be despised by God. The act of confession was intensely painful and thoroughly liberating.

It's helpful here to make a side trip to Psalm 32. In verse 5 David looks back at his painful prayer of confession, and he makes this observation about it: "I acknowledged my sin to You, and my iniquity I have not hidden. I said, 'I will confess my transgressions to the LORD,' and You forgave the iniquity of my sin."

David is describing a breakthrough moment—the moment in which we come clean, acknowledging the awful truth. Finally we can say we have done something right. Finally the door is open again to transactions with our heavenly Father.

In 1973 Dr. Karl Menninger, a psychologist, wrote the book *Whatever Became of Sin?* But his prophetic title is truer now than it was nearly thirty years ago. The word is out of step with the times, isn't it? There are no sins, only "personal decisions." Actions once forbidden are now the subjects of TV sitcoms. And if someone does happen to do something our culture can't accept, then it's shrugged away as a result of nature or nurture. In every era between the biblical world and this one, sin was despised. One might be so conscious of a serious sin that he agonized over losing his salvation. If those generations needed a better grasp of grace, it is our time that needs a better sense of *sin* — its blackness, its filth, its ability to exile us from the presence of our loving Father.

Sociologist James Davison Hunter observes that schoolteachers no longer say things like, "Stop it, please! You're disturbing the class!" No, that would be too "judgmental" by current standards. If Johnny is involved in some destructive activity in the classroom, today's young teacher is more likely to say, "What are you doing? Why are you doing it? How does doing it make you feel?"[1]

We can only grimace when Hunter points out that the word *sin* has retreated mostly to dessert menus. Butterscotch Binge and Fudge Fandango are *sinful*, according to the menus. And that's supposed to be a *good* thing. But when it comes to lying and adultery — we *fudge*, of course. We choose careful euphemisms for discussing our iniquities. "I didn't lie. I presented a subject interpretation," or "I ended the marriage so we could better fulfill our independent goals."

By scrubbing the word *sin* out of the vocabulary of everyday life, we've actually deprived people of the doorway to healing. There's no way to be made well unless we first acknowledge the reality of sin. Apart from this, your situation is hopeless.

He Addresses His Confession to God

David then addresses the true victim. He writes:

Against You, You only, have I sinned, and done *this* evil in Your sight.
(Psalm 51:4)

That prayer is very wise. After acknowledging the reality of sin, the second step is to turn our face toward God. All sin is an offense first and foremost against Him, even when there's a human victim.

David knows painfully well how Bathsheba has been manipulated — used sexually, made a widow and subsequently the bride of her husband's killer. David knows that Uriah has been deprived of his very life. Even Joab has been wronged, for he was forced to compromise his integrity by following the orders of his king. And we must also mention the little boy born to David and Bathsheba, who was yet another victim of David's ruthlessness. All of these have borne the brunt of David's sin.

But confession must first be directed above. David recognized that at the root of every sin, from the pettiest offense to murder, is an insult to the God who created us and sustains us every moment of our lives. Before the sin claims any victims, it has already been an injury to the person of God, who set out laws to guide us. David therefore said to God, "against You and You only I have sinned." At the deepest level it's "only God," and that's why, when it comes to forgiveness, it's *also* "only God." No one else can redeem except Him. If you sin against me I can forgive you personally, but I can't remove your guilt. I can't give you that deeper level of forgiveness, because I can't remove the offense against the Lord. Only He can do that.

David acknowledged his sin; he addressed his confession to God.

THE ANSWER TO GUILT: PSALM 51:2-12

Removing the Sin

Now David turns his attention to the issue of cleansing.

Wash me thoroughly from my iniquity, and cleanse me from my sin. (Psalm 51:2)

Five verses later, he adds, "Purge me with hyssop, and I shall be clean; wash me, and I shall be whiter than snow." Have you ever been out after a day's outdoor work in the summer heat, and you long for a bath or shower more than anything else? David feels that way inside. He knows the full extent of his filthiness, and he knows that only God can wash the filth deep within.

"Blot out all my iniquities," he pleads in verse 9. Again and again he repeats this idea. This is more than lip service—this is genuine, remorseful petition. He speaks of his sin and God's forgiveness with the same depth of intensity. If moral degradation is unthinkable, then forgiveness is all the more blessed. David is humble, honest, and wholehearted. Sin is a stain to the soul, and the king uses the same Hebrew word for *cleanse* that might have been applied to the cleansing of a leper—serious cleansing indeed. "I'm a leper of the soul," he says of himself with relentless honesty. "Make me clean again."

In verse 7 we find this word *hyssop*. An interesting Old Testament custom is worth relating here. Purity, as we know, was a crucial issue to the Jews. The law required that when a person came into contact with a corpse, he had to be ceremoniously cleansed with hyssop. David is thinking of Uriah. He has been dealing in death, and he must be cleaned to satisfy the fullest demands of the law.

"Lord," he continues, "blot out all my iniquities." Why *blot*? Most sins were handled in the manner of transactions. If you committed some offense, you could perform some kind of sacrifice to make atonement. But there were two sins with no remedy: adultery and murder. David had committed both of these, and they were written in God's great book in red letters. There was nothing David could do, no sacrifice to make, no atonement to seek. The accusing page was beyond his reach. All he could do was fall upon the mercy of God to blot out that red ink. *Wipe it away completely, Lord!*

No priest, of course, could do that. Only God had the solvent, then and now.

Restoring the Joy

Unfinished business of the soul takes its toll on our lives. David had not, prior to now, confronted the demons within him. He had not come to terms with them, and he had paid the price in misery for a year. For twelve months, the very vitality of his life had been seeping away. Now he comes to God and asks Him to do more than offer forgiveness. He asks God to restore his joy. In verses 8 and 12 he writes, "Make me to hear joy and gladness, *that* the bones which You have broken may rejoice . . . Restore to me the joy of Your salvation, and uphold me with *Your* generous Spirit."

Notice David doesn't ask for his salvation to be restored; that will come next. What he wants back is the *joy* of it, the liberation and freedom of living the redeemed life. We can't lose our salvation, but we can certainly lose some of the fringe benefits. Some of us do things that displease God, and we never face up to them. The time comes when we realize our lives are grim and joyless. When that happens, we need to check the backlog for unconfessed sin. Something is standing between God and us, and we need the joy of our salvation restored. The non-Christian, of course, would never know the difference; he or she has *always* lived without God. But the believer who "backslides," as we used to say, is aware of something missing—the unique, boundless joy of walking in the Spirit.

Renewing the Fellowship

"Do not cast me away from Your presence," David writes in verse 11, "and do not take Your Holy Spirit from me."

Imagine it: *cast away from the presence of God.* This would be the description of a soul eternally lost—a soul castaway! David prays to avoid such a destiny. He pleads with God not to remove His Holy Spirit from him.

The Bible tells us that on the day when David was crowned king, God removed His Spirit from Saul and filled David instead. The new king was mindful of Saul's great sin and the ugly consequences. Saul had become a soul castaway, and God had finally set him adrift. You can imagine that these things are running through David's mind as he offers this prayer. *Please, Lord. Don't let me go the way of Saul. Don't set me adrift! Don't take Your Holy Spirit from me.*

Refocusing on the Future

"Uphold me *with Your* generous Spirit" (v. 12). David is asking God to bolster him in the future, to help him learn from his tragic mistakes. He never wants to go through this again. Having dealt thoroughly with the sin, brought it before God, experienced cleansing, and sought the restoration of joy, the time comes to look to the future.

There's a beautiful spiritual principle known as a *covenant.* Covenants often follow times of forgiveness and restoration. We say, "Lord, I can see the folly of my ways. You've saved me from myself. Now it's time for me to make a solemn promise that I'll be responsible for my actions. I'll never let this happen again." It's a time to put it into words. It's a time to write it on paper. It's a time to hold yourself accountable. But it's also a time to seek deeper strength from God. *Uphold me, Lord. Let me depend so thoroughly on Your guidance that such a failure will be unthinkable in the future.*

In Psalm 32, we see how David's thinking has changed. "Blessed is *he whose* transgression is forgiven, *whose* sin *is* covered. Blessed *is* the man to whom the LORD does not impute iniquity, and in whose spirit *there is* no deceit" (vv. 1–2).

The word *blessed* is another word for *happy*. *Happy* is that man whose sin is forgiven. The truth here is so incredible, so revolutionary, that your life is bound to be changed forever if you will only grasp it. *No sin outweighs the forgiveness of God.* If I were you, I'd read that sentence slowly, several times; I'd contemplate it carefully.

Someone reading this book might have committed a murder in the past—you could be reading from a prison cell. Some of you have committed adultery. Many of you have damaged and betrayed those closest to you, just as David did. The only two things I know for certain about you are that you've sinned seriously and that God's mercy is even more powerful. It's a great, boundless sea that will engulf the worst atrocities we can imagine. It doesn't matter what others may tell you or how they may make you feel. It doesn't matter how you yourself feel about it.

What matters is God's response, for He's the ultimate victim of every sin ever committed. And He sent His Son to pay the price for each one of them. His message to you is, "I no longer know your guilt. I don't want you to know it, either. I want you to live in a new way with Me, in a fellowship so rich that it will overflow and overcome your old sinful tendencies."

THE BURDEN OF A LIFETIME

When we read David's appalling story, we react as he did when he heard the sheep tale. We say, "This is an outrage! The man must die!"

And then, like David, we realize with a shock that we're talking about ourselves. We, too, have multiplied our transgressions. We would do well to face up to the full magnitude of our guilt, as David has, and embrace the full magnitude of His forgiveness. I learned that lesson in the school of experience.

As a high school student, I worked for a hardware store in Cedarville, Ohio. Fred Lutenberger ran the store—a fine man and a tough taskmaster. He sent me to the attic to clean the oily metal shavings from pipe threading, and each night I came home filthy. The work wasn't fun; I felt I was getting the lowest assignments.

One day I was hard at work when a customer came in to make a purchase. No one was there to help him but me, so we made the twenty-dollar transaction. Stuffing the bill into my pocket instead of the cash register, I returned to my labor. I was in a hurry to be finished. When I arrived home, I found the store's twenty dollars still in my pocket. It hadn't been theft on my part—just an honest mistake. And yet, I got to thinking. This was a lot of money for those times. I was a teenager without much, and here was this boss underpaying me for hard labor. Why, he required overtime and didn't pay me for it. I was able to create in my mind a complex rationale for keeping the money.

So I kept the money and went on about my life. But the strangest thing happened. I didn't think about the money except in those times when I wanted to do something for God. And then the issue of the twenty dollars always sprang into my mind. It weighed upon me. But the problem was that any way I could think of to make restitution would embarrass me, as well as my father, who was the president of a local Christian college. Like David, I had entangled myself in a mess. My new rationale was that I was protecting my father from embarrassment by not returning the money.

Time passed; I attended seminary and married. Soon we accepted our first ministerial calling in Haddon Heights, New Jersey, working with youth. One day I received an invitation to speak to the young people at a Bible Club camp. So I set off alone for Upper Darby, Pennsylvania, in my car. During that trip, the old incident of the twenty dollars arose from the grave where I'd attempted to bury it. All the suppressed guilt came back, and I was over-whelmed with remorse. On a car trip alone there's a lot of time to think and nowhere to hide. You can't turn the radio loud enough to drown out a con-science.

I found myself computing the interest on twenty dollars over the inter-vening years. Soon I pulled over in a small town and pulled sixty dollars in traveling money from my pocket. I stuffed it all into an envelope and made out the address, without any note, to that old hardware store in Cedarville. An anonymous restitution. *Now*, I thought, *I can have peace.*

I'd repaid the money. I'd even been on the generous side in estimating the interest. But there were things I hadn't done, too. I hadn't confessed the sin. I hadn't asked for forgiveness. I hadn't moved through the steps that David laid out for us in these psalms. I found that the blot on my hand hadn't washed away.

More years passed, and I became a pastor in Fort Wayne, Indiana. One day the hardware dealers came into town for a convention. So there I stood at the pulpit when the sanctuary door swung open and in came Mr. and Mrs. Fred Lutenberger. It was as if Nathan himself were coming down the aisle of my church, pointing his bony finger right at me.

The Lutenbergers found a seat in the third row. I can assure you I didn't do my best preaching that day. I couldn't help wanting the service to be over as soon as possible. After the sermon, there was a brief invitation. Then I came down and found the couple. "Come with me," I whispered as I took each of them by the hand. I led the Lutenbergers to my study and asked, "Do you ever remember receiving an envelope with sixty dollars and no explanation?"

Fred Lutenberger nodded and looked at his wife. "Yes, as a matter of fact. That was a strange thing."

Then I lost my composure. I began to weep as I told them the whole story. I'd been carrying the burden for all these years. A little thing—a few dollars—is enough, over time, to bring about misery, even destroy a life. I confessed everything, and begged for the Lutenbergers' forgiveness. They quickly wrapped their arms around me and told me they loved me. They thanked me for doing the right thing. And I felt such joy that it's difficult to put into words. I felt light enough to dance. An old, heavy weight had been lifted, and I was free.

> Blessed is *he whose* transgression *is* forgiven, whose sin is covered. (Psalm 32:1)

In a little cell in Detroit, Robert Garth, former track star and confessed murderer, marked time. He was at peace even as the detectives were in turmoil, racing around to check facts and pore over old files.

Robert's shocking story did check out, of course—every detail. Only one element made no sense to the detectives: Why would a murderer, who'd committed a perfect crime, come forward to implicate himself fifteen years later? He'd pulled it off; *no one* had known.

But someone had known, of course; the person who mattered most of all. Now that person was free, at least from the solitude of the secret. He was actually able to concentrate on the book that someone had handed him: a Bible. The section of the Book that drew him irresistibly was the book of Psalms. It was as if someone had been recording his thoughts over the years, an x-ray of his soul. This King David had wandered down the same dark alleys of guilt, the same boulevards of despair—but he had found a way out. Robert read about a God of forgiveness who could shoulder the heaviest, deadliest burden. He found the promise of true liberation. David was a murderer like himself, and God loved him nonetheless.

It was too good to be true, but Robert knew in his heart it *was* true. He couldn't contain his joy, and finally his feelings overflowed in a great shout that echoed through the barred corridor. He'd have to be careful about that—they already thought he'd taken leave of his senses just for confessing. He didn't want to be moved to a psychiatric ward.

The trial judge, seeing Robert's remarkable remorse, was lenient. This defendant was his own accuser; he might have escaped, but he had made a full confession and accepted the consequences. The sentence was a short one for a murder case.

"My time in prison," Robert would later say, "was easy—compared to the fifteen years I lived with that crime in my mind . . . Nothing they could ever do to me, even incarcerating me for the rest of my life, could measure up to the imprisonment of my own guilt during the fifteen years of hiding my sin."

Guilt is a giant of terrible weight. But Robert finally brought down that giant with a shout of joy. For the first time in years, his feet felt light again— light enough to sprint all the way to the throne of the One who forgave him.[2]

Now he was truly ready to run the race and claim the prize. Let's you and I run beside him.

6

Taming Your Temptation

YOU CAN WIN THE BATTLE AND
LIVE VICTORIOUSLY

An honorable life is a precarious thing, constructed throughout a lifetime by the bricks of integrity and the mortar of self-control. From the outside, it appears sturdy enough to withstand a tempest. But the weak spots are found within; it can all come toppling down in one weak moment.

Tyrone can quote you chapter and verse on that subject, and with a touch of poetry. Tyrone is an eloquent young man; he has the wistful soul and observant eye of a writer. But there's not much to observe from the confinement of a prison cell. Mostly he sees the same old story played out in countless variations on an ancient theme. The title of that story is "I Didn't Walk Away."

Take the case of J. W., Tyrone's old cellmate. "He strutted in here thinking this place is a weekend retreat," Tyrone says. "He still had his homeboys. His girlfriend sent money. His mom visited regularly, and he sported Air Jordans, DKNY gear, and Ray-Bans. He pumped gangster rap all day, and for a couple of years he experienced little pain."

J. W. didn't appear concerned when his family couldn't afford an attorney, nor when he got the news about the public defender's office being so backed up that his appeal was unlikely to see the light of day. J. W.'s ice-cold demeanor melted only a degree or two when his girlfriend stopped answering his letters and calls. He simply shrugged when his parents and siblings resumed their lives and put him out of their minds.

But time alone has the power to erode a young man's surface—time and the sameness of the walls, the drudgery of dollar-a-day labor, and the daily struggle to survive the other ice-cold customers. In time, J. W. would be just like the rest: a lost child, a broken soul with little more than regret.

Shifting forward on his cot, Tyrone looks into your eye and offers the message straight up: "I'm serving time in maximum security because I had too much pride to walk away," he says. "I can only hope that God Almighty will have mercy on me and allow me to one day be a father to my children; to treat my mother to dinner on her birthday; to taste soft ice cream—the simple joys of life.

"Whatever you may be facing," he says, "it isn't worth the price of your freedom. Learn to walk away—unless, of course, you want to be my next cell-buddy."

Tom was just the kind of guy any church would appoint to teach college Sunday school. A gifted minister, he had never attended high school; he had dropped out to play in a rock band. Years later, as a believer with more maturity, he had amazing chemistry with young people. He was a vocational minister specializing in college ministry, and a good one. Students would often bring their friends to hear him teach and to meet him after class.

Tom labored to build an honorable life and ministry. But one day a threat loomed on the horizon. One of the young ladies introduced a friend, they chatted briefly, and Tom felt it immediately: a powerful physical attraction. He was almost certain an invitation flickered in her eye, and he worried about what might be revealed in his own. Tom didn't like the thoughts and what-ifs that quickly seeped into his head. He cut off the conversation politely and turned his attention toward others in the meet-and-greet circle.

But the rest of the day, those thoughts kept returning. Well into the next week, he found himself thinking of the attractive girl. Tom was married, mature, and proud of his ability to minister to college kids of *both* genders. He spent time daily with God; how could he doubt his ability to handle such basic relationships? He had a daughter not much younger than some of these coeds. These students could practically be his own children; in a sense, that's exactly what they were.

And yet, in the very face of reason and wisdom, the thoughts persisted. Tom couldn't dispel his fantasies, even when he shared them with God, even when he avoided the presence of the girl in question, even when he recited the appropriate Bible verses. Intentionally trying not to think about her was like trying not to think of a polka-dot elephant. He couldn't master his mind.

Tom wondered if he would be able to master his actions.[1]

The deceiver was once among God's most beautiful creations. But he fell, and now he spends every moment contemplating revenge against his punisher. There is one simple way, he knows, to break the heart of God. Cut Him off from His own children. And he has one deadly weapon for that one demonic goal. It's called temptation, and the devil uses it over and over like a battering ram, hammering at the fortresses of our lives until he can finally create a breach.

All he needs is a small opening; that's all it takes to topple a life of honor. That's all it takes to poison the well of living water in our souls. That's all it takes to send a message to the world that one more so-called believer has fallen, and the rest of us might as well give up and give in to the pleasures of the world.

TEMPTATION'S TARGET

We should never be surprised when temptation knocks at the door of the church. That's Satan's most strategic target. He hammers at the pastor, hammers at the deacons and other church leaders, hammers at the ordinary Christians who sit in the pews and seek godly lives. We admire and aspire to be like the first Christians, but they struggled just as we do. For evidence of that we need only open our Bibles to 1 Corinthians. There we find the story of a church plagued by moral failure—a church filled with men and women who didn't know when to walk away. Paul's words for those people are words for you and me.

> Therefore let him who thinks he stands take heed lest he fall. No temptation has overtaken you except such as is common to man; but God *is* faithful, who will not allow you to be tempted beyond what you are able, but with the temptation will also make the way of escape, that you may be able to bear it. Therefore, my beloved, flee from idolatry. (1 Corinthians 10:12–14)

The town of Corinth was a fine target. The devil must have laughed. Here was one of the most wicked cities in the first-century world. The Christians were starting up one of their churches, but these churches were composed of people who were products of that culture of decadence. If they wanted to follow the way of Jesus, just look at the habits and customs they would have to give up!

It's easy for me to imagine that one day Paul must have received a letter from some young man in Corinth. The letter may have said something like, "Sir, I gave my heart to Christ, just in the way you taught us. I made the commitment, and I understood that Jesus would come into my heart and mind—that I would be a new creature. Then why is it that I still want to do all the old things? My mind and my appetites are the same as they ever were. Frankly, I'm disappointed. I thought Jesus would make me strong."

Perhaps there was a young man like that, and perhaps Paul had him in mind when he wrote this section of his letter dealing with new life and old appetites.

THE COMMON EXPERIENCE OF TEMPTATION

Before anything else, we must see Paul's point: "No temptation has over-taken you except such as is common to man." These are words of reassurance: Whatever you're going through, please remember that you're not the only person to pass that way. You're in good company. Countless people have felt the pull of the temptation that now tugs at *you.*

That's something we tend to forget in the heat of the moment. We feel isolated. Our universe is reduced to an appetite and an object. The devil has a way of slipping the blinders onto our heads so that we see nothing else. But Paul is saying, in essence, that temptation is the oldest trick in the book. It's a "humanity thing," it comes with the territory, and we simply need to rely on God's power. There even happens to be an encyclopedia of every conceivable temptation, and it's called the Bible. Throughout its pages are woven the stories of men and women struggling with tempta-tion—some, like Samson, who were consumed; others, like Daniel, who stood firm.

What about Jesus? He was tempted, too. Hebrews 4:15 tells us that "we do not have a High Priest who cannot sympathize with our weaknesses, but was in all *points* tempted as *we are*, yet without sin." That means the holiest Man to ever walk this earth felt every urge we feel. But He never gave in— He never sinned. Temptation, you see, is not sin. That's a very crucial point that many of us manage to miss. I counsel people who feel defeated before they begin, simply because temptation knocked upon their door. Again, that's the devil's doing. He's saying, "You're already beaten," when the truth is that temptation itself is neutral. The sin comes in the yielding.

J. Wilbur Chapman once said, "Temptation is the tempter looking through the keyhole into the room where you're living; sin is your drawing back the bolt and making it possible for him to enter." You can't avoid someone coming to your door or looking through the keyhole—but you do control the deadbolt.

Temptation is a fork in the road. It's the presentation of a choice of which road to travel: the high one or the low one. Wouldn't life be easier if there were no forks, no decisions to make—if the road were simply a straight and narrow path? But the Bible gives us no magic formulas for that kind of life. It assures us that we'll come to those forks regularly, and we must choose where to step. Some forks will lead down roads of sexuality, some of gluttony, some of materialism, of revenge, and there are too many more to name. If we could see the road map, it might look like a plate of spaghetti.

As a matter of fact, the wiser and more mature in Christ we become, the more treacherous and subtle are the choices. They don't become easier but more difficult, for the devil is no fool. The advanced level earns you advanced opposition. The important thing to remember is that you're walking with the Lord on that journey. He will hold your hand, and He will never fail to point out the direction that's right and true.

It never becomes easier, but it becomes more rewarding. The founder of Dallas Theological Seminary, Dr. Lewis Sperry Chafer, used to say that committed Christians are placed on the front lines of the battle. It's the place where the enemy's fiercest pressure is felt, but it also offers the best view of his crushing defeat. You'll never grow beyond the power of temptation. You'll see it in ever-new, more devious forms. But your eyes will be filled with the glorious sights God reserves for those who follow Him with the utmost devotion.

We may walk an uphill road, but we walk it with plenty of company—with fellow believers, a cloud of witnesses from the past, and with God Himself.

THE CONTROLLED ENVIRONMENT OF TEMPTATION

Notice Paul's words: "But God is faithful, who will not allow you to be tempted beyond what you are able" (1 Corinthians 10:13). A crucial contingency is set out for us here.

It's clear that God allows temptation in our lives for many reasons. But as He does so, we have His promise that He places a limitation on the intensity of the temptation. He knows our capacity in every area; He knows what we can bear, and exactly where the limits to our endurance lie. If you hear someone say, "I was overcome by temptation; it was more than I could withstand," don't believe a word of it. That person had better come up with some other excuse, because the clear biblical truth is that God allows only temptations we *can* handle. The issue is not based on our impression of our limits, but on His precise understanding of them. He's the One who set the valves on them, after all.

If we're planning to give in, we have to concede that we do so by free will. It's never out of our control. As a matter of fact, Paul reveals the secret of that in another passage, written to the same church. In his second letter to Corinth, he says:

> For we do not want you to be ignorant, brethren, of our trouble which came to us in Asia: that we were burdened beyond measure, above strength, so that we despaired even of life. Yes, we had the sentence of death in ourselves, that we should not trust in ourselves but in God who raises the dead, who delivered us from so great a death, and does deliver us; in whom we trust that He will still deliver *us*. (2 Corinthians 1:8–10)

"Burdened beyond measure . . . above strength." Paul tells us that you may reach the point when you would just as soon die, but we happen to be under the care of a God who raises the dead. The trouble may be intense, but God's love is immense. Never worry about the limits of your strength—it's all about *God's* strength. You'll never be tested beyond your endurance because you can rely on *His* endurance.

When you're facing temptation, stand firm. Know that Christ has been there, that His Spirit is with you now, that God is strong enough to pull you through it. With those truths in your grasp, you'll experience victory over temptation every single time.

Remember also that we actually need these tests. Did you know that? Yes, we need them because they help us demonstrate our love for Christ. In school, you need to take a test occasionally to prove what you've learned. Otherwise there'd be no measure; otherwise you wouldn't even have to study and grow wiser in the subject. Life is the same way. Without the occasional test, how could we measure our growth in Christ? Why would we even need to depend on Him? Every one of us could run the perfect race, and what would it mean? Nothing at all. But when we have every possibility of stumbling, every possibility of choosing the wrong path, and we stand tall and walk wisely just the same, God is glorified in this world and in the next. The angels stop, put down their harps, and applaud!

No wonder God allows us to walk through these valleys.

THE CERTAIN ESCAPE FROM TEMPTATION

"But with the temptation," Paul writes, "[God] will also make the way of escape, that you may be able to bear it" (1 Corinthians 10:13).

When it comes to temptation, God begins with the end in mind. He already knows exactly how we can escape. We tend to think of Him as watching us anxiously, perhaps ready to throw down a rope ladder if things become tense. But in truth, God has it all mapped out—and He had it done long before you and I were born. He knows our circumstances; He knows our character; He knows the plan that will provide victory and new maturity. As your crisis unfolds, God has already provided the way of escape you need. Please engrave that into your heart so you'll remember it the moment you're tempted. The escape hatch is nearby, and the door is open.

And why? Hebrews 2:18 tells us that as Christ suffered, He can help us through our sufferings. Because He walked the road of temptation, He knows the right and wrong turns. "I know exactly what you're facing," Jesus says with an arm around your shoulders. "Follow Me—let Me show you a way out of here—that I found myself."

Over time I believe I've discovered that temptation isn't so much a matter of what we *do*, but of whom we *love*. Knowing Christ—really knowing Him, not simply knowing *about* Him—changes everything. More often than not, power in the time of temptation comes because we've filled our minds with His magnificence, and there's no room for the world's shabby offerings. There's power in the name of Christ, and there's power in His presence as well.

Worship and fellowship with God in the morning actually make it difficult to walk right out into the world and commit some transgression. Knowing that we've just been in the presence of the Lord of creation, and that we're carrying Him with us, makes it very difficult to sink to our lowest levels. The best escape Jesus provides is His own embrace.

I challenge you to think about the times when you've been tempted. Perhaps it was a serious moral issue, or only a second helping of dessert you didn't need. Whatever the gravity of the iniquity, I submit that you were aware of a defining moment in the instant of decision. The way of escape was, in that moment, made clear to you. Can you remember? There's always a point at which the still, small voice whispers to us with the directions out of the maze. A thought rushes through the head: *This is wrong. I can avoid this.* And right there, we have our best opportunity to walk away. But if we push that moment aside, if we permit the birds of temptation to nest in our hair (in Martin Luther's memorable analogy), then victory becomes more and more difficult.

When you see the Exit sign glowing in the dark, push it open and make tracks. Missionary Jim Elliot said, "Don't put yourself in a position to see how good your resistance is. When you feel temptation coming, get out of there!"

The Greek word for *escape* in 1 Corinthians had the connotation of a narrow passage out of a treacherous canyon. In California, where I live, we have a few areas of rugged landscape, so I have a good mental picture of this idea. You might climb down into a canyon and find yourself trapped. You're grateful to find the narrow way out. Paul says that if you see that little path, don't walk past it! You'll never pass this way again, but will sink deeper and deeper into the abyss.

Those drawn to the possibility of adultery will affirm the defining moment—the window of best opportunity for escape. In your business, perhaps you've had a working relationship with someone of the opposite sex. You're married; perhaps he or she is, too. It all begins with a friendship that moves a bit too far, too close, too fast. The time comes when you realize where this thing is heading. So does the other person. It's there in the eyes, in the body language, in what is said and what is not said. You have that moment when you know you can walk away safely—and if you ignore the warning lights, it will be that much harder to put on the brakes later. So often, this is your way of escape, provided by God, prompted by His Holy Spirit. Ignore it at your own peril—but never claim that you didn't see it coming.

TEMPTATION-TAMER'S CHECKLIST

Let's be very practical. I'd like to offer you an arsenal of weapons to use against temptation, right there on the battlefield.

✓ Recognize the Possibility of Temptation

Forewarned is forearmed. Never fall into the trap of false security. If I've heard this once, I've heard it a thousand times: "I can't believe it happened to me!"

Oh, really? Why *not* you? If the Son of God could experience every single temptation known to man, that should be a clue that you're not bigger than the system. People believe that their commitment to Christ, their spirituality, their knowledge of the Bible, or their church attendance will place them beyond temptation. It simply isn't true. In battle, the enemy's best weapon is surprise. Don't let the devil sneak up on you.

Remember the first words of our passage? "Therefore let him who thinks he stands take heed lest he fall" (1 Corinthians 10:12). In other words, as soon as you flex your muscles and begin to admire yourself in the mirror, that's the best moment for someone to pull the rug out from under you! Remember the advance billing of the *Titanic*? "Even God couldn't sink it." The truth is that if you drift into arrogance, not even God can get through to you. So avoid those delusions of spiritual grandeur.

Dr. Howard Hendricks was my professor at Dallas Seminary, and he remains a close friend today. He used to carry a little notebook around in his pocket. It listed the names of ministers and students from his classes who had fallen into sexual temptation and out of the ministry. At one time, he said, there were more than a hundred names on that list. One day as he was looking through the list, he began to wonder what all those poor souls on the casualty list had in common. These were names he knew—friends, students. He pored over them again and concluded that *all*, with the exception of two, shared in common a spirit of pride and arrogance.

Proverbs 16:18 tells us that pride precedes destruction, and a haughty spirit leads to a fall.

✓ Request Help in Time of Temptation

Twice in the New Testament, Jesus tells us to pray about temptation. We're well-advised to take those two admonitions seriously. First we have the Lord's Prayer, which includes, "And do not lead us into temptation, but deliver us from the evil one" (Matthew 6:13). Second we have Matthew 26:41, in which Jesus said to "watch and pray, lest you enter into temptation."

Watch and pray. The idea is to be alert. We need to begin every day asking God to sharpen our antennae toward the devil's ploys. We want God to help us see through the devil's bait-and-switch tactics, and to discern the spiritual reality and its consequences. We should also ask God to make us sensitive to that moment of awareness, the escape hatch that offers safety.

Otherwise, temptation springs upon us without warning. It will catch us at our very worst. If we knew that heavy anvils were falling out of buildings today, we'd walk down the city street with our neck craned, watching the windows. Every day carries hazards for the Christian. We need to pray constantly for awareness and strength.

✓ Resist the Devil and He Will Flee from You

The Bible tells us to stand firm and hold out. James 4:7 promises us that if we resist the devil, he will flee. There is a variety of ways to see that delightful sight of the enemy hightailing it away.

First, we can take into our hands the sword of the Spirit, which is the

Word of God. That's what Jesus did, if you remember His wilderness temptation with the devil. As I study that passage, I smile because Jesus fired Scripture at the devil—but He only used ammunition from Deuteronomy. He defended Himself with only one book!

The result of it, as the Scriptures tell us, is that Satan departed from Him. That's another word for *fled*. Resist the devil and you'll be treated to the sight of his back as he runs away. Recognize, request help, resist.

✓ Retreat from Certain Kinds of Temptation

Wise believers recognize that there are degrees of difference in the perils we face. Good military leaders recognize this same principle: There is a time to resist and a time to *retreat*. Sometimes we need to see the devil flee; sometimes we need to do the fleeing. "There are several good protections against temptations," Mark Twain said, "but the surest is cowardice." There are times when *cowardice* is another word for *wisdom*. The Bible gives us three kinds of sins to flee.

1. *Flee from idolatry.* "Therefore my beloved, flee from idolatry" (1 Corinthians 10:14). This is from the very passage we're studying in this chapter.

An idol is anything that comes between you and God. Anything of value to you could be an idol. When you begin to realize that something is taking the place of God in your life, you don't need to sit and ponder it. You don't need to write a thesis or call a meeting about it. You need to flee! Every moment of personal idolatry is a moment of spiritual danger. It is wear and tear on your soul. Flee from idolatry.

2. *Flee from immorality.* Twice in the New Testament we are told to turn tail and run when confronted with immorality:

Flee sexual immorality. (1 Corinthians 6:18)

Flee . . . youthful lusts. (2 Timothy 2:22)

Sexual temptation is a demonic trump card; there's something unique and terrible about its power. The devil uses it for those in ministry, those in marriage, those maturing. He uses it particularly for those perched in precarious positions—those in transition, whether through the storms of adolescence, the trials of marriage, or the temptations of business travel.

The story that immediately comes to mind, of course, is that of Joseph in Genesis 39. He was in a crucial transition between slavery and the respect that could be available through a better position in life. But he caught the eye of his master's wife, and she dismissed all the other servants one day in order to set her web of seduction. When she approached Joseph with her offer, he did just what the Bible prescribes—he fled. He turned to run so quickly that the woman was left holding his coat in her hand. It's a good thing that God made young feet swift; they need to be ready to flee from temptations to dishonor God through sexual immorality.

3. *Flee from greed.* Only in recent years have I discovered this third "flight advisory." I knew that we should flee from idolatry and immorality, but I hadn't noticed that the Bible also commands us to run from greed:

> For the love of money is a root of all *kinds of* evil, for which some have strayed from the faith in their greediness, and pierced themselves through with many sorrows. But you, O man of God, flee these things. (1 Timothy 6:10–11)

This is really another form of idolatry, isn't it? But I know you'll agree that it's a form that deserves its own special category, because it's so pervasive in our society. I wonder how many people reading this book see materialism as an issue in their lives. The Bible spares no words about the seriousness of that—"a root of all kinds of evil."

This is so pervasive in our society. All kinds of evils proceed from the mouth of materialism. Don't let greed get its hooks into your life or the lives of your children.

Now let's move on to our fifth checklist item for taming temptation.

✓ Remove Any Means of Sin Far from You

There is a story about a man who was overweight. He became very serious about maintaining a diet, and he worked out every detail, planning his life accordingly. He even changed his route for driving to work because he didn't want to drive by the bakery.

For about a week, he did marvelously. Isn't that always the way with diets? All his coworkers were proud of him. One morning, as they stood around the coffeepot talking about his progress, he came in carrying a dozen doughnuts and a cheesecake. Everyone was aghast. They asked him what happened, and he told them, "I forgot and drove my old route to work today." He smiled. "And I decided that if God wanted me to stop at the bakery, He'd give me a parking space right in front of the main entrance. And you know, He did just that on the eighth trip around the block!"

It's easy to find ways to force our faith into the cookie cutter of our desires, isn't it? But the Bible tells us to take a different road entirely. The doughnut lover should read Proverbs 4:14–15: "Do not enter the path of the wicked, and do not walk in the way of evil. Avoid it, do not travel on it; turn away from it and pass on."

A man told the doctor his arm was broken in two places, and the doctor said, "Well, stop going to those two places." Good advice, but Paul put it even better: "Make no provision for the flesh" (Romans 13:14).

Go home by another way.

✓ Replace Bad Influences with Good Ones

Again we turn to the wise words of Solomon. Proverbs 13:20 says, "He who walks with wise men will be wise, but the companion of fools will be destroyed."

This is a touchy point for some of us. Yes, we need to be salt and light in the world. We need to know nonbelievers in order to share Christ with them. But there are also times when we need to stand back, take a hard look, and decide who is influencing whom. Try standing on a stool, attempting to pull someone up alongside you. It's much easier for the other person to pull you down. We must always be busy with the work of evangelism Christ set out for us, but let's take care not to use evangelism as an excuse for unhealthy friendships. We don't need to place ourselves under the influence of those who don't know God.

"Do not be unequally yoked together with unbelievers. For what fellowship has righteousness with lawlessness? And what communion has light with darkness?" (2 Corinthians 6:14). Nobody would accuse Paul of lacking evangelistic zeal, but he was also wary of the power of unhealthy influences on Christians.

Let's focus on the positive here. The answer is to replace poor models with strong ones. Find people who will point you to Christ, make you spiritually stronger, and hold you accountable. Look for wise believers to pull you up alongside them.

✓ Resolve to Take the High Road

This seventh resolution is a key one. I believe that most people, whether they realize it or not, have looked at the map, thought about the journey, and decided on their route. They know whether they intend to take the high road, the low road, or the great, wild forest in between. I know many good people who have made a Christian commitment and manage to fill most of the expectations that come with it. They attend church, volunteer as workers, perhaps even read their Bibles regularly. But there's something missing. They haven't given God their all. They're quite content to take the middle road and to serve God with halfhearted commitment. They see it as a kind of minimum requirement to acquire the free pass for heaven—without placing inconvenient demands on daily life.

Such people don't realize they're choosing the most treacherous road of all. They'll find that out when the tests begin to come. The path of lukewarm faith is not a road at all, but a jungle between the two paths. And it's filled with the briers and brambles of a life lacking consistency. When the big decisions come, there's just enough faith to provide conviction, but not enough to sustain courage. The result is a miserable soul.

They could, of course, take the high road. They could say, "What other choice is there but to take the hand of Christ Himself and press on the upward way? I'm going to realign my whole life in consistency with that walk. I'm going to clean out every hindrance that would keep me from hearing His voice. I'm going to wipe away every obstruction that would keep me from seeing His face. And I know that when the temptations come, as they will, I'll be prepared."

In his book *Unhappy Secrets of the Christian Life*, Tim Stafford tells how the nuclear submarine *Thresher* went too deep into the sea and collapsed under the weight of the water. The sub was crushed into such tiny bits in the ensuing implosion that almost nothing could be later identified. You see, a sub needs thick steel bulkheads to withstand the pressure of the water as it dives. But there are few walls we can build to withstand the pressure of the deepest oceans; even steel gives way, as the crew of the *Thresher* tragically discovered.

And yet isn't it fascinating that, in those same deep waters where that steel submarine had been crushed, little fish swim without a care in the world? What is their secret? Why aren't they crushed? Are they made of some new indestructible iron?

No, they possess only the thinnest layer of skin, measured in micrometers. The little fish, it seems, have an internal pressure that perfectly corresponds to the pressure from the outside. God gave them what they need to swim in the deep places.[2]

You and I can spend our lives building walls to block out the temptation. We can make walls of steel, but they'll never be enough—the pressure comes from inside anyway. So what happens when we have a power inside us that corresponds to the pressure from outside? The inner man, Paul tells us, is being renewed every day. When we give ourselves wholly to God, we have the inner answer to the outer pressure.

So build the inner man, the inner woman. Let Christ renew your heart and your mind. Cultivate the ministry of the Holy Spirit daily. Read the Word of God. Be strong in the Lord so that the pressure within you can withstand the pressure outside you. Then you'll encounter temptation and brush it away. You'll be able to move into the deep places of life with a lightness of being. God has given you what you need.

I like the way *The Amplified Bible* renders Philippians 4:13: "I have strength for all things in Christ Who empowers me—I am ready for anything and equal to anything through Him Who infuses inner strength into me."[3] That's Christ in you—a power for the deepest places and the most intense pressure; your strength when the world presses in.

Tom, the college Sunday school teacher, learned something about pressure in the depths. He found himself physically attracted to a young girl, but he committed to avoid the road that would surely lead to the destruction of his marriage, his ministry, and his life of honor.

Tom did the right things. He went to a trusted friend who worked in the college ministry with him, and he confided his temptation. Surprisingly, the friend responded that he, too, was struggling with the same feelings about the same girl. Obviously God had led these two men together. They prayed and committed to hold each other accountable. Tom even had the courage to confide in his wife. She affirmed him for his honesty and prayed with him. It strengthened their marriage.

In the days that followed, Tom sensed that he had come through the storm. He could feel the devil fleeing; the temptation lost its power over him. While he didn't drop his guard, he gave thanks to God for his deliverance.

Later, he began to comprehend something of the bigger picture—the spiritual perspective. At an evening meeting, the young woman began to weep after a Bible study. She accepted Christ on the spot and confessed that she was under deep conviction; she was being led by God's Spirit to adopt a lifestyle of greater purity. No one had even realized that she wasn't a believer. This had been about more than Tom's personal passions; this was a struggle for a young lady's soul, fought across the battlefields of other men's weaknesses.

It was a battle the devil lost.

Praise God for that. Praise Him that He will always be faithful if we'll only turn to Him in our trials. Praise Him that He makes all things new, in the darkest regions of the soul, in the deepest waters in which we swim.

7

ATTACKING YOUR ANGER

YOU CAN WIN THE BATTLE AND LIVE VICTORIOUSLY

PETER CAME FROM GOOD STOCK—Bible-believing, churchgoing people. But there was something in him, some indefinable spark of rebellion, that began to appear in his adolescence. When Peter went off to college, he basically swept God from his life. He fell into a life of moral laxity, hung out with poor influences, and built a lifestyle that made for a troubled marriage by the time he was halfway through his twenties.

Why, then, did he become a policeman? It may have been the course correction of a life flying out of control. Perhaps he fled from a life of lawlessness to one built around enforcement. Whatever the case, the change meant something to Peter. It symbolized a new order and discipline. Life was on the upswing for him; above all, he would build a strong marriage and a tightknit family. To that end, he put in the necessary hours and gave his best. When Peter's wife became pregnant, this was only a confirmation that all his dreams were on the verge of fulfillment.

That's when the bomb hit. That's when the pink slip arrived.

Peter stared at the little note in disbelief. There had been no warning, and the chief offered no explanation whatsoever; Peter was being given his walking papers. His services were no longer required. All the years of devotion to police training, all his loyalty and commitment, and now—with a pregnant wife, huge debts, and no prospects—Peter was rejected, discarded like dirty linen.

As he stared at the dismissal in his hands, the pink slip became purple rage. The slip crumpled; the hands clutched like claws. They were strong hands; now they were itching for vengeance.

Peter went home and tried to make the best of things, but there was no "best" to be found. At night he lay awake, thinking only of his chief. He tried to focus on the future, but his rage kept pointing back to the smug face of the man who had fired him. Late at night, the mind of an insomniac will move in many strange directions. Only days earlier he wouldn't have believed it, but now Peter found himself plotting a murder—and the purple rage deepened to black.

Perhaps it began as a mental exercise, just a way of coping with his feelings. But fantasies often create their own reality. Peter began to rehearse in his mind the details of premeditated murder. He had the guns; his employment had trained him well in their use. He'd also been taught about criminals and the mistakes that got them caught. Peter could avoid those mistakes. Who else but a well-trained cop was equipped to commit the perfect crime?

But the odds of apprehension were a moot point. In truth, he didn't care. So black was his rage that he was willing to pay any price—prison, execution, the loss of his family. None of those things dwelt in the forefront of his mind.

His mind had no room for anything but rage.

The world is an angry place. Who can say why the word *rage* has developed so many qualifiers? I'll leave that to the sociologists, but you need only pick up your morning newspaper to read about the following manifestations actually credited in news stories: road rage, parking rage, air rage, boat rage, surf rage, fishing rage, river rage, pedestrian rage, pavement rage, jogger rage, biker rage, trucker rage, cell phone rage, shopping rage, grocery cart rage, and checkout line rage. I'm told there's such a thing as pew rage, though I haven't actually witnessed it at our church—*yet*. We might observe that rage is all the rage—but of course, we're talking about a serious matter.

What makes anger so elusive and so incredibly dangerous is that it flares suddenly, powerfully, and irrationally. It takes no counsel of the future. It takes no counsel of personal safety, even one's own. If we were dealing with a *lengthy* fuse, there would be no problem at all, would there? We'd think,

Wait—I smell smoke. I hear that the fuse has been lit. I'll go get a bucket of water to douse the flame.

But it's not a lengthy fuse. It's a short fuse that you and I have to contend with. And when someone with a short fuse is behind the wheel of a car moving at seventy miles per hour, or within reach of a handgun, or even simply in possession of a balled-up fist or an eloquent tongue, then anger becomes a harmful thing. It's as old as sin itself, of course—certainly as old as Cain—but I believe we've seen toxic anger climb to new levels in our generation. Until recently, I hadn't been followed off the freeway by an angry driver after I had accidentally cut him off. I hadn't counseled junior high students who had seen their friends murdered in school hallways. I hadn't seen rage—*life* rage—flame out of control to the point that we're afraid to venture into public.

But there we have it: *life* rage. There are people who spend their entire adult lives in anger. And we all know that explosive substances are a danger not only to the targets but also to those who set them and to innocent bystanders. Anger is the acid that can harm the vessel in which it is stored even more than the person on whom it is poured. If you struggle with toxic anger, then you're in more danger than anyone else.

We have much to learn from God's Word about the anger epidemic.

RECOGNIZING SINLESS ANGER

Ephesians 4:26–27 is simple and profound—and a bit of a surprise:

> *"Be angry, and do not sin"*: do not let the sun go down on your wrath, nor give place to the devil.

We don't expect a biblical command to be angry! We've seen all the damage anger can cause. We recognize it as a product of sin. So why does Paul tell us to "be angry"—especially when he is about to write, in verse 31, that we should put all anger *away* from us? Is this some kind of contradiction?

No, of course not. The indication is that we're dealing with a different kind of anger. Could there be some positive or sinless form of it, if Paul is advising us to "be angry"? That's exactly what Paul is talking about when he tells us to be angry but not to sin. We're going to take a close look at the ultimate model of that principle: Jesus Christ Himself. It's possible to use anger positively, and He showed us how. On the other hand, let's be clear on one point about anger. Some people use this passage to justify "venting" their anger—acting it out physically—as a positive and therapeutic thing.

Pop psychologists love giving this advice, particularly that new breed known as the radio therapist. "Don't hold it in!" they say. "Go let it out! Find the person who has ticked you off, and give them an earful!" And it's no wonder, of course, that these radio doctors are popular. They tickle the ear with pleasing prescriptions. Let's remember, they'd rather have high ratings than high righteousness. Television, radio, and the movies understand that we savor anger (as we'll see), and they love to egg people on to play out their carnal passions.

Biblical Anger

The Bible, of course, offers no option for acting out anger. As a matter of fact, the Bible forbids us from even indulging it in our minds! In his popular paraphrase *The Message*, Eugene Peterson renders Matthew 5:21 this way: "You're familiar with the command to the ancients, 'Do not murder.' I'm telling you that anyone who is so much as angry with a brother or sister is guilty of murder."[1]

And there are many other scriptural condemnations of anger:

- In Galatians 5:20, fits of rage are listed as sins of the evil nature.
- Proverbs 29:11 tells us, "A fool vents all his feelings, but a wise man holds them back."
- James 1:19–20 adds: "Therefore, my beloved brethren, let every man be swift to hear, slow to speak, slow to wrath; for the wrath of man does not produce the righteousness of God."
- Psalm 37:8 instructs, "Cease from anger, and forsake wrath . . . it only *causes* harm."

We've come to a point at which secular experts are beginning to rethink the conventional wisdom about the healthiness of anger-venting. In her book *Anger: The Misunderstood Emotion*, Carol Travis writes that the psychological rationale for acting out our anger does not stand up under experimental scrutiny. The weight of the evidence, she claims, indicates precisely the opposite: that expressing our anger only increases it, solidifying a hostile spirit and a harmful habit.[2]

Why, then, does Paul tell us to "be angry"? Is there such a thing as anger without sin? I believe we find that answer by investigating the life and emotions of Jesus. He is our model in all things, anger included.

The Anger of Jesus

Jesus expressed anger on more than one occasion. You may already be thinking of the most famous of these—His encounter with the moneychangers at the Temple. The apostle John places the account of this event right at the front end of his Gospel, in chapter 2. We learn that Jesus came to the great house of God and found a thriving business venture in process—the selling of sheep and oxen, the exchange of money, and the making of fortunes. Jesus carefully constructed a whip made of cords, and He set about driving out all the purveyors of the sacrifice industry. Not only that, He overturned the tables and let all the money fall to the floor (John 2:14–15).

This passage, of course, is a wonderful antidote to the "Gentle Jesus, Meek and Mild" conception popularized by Victorian art and certain old songs. There's nothing meek and mild about a man walking through the Temple with a whip, terrifying humans and animals alike.

To understand Jesus' anger, we have to understand the moneychangers. They were practicing a kind of ecclesiastical extortion on the holiest ground in the world. This was the only place where people could come to worship God on the high holy days, and they were instructed to bring a sacrifice. They would bring the best from their flocks, their most unblemished lambs, only to be turned down by the priests' inspection. The priests, of course, had a sweet deal with the men over at the money tables who happened to have "acceptable" stock, guaranteed to pass inspection. The prices were like concession prices in a modern-day stadium or theater—sky-high in the absence of competition or controls. So people were coming to worship God, and they were being institutionally cheated.

But there was more that raised the ire of Jesus. The merchants had set up shop in the Court of the Gentiles. This was the outer court of the

Temple, and the only place provided for non-Jews to worship. Needless to say, it was a special thing to have Gentiles come to worship the one true God, and historically this court was specially set aside and protected. But the merchants had cut it off. They had filled it up with all the supplies and baggage and essentials of their trade. The Gentiles had no other place to go. And Jesus, who knew He had come to seek and to save the lost—including lost Gentiles—could in no way accept such a thing.

Now we can see why the anger bubbled up inside the Son of God. But what was remarkable about His anger? What sanctified it as compared to yours or mine? The key is in the object of His wrath. Jesus was not angry at injustices done to Him (we see no anger at all when He was hauled before Herod or Pilate, when He was beaten or mocked; we see no anger when a crowd backed Him up to a cliff at the beginning of His ministry). His anger was a righteous anger directed at injustice against people and against God. His anger was not about self but about God. How often can we say that about our own anger?

Sadly, we have plenty of anger about our own issues, but very little about the things that concern God and the issues He cares about. We feel very little emotion over starving or homeless children, persecution of Christians abroad, or people dying without hearing the gospel. Righteous anger is never about ourselves; it's always forgetful of self.

We can also observe that Jesus had a measured, rational response—not a temperamental one—to the injustice He saw. He carefully constructed the cords, then brought about a practical resolution by clearing the Court of the Gentiles. This was not an uncontrolled tantrum but a redemptive action.

There's another illuminating example of Jesus' anger. One day a man with a withered hand was brought before Him. Jesus felt immediate compassion for the handicapped man and healed him on the spot. But controversy was aroused because it was the Sabbath, and this would be a technical violation of its ordinances. Mark 3:5 tells us in no uncertain terms that Jesus "looked around at them with anger . . . grieved by the hardness of their hearts." He was frustrated because the people didn't get it—they didn't comprehend what the Hebrew laws were truly all about. They didn't comprehend compassion and a redemptive love that could override the fine print of the Hebrew law. And they didn't comprehend what Jesus Himself was all about. So He was angry—*righteously* angry.

Aristotle phrased it well: "A man who is angry on the right grounds, against the right persons, in the right manner, at the right moment and for the right length of time deserves great praise." The anger of Jesus embodied every clause in that statement.

There is such a thing as righteous, sinless anger. But approach it with care; look deeply into your heart before accepting it in yourself. The right kind of anger is admirable, but the wrong kind is an abomination.

RENOUNCING SINFUL ANGER

Now we come to the other face of anger—the kind Paul refers to later in the same chapter. He describes this kind in more detail, offering some of the forms it's likely to take:

> Let all bitterness, wrath, anger, clamor, and evil speaking be put away from
> you, with all malice. (Ephesians 4:31)

This is the kind of anger you and I know so well. We all claim to be expressing "righteous indignation" from time to time, but most of the time what we're really talking about is garden-variety anger: bitterness (grudges), wrath (rage), clamor (tantrums), and evil speaking (a tongue dipped in poison). We all have our weak spots—our "pet peeves" that get inside us and work on our emotions until we're struggling with anger. We have to live in a hurtful world. There is so much to be angry about. So what can we do about it? How can we handle our anger? Let's look at some positive prescriptions.

Don't Nurse Your Anger

Remember that anger is, at some point, a choice. We saw this same principle with temptation in the preceding chapter—the moment when the "escape hatch" swings open. In one defining moment, we can choose to put away the impure feelings, as Paul counsels us to do, or we can build a little nest. The moment we take note of an angry impulse and refuse to send it away, we've put the first twig into that nest. And we all know what happens in a nest sooner or later: Something hatches and flies out.

The Bible tells us not to let the sun set on our anger. That's simply an eloquent way of saying to clear all your accounts before the day is over and to start each day with clean books. Enforce a twelve-hour limit on feelings of resentment; after that, they should be wiped as clean as God wipes your own sins. I'm not aware of a Bible paraphrase authored by Phyllis Diller, but I know she has said, "Never go to bed mad. Stay up and fight!" I *hope* she means to bring things out in the open and come to a righteous resolution. Wiping the slate clean isn't the same as sweeping things under the bed.

If only it were easy to take this advice. But you may have noticed that of all the seven deadly sins, anger is the one that tastes the best. This is the one we actually enjoy; perhaps the word is that we *savor* our anger. We take it in, welcome it, build the nest—then we begin fantasizing speeches, thinking about how to get even, devising plans of attack. Peter, the policeman who opens this chapter, illustrates the danger of nurtured anger.

What happens when those fantasies take on a life of their own? They may conceivably become more than fantasies. Think of all the angry speeches you've devised as you lay tossing and turning in bed. What if you really said all the things that passed through your mind? Would you like them to be published in a book for your friends and family to read? I'm glad this publisher hasn't done that little favor for me—*that's* not a book I'm eager to put into print. It would cause me great sorrow and distress. Yet we enjoy composing those covert, undeliverable speeches; we savor our anger. It's so hard to let go.

A ministerial friend counseled a woman who had been divorced for many years. After all this time, she was still attending divorce recovery seminars. She was still spouting off all her rage and bitterness about the husband who had abandoned her for another woman. The leader asked her, "Why can't you move on with your life? Why can't you let go of your anger?"

She replied, "Because it's the only story I have."

That's a sad commentary. Sometimes we need to write "The End" on the story, unhappy ending and all, and begin a new and fresh chapter. Nurtured anger is no way to live. The grudge is a kind of cancer that attacks the soul, bringing with it feelings of dark cynicism. This is why we say anger is *toxic*—it becomes a poison that will eventually kill the spirit. Hebrews 12:15 warns us to be careful gardeners: We're not to let any root of bitterness spring up and cause trouble, defiling the garden of our relationships.

Clear all accounts when the sun goes down. Realize that if someone owes you, you're probably in debt as well—and be content to break even on the relationship books. We have to remember the Bible tells us to avoid any debt other than the debt of love.

Don't Rehearse Your Anger

You and I know people who love to tell us all about their anger in great detail. They're practically artists of anger, with resentful words as their medium. Perhaps it's the only story they have—or perhaps their anger is preventing them from having any other stories. "Wait 'til you hear the latest!" they say as they hurry to your side in the hallway. Their anger so consumes them that they've lost sight of how thoroughly unattractive anger is in a person.

When I was a young man just beginning my ministry, I heard a speech by Henry Brandt on this topic. He believed that it's a fallacy to say that some other person "makes us angry." According to Brandt, that's something that can't be done. If we become angry it's because we had anger already within us, and we allowed someone else to pull it out of us. But no one can *make* us angry.

As time has gone by, I've seen the wisdom in his words. There are people who maintain their own little anger factories within themselves, and they keep a steady supply on hand. Nearly anyone can make them angry; the same thing done or said to someone else wouldn't even bother them. Some people simply have more buttons to push. Some people are nothing *but* buttons.

The main process in the manufacture of anger, of course, is the *rehearsing* of it. We go over and over what someone said. We begin to find new meanings in it. We build it up to something that may not have even bothered us much at the time—but we've fed the fire until the flames are high.

The rehearsal of anger is a dangerous thing.

Don't Converse About Your Anger

The mouth is a deadly weapon; don't let it be a promoter of anger. Ephesians 4:29 tells us, "Let no corrupt communication proceed out of your mouth." That word *corrupt* carries the idea of cutting—don't let any *cutting* remark escape you.

Unfortunately, that's almost an indoor sport in our contemporary culture. It's a cynical, smart-mouth age we live in, haven't you noticed? We use so much disrespect that we've abbreviated the word into "dis." "Don't dis me, man!" We spend plenty of time cutting the boss, the pastor, the children, the parents, the neighbors—the list, of course, is limited only by the number of acquaintances we have. Some today are willing to make cutting remarks in public about their spouses. As widespread as sarcasm is, there's no place for it in the Christian vocabulary—not if we're to hold the New Testament as our authority.

At one time I had a friend who was a master of the cutting comment. He kept his blade plenty sharp. We'd have a lunch date, and he would begin cutting into me. I took it with good humor, because that's the way it was meant. As a matter of fact, I decided I might as well fight fire with fire. I began to cut him right back—all in fun. But time went on, and this mock-adversarial exchange became the pattern for our relationship, and finally I began to sense a change in my friend's spirit. One day I noticed he didn't seem to want any part of me; I couldn't even get him to look me in the eye. He was now too busy for the lunches we used to share. Finally I confronted him about it.

My friend immediately pointed me to a conversation I'd completely forgotten. I'd made some joking observation of him without meaning it at all. But I'd hit a nerve. He took it very personally, nurtured it in his heart, and developed a spirit of bitterness. The remark, innocent as it was on my part, had poisoned our friendship.

On that day I vowed before God that, as much as it was possible on my end, I'd clean that brand of conversation right out of my life. Words are too powerful to be used carelessly. From then on I began to use words to say what I really meant—nothing more, nothing less. When it comes to words and you fight fire with fire, someone always ends up getting burned.

I'm grateful there's something better for us. According to Ephesians 4:29, our alternative is to say "what is good for necessary edification, that it may impart grace to the hearers." That sounds much more attractive, doesn't it? Rather than running down people, we can spend the same time edifying them, using the tongue as a vessel of grace. That's one of the marks of the Christian.

We also need to keep in mind that conversation is infectious. If you hang out with a sarcastic crowd, that spirit will seep into you sooner or later. That's what Proverbs 22:24–25 is trying to tell us: "Make no friendship with an angry man, and with a furious man do not go, lest you learn his ways and set a snare for your soul." Have you ever considered this? The relationships you choose may be setting a soul-trap.

Don't Disperse Your Anger

Proverbs 19:11 says, "The discretion of a man makes him slow to anger, and *it is to* his glory to overlook a transgression." Sinful anger isn't about offering a rebuke; it's about indulging in a tantrum.

Temper tantrums, of course, are identified with little children. My grandson is angelic, and I wish there was room for my snapshots of him here in this book—but I've seen a few tantrums, too. Occasionally David Todd wants something that isn't available to him. So he does what every child his age does: He squeals, he pounds his fists, he kicks his feet, he rolls on the carpet. He expresses every ounce of the anger and frustration within him, because he hasn't yet reached the age where self-control is possible.

Most of us do reach that age. We do master our emotions—to differing extents. There are some adults who indulge in very adult temper tantrums. They may not roll on the carpet or squeal, but they act out their emotions on their own terms.

When you must deal with anger, don't nurse it; don't rehearse it; don't converse about it; don't disperse it. Instead, you must reverse it.

Reverse Your Anger

Anger in reverse? What does that mean? We've all done things we've wished we could reverse. We've broken something or said something or done something, and we've wished we could rewind the film of life and reverse the damage. But time is irreversible. The Bible offers an alternative way to reverse things.

As a matter of fact, the Scriptures are filled with this prescription. It seems like sheer foolishness to the world—on those rare occasions when the world sees it. If someone makes us angry, we offer love in return. If someone threatens harm, we feel compassion for the forces that made him or her that way. Instead of retaliation, we offer redemption. Romans 12:20 says, "If your enemy hungers, feed him; if he thirsts, give him a drink; for in so doing you will heap coals of fire on his head."

That's a verse that used to puzzle me. I'm supposed to offer *comfort* to the enemy—and for the purpose of *what*? Heaping burning coals on his head? I decided to get to the bottom of this passage, and what I discovered fascinated me. I found out about an old Egyptian custom. A person committed some kind of misdeed, and he felt the need to express his shame and contrition. To show everyone the burning shame within his heart, this person would place a pan of hot coals on his head.

That's the actual background of this misunderstood New Testament passage. If someone wrongs you in some way, see what happens when you return right for wrong. The other person's shame becomes as visible as a pan of hot coals sizzling on his head. As a matter of fact, that mental image may itself be enough to turn your snarl to a smile!

This is what we mean by reversing our anger. We turn base human reactions on their head. We pay out the reverse of what we might feel, or of what has been done to us. Is this an easy thing to do? No, not at all. It takes healthy doses of wisdom, maturity, and self-control. But the results are well worth it. I found that out one day not too long ago.

It was a busy day. I had to eat lunch on the run, so I drove up to the drive-through window of a local fast-food restaurant. I suppose I had my mind on my order, and I didn't see the woman who was approaching the line of cars from the other direction. Apparently I cut off her intended route. It was completely unintentional, but she didn't see it that way; she was furious. The woman rolled down her window and gave me a piece of her mind—more than a piece, she served me a second helping.

She shouted some obscenities I hadn't heard in a long time, she used hand gestures, she honked her horn—it was a multimedia presentation, to say the least, one of the most *detailed* dispersals of anger I'd ever seen. And by the time her volcano was out of molten lava, there she was behind me in line, and we were both waiting for lunch. I admit that I reached over and locked my doors.

But I also had a sly idea. As I was getting my food, I asked for the total bill for the woman behind me. The waitress asked, "Is she one of your relatives?"

"Certainly not!" I said. That thought sent a cold chill up my spine. "But still, I'd like to pay for her dinner."

"Well, that's very nice," said the drive-through waitress. So I paid for both of us.

I confess that I couldn't help but wait around and furtively adjust my rearview mirror, because I wanted to see the woman's response.

She was in total shock when I saw her again. It was as if she had seen the supernatural—and maybe she had. She had just attacked some stranger with all her claws, and he had bought her lunch! It was a full-scale reversal.

We reverse not only what we might have done, but certainly how we're going to feel about it afterward. I don't know how she feels about it today—whether it's hot coals or hot lava—but I feel good about the incident. I feel that I proved the truth of the biblical prescription. Any armchair quarterback can tell you that when you feel pressure up the middle, you call a reverse.

We show that we don't have that molten stuff inside us; we're all out of worldly wrath, but we have plenty of loving-kindness, tenderness, and forgiveness in stock. We go heavy on the grace and the benefit of the doubt. We find some way, some action, to encourage the aggressor. And in the process of doing all this, I can guarantee you there's no anger your soul can whip up that won't be dissolved by the power of godly grace.

PUNCTUATING THE SENTENCE

Grace isn't the natural way to behave; it's the supernatural way. The world should be able to expect Christians to do something beyond the natural thing. To be able to take all the wrong and evil and persecution the world can dish out, and to meet it with a double dose of love and compassion—this is the visible evidence of God. It's the most powerful witness you can possibly offer. It's a living picture worth a thousand words.

Rubin "Hurricane" Carter was a boxer who went from the headlines to Hollywood. He was wrongly convicted of three murders. He spent two decades in prison, paying the price for someone else's crime, before he finally won his freedom. A book and a movie told the story of his troubles.

How would you feel if it happened to you? Sitting in that cell alone for twenty years, what thoughts and emotions would be likely to circulate through your mind? I'll let Rubin offer you these thoughts about his night-marish experience:

> The question invariably arises, it has before and it will again: "Rubin, are you bitter?" And in answer to that I will say, "After all that's been said and done—the fact that the most productive years of my life, between the ages of twenty-nine and fifty, have been stolen; the fact that I was deprived of seeing my children grow up—wouldn't you think I would have a right to be bitter? Wouldn't anyone under those circumstances have a right to be bitter? In fact, it would be very easy to be bitter. But that has never been my nature, or my lot, to do things the easy way. If I have learned nothing else in my life, I've learned that bitterness only consumes the vessel that contains it. And for me to permit bitterness to control or to infect my life in any way whatsoever would be to allow those who imprisoned me to take even more than the 22 years they've already taken. Now that would make me an accomplice to their crime."[3]

Rubin Carter might have whirled up a hurricane of emotions inside him-self—most people would have done so. But he knew that one crime was enough. Why perpetuate it? Somewhere all evil, all wrongdoing, must be punctuated. Someone must put down a period instead of a comma—other-wise life is one long sentence without parole. Rubin Carter felt his sentence was long enough. So he walked away a free man—free not only of the bars of steel, but also of the ones we impose on ourselves.

Anger can be punctuated. We do so when we reverse it and release it to God. One day, many years ago, a man was beaten and tortured. He was spat upon and robbed. He endured every insult imaginable, then He was nailed to a cross. Hanging there in darkness and mockery, blood flowing from nearly every part of His body, He might have yelled out curses to all His killers. As a matter of fact, He might have done much more than that. Awesome power was in His grasp.

But Jesus reversed the evil. He took it all within His aching body and offered a prayer of forgiveness. "They know not what they do," He said. And isn't that almost always true when we've been wronged? People know not what they do.

When Jesus chose that reaction, the greatest of all miracles occurred. Sin wasn't ignored; it was healed. Death itself was destroyed. A long chain of evil dating all the way from creation was broken. And even more—a new pattern was established. You and I are to live out that pattern. *Good* for evil. *Blessings* for curses. *Compassion* for aggression. The day we do this, the miracles begin. The day we do this, we're liberated from a self-imposed prison and granted the freedom to live in peace and joy.

Peter stood before his gun cabinet, oiling, polishing, plotting. His plans had been destroyed, and someone had to pay. He was on the verge of becoming the very thing he had sworn to fight—of violating the most sacred law he had sworn to uphold. Peter heard the metallic click of the gun shells rolling into the chamber. His mind was filled with angry voices, urging him on—except for one voice. It was different from the rest.

What was this? There was the sound, the feel of *prayer* within the buzzing of his head. It made no sense at all. Somehow, some part of Peter was *praying* as the rest of him was plotting. He stopped, listened, and found himself embracing the words that seemed to come directly from his soul:

Please, God, stop me! Don't let me take this man's life. Don't let me dishonor my wife and my unborn child. I ask You now, Lord—restrain my hand.

And just like that, the spirit of vengeance was broken. Whatever there was in Peter that had been bound for evil, now it had taken flight. Peter knelt, and trembled, and wept. Then he put away the guns and the plans and the rage. And he walked out the door to find a new job.

But no job was to be found. And, to be honest about it, there was still a fair amount of bitterness within Peter; it was a more *rational* bitterness, that was all. He still hadn't made things right with God. In the weeks to come, as he continued searching for a new career, his wife finally went into labor. Like many firstborns, this one came with a great deal of pain and struggle. Labor lasted the longest twelve hours Peter had ever spent, and he prayed nearly every moment of it. *Help my wife, Lord! Help my child!* As he talked to God simply and honestly, it seemed as if God was saying something back to him. He suddenly came to understand that he hadn't known God at all and that without Him, there could never be any peace in his life. There in the hospital, he committed himself fully to the Lord.

After the baby came, Peter was making phone calls to share the news. Trying to call his parents, he accidentally dialed his own number and decided to go ahead and check messages. A man was trying to reach him, to offer him a job. The work began the next day. Was Peter interested? Of course he was.

Peter's trainer turned out to be a man who loved the Lord intensely, a man who quickly perceived what was happening in his young coworker's soul. He trained Peter in much more than work over the next few weeks. The same God who had restrained Peter's hand had sent an angel to nurture his soul. *God must love me a lot*, Peter thought. It was hard to take in.

Today Peter is a new man. He's a committed husband, a loving father to his children, and a growing child of God. Every aspect of his life is flourishing. There is a miracle in every corner. And every bit of it was almost destroyed by the demons of anger.

Are you angry? Release your anger to God. See what miraculous thing can be wrought from it. He loves you as much as He loves Peter.

8

RESISTING YOUR RESENTMENT

YOU CAN WIN THE BATTLE AND LIVE VICTORIOUSLY

LEONARD HOLT WAS AN OLD-FASHIONED "company man." He had put in nineteen years of hard work at the same Pennsylvania paper mill. When he wasn't on duty there as a lab technician, you could find him in town leading a Boy Scout troop. Or spending time with his children. Or volunteering at the local fire brigade. Leonard was an active church member and all-around model citizen, the very embodiment of caring and community.

Everyone in town admired Leonard—until the day he stuffed two pistols into his coat pockets, drove to the mill, and walked through the plant methodically gunning down friends and coworkers of long standing. Before the attack had run its bloody course, Leonard Holt had fired thirty deadly bullets and left a number of casualties.

The community could only respond in shocked bewilderment and grief. Why would their church leader, their scoutmaster, their loyal neighbor do such a thing? If a man like Leonard Holt was capable of this, who then could be trusted?

It took some time to begin to understand the complex puzzle of Leonard Holt's meltdown. Detectives, friends, and neighbors began reassembling the pieces of a life that bolstered a town before tearing it to pieces. Who or what was the demon that had taken hold of Leonard Holt? As the people of the town talked, compared notes, and put all the pieces together, they saw a picture that had been there all along; they simply hadn't chosen to see it. There was something beneath all the hard work, neighborly smiles, and volunteerism.

They found the demon, and its name was resentment.

The key puzzle piece was Leonard's job. In nineteen years at the mill, he had always given his best—yet there were men beneath him who had been promoted ahead of him. Nobody had paid much attention to Leonard's feelings about that, but now, many of the promoted men were the very ones who lay buried in the cemetery. Another puzzle piece was provided by Leonard's carpool, of all things. Some coworkers had opted out of it because Leonard's driving was reckless and dangerous. Now it seemed clear that something had been eating away at him on the way to work, back home again, and probably all the hours in between. No one had suspected the demon of festering bitterness that had taken hold of the man's soul.

After all, Leonard Holt was just another face in the crowd—a face that eventually appeared in *Time* magazine over this caption: "Responsible, Respectable, Resentful."[1]

Perhaps the best caricature of the power of resentment was penned by the author Charles Dickens in his novel *Great Expectations*. There we meet the immortal character Miss Havisham, jilted at the altar many years before. Long ago, she was dressing for her wedding, waiting for the hour of nine when her groom would arrive and the blessed event would begin. The immense wedding cake, along with a sumptuous feast, lay in wait.

At precisely ten minutes before nine, a message had arrived. The groom would not be coming; he had run away with another woman.

At that moment, time had ceased to move forward in the mansion of Miss Havisham. Every clock in the house registered ten minutes to nine from that day on. Neither did old Miss Havisham's wardrobe ever change: she still wore the wedding dress and the veil, now faded, yellowed with age and tattered. The windows of the ruined mansion stayed heavily draped so that sunshine might never enter. For decades the cake and the feast had rotted on the tables, mostly carried off by rats and spiders. The rats could be heard moving behind the wall panels. "Sharper teeth than those of the rats have been gnawing on me," said Miss Havisham.

And of course she was right. The teeth of resentment cut sharp and deep, and can lay waste to the life that God designed as a feast and a celebration of abundant living. Resentful souls draw the drapes and purposely block out the sunshine. In the previous chapter we explored the emotion of anger; resentment is anger multiplied by time. It doesn't dissipate like anger, but lurks beneath the surface, undetected by any sonogram. Author Lewis B. Smedes wrote, "We make believe we are at peace while the furies rage within, beneath the surface. There, hidden, and suppressed, our hate opens the subterranean faucets of venom that will eventually infect all of our relationships in ways we cannot predict."[2]

My good friend Gary Inrig has told the story of a man bitten by a dog later discovered to be rabid. Hospital tests confirmed it: The man had contracted rabies. This was at a time when there was nothing much to be done after rabies had set in; no cure had been developed. The doctor had the bleak assignment of bringing the bad news to his patient.

"Sir," he said, "everything possible will be done to make you comfortable, but we can't offer any false hope. My best advice to you is to put your affairs in order as soon as possible."

The dying man sank back in depression and shock, but finally he rallied enough strength to ask for a pen and paper. He began writing furiously.

An hour later, when the doctor returned, the man's pen was still flowing. The doctor said, "Well, it's good to see you've taken my advice. I take it you're working on your will."

"This ain't no will, Doc," said the man. "It's a list of people I plan on bitin' before I die."[3]

The resentful are those who have been bitten and thus channel their energy into snapping at others. Resentment makes us permanently angry; it carves deep lines on our faces. It adds a heaviness to our very steps. This is no way to live; why do people choose it as a lifestyle?

The Bible paints a detailed portrait of the malignant giant called resentment. Let's take a closer look.

THE EXAMINATION OF RESENTFULNESS

You won't find the word *resentment* in the concordance of your Bible. It's a modern term, but the idea is nothing new. Paul does use a phrase that comes very close to the meaning of it. We find it in a surprising place, and we discover it has a surprising meaning.

It's found in 1 Corinthians 13—the classic chapter on love. As you may remember, Paul describes *agape* love like this: "[Love] . . . thinks no evil" (v. 5). The portion of that phrase that gives us *thinks* is the Greek word *logizomai*. You'd be unlikely to guess where this word originated. It came from the bookkeepers. It actually means "to calculate or reckon." The first-century certified public accountant might be entering a tally into the ledger book, and he would calculate or reckon that he had a certain number of items. The word for his computation would be *logizomai*.

So *logizomai* has to do with working over your ledger, making an entry in permanent ink. In the New Testament, this is generally a *good* thing. We're organized when we keep good records. But there are records we'd rather not see in the books. In Romans 4:8, Paul declares, *"Blessed is the man to whom the LORD shall not impute sin."* The idea is that God keeps a ledger book, and you're truly blessed if God has no entries beside your name. If you've committed yourself to Christ, of course, His blood has washed across the line with your name on it anyway—and yes, you're truly blessed.

In 2 Corinthians 5:19 we find, "God was in Christ reconciling the world to Himself, not imputing their trespasses to them." He throws out the ledger book. For many of us, the image of God with such a book isn't a novel idea at all—some people have the conception of God working away, recording every little sin. You need to know that He has removed your sin from you as far as the east is from the west. We deserve to have the book thrown *at* us, but instead it's thrown away *for* us.

When it comes to your tax records, your business papers, and your household transactions, record keeping is highly recommended. But when it comes to the transactions we call relationships, we need to throw away the books. The practice of *logizomai* is poison when it comes to husbands and wives, parents and children, friends and companions. Love, Paul tells us in 1 Corinthians 13, keeps no books. It posts no scoreboard. It makes no list of whom to bite. Love remembers to forget.

Chrysostom, the leader of the fourth-century church, once said that a wrong done against love is like a spark that falls into the sea and is quenched. Resentment douses the flames of life and love. It enshrines failure and evil, and it lets no one else forget.

THE EXAMPLE OF RESENTMENT

David, the textbook example of so many matters of the heart, is naturally a model of resentment as well. He was the man after God's own heart, but he had many failures. On his deathbed, King David brought his son Solomon into the room for final counsel. In 1 Kings 2:5–6, we have a record of their words.

> Moreover you know also what Joab the son of Zeruiah did to me, *and* what
> he did to the two commanders of the armies of Israel, to Abner the son of
> Ner and Amasa the son of Jether, whom he killed. And he shed the blood
> of war in peacetime, and put the blood of war on his belt that *was* around
> his waist, and on his sandals that *were* on his feet. Therefore do according
> to your wisdom, and do not let his gray hair go down to the grave in peace.

Think of this: the greatest man of his time in all the world, preparing to meet his God. And what wisdom does he share? An old grudge dating back many years, an item from the mental ledger of a king, and the generational perpetuation of a character flaw. For David is passing a legacy of vengeance on to his son—the same son he wants to be a wise and godly king. "Don't let Joab die naturally, whatever you do," he is saying. "See that he pays with his life for the pain he caused me."

This is the side of David we'd rather not see. Perhaps it's a side of ourselves we'd rather not face. Resentment is an ugly, deformed creature. Poet Stephen Crane described it this way:

In the desert
I saw a creature, naked, bestial,
Who, squatting upon the ground,
Held his heart in his hands,
And ate of it.
I said: "Is it good, friend?"
"It is bitter-bitter," he answered;
"But I like it
Because it is bitter,
And because it is my heart."

Too many people become that ugly, stooped character, eating away at their hearts and believing they like the taste. But what they don't realize is that the resentment inside them doesn't stay the same. It's actually more like a cancer that takes hold—then takes charge. As Helen Grace Lesheid has written, "It grows. It distorts reality. It keeps us chained to the past. Like bad air, it pollutes not just the bitter person, but those who come in contact with the person."[4]

A chain, a cancer, an ugly little creature, poisoned air. Bitterness and resentment are described through many word pictures, but perhaps the most enduring is the one found in Hebrews 12:15. It is the metaphor of the malignant weed: "Looking diligently lest anyone fall short of the grace of God; lest any *root of bitterness* springing up cause trouble, and by this many become defiled" (emphasis added). Ask any gardener about weeds. The gardener will tell you that once weeds take hold, they can be very difficult to drive out. Weeds will move in and choke away the beautiful grass and flowers that were intended for this plot of land. That's exactly what resentment does.

"Let me have my bitterness," someone might say. "It's nobody's business but my own." Why not ignore that stray weed? If you don't look too closely, it can pass for grass. The answer, of course, is that both of these spread out and poison their environment. Your bitterness against an ex-husband or the boss at work will color all your relationships. It will spread into your marriage, your friendships, even your relationship with God. It chokes out whatever it touches.

THE EXPENSE OF RESENTMENT

Psychologists tell us that the weed of bitterness is cultivated at great price. When we choose to hold on to our resentment, we relinquish control of our future. We trade the freshness of the new day and all its possibilities for the pain of the past. Quite often we eat away our hearts, one bite at a time, over someone who may be far away and totally unaware of our thoughts, totally forgetful of what happened, and—certainly—totally unaffected by anything we're thinking or doing. Resentment, someone said, is swallowing poison and waiting for the other person to die.

We've jeopardized not only our spiritual but our physical health. As a matter of fact, Dick Innes has written about a doctor whose patient was suffering through all kinds of symptoms—stress, ulcers, high blood pressure. "If you don't cut out your resentments," said the doctor to the shocked patient, "I may have to cut out part of your intestinal tract." That got the man's attention. He went home and cut way down on his resentment intake, making every arrangement possible to get his relationships and feelings in order. During his next appointment, the doctor was able to tell him that his condition had cleared up; he was now a healthy man.[5]

When we opt to cling to bitterness, it's as if we've placed ourselves under an evil spell. Only the ancient and godly remedy of forgiveness will remove that spell. In our time, the definitive book on that subject is by Lewis Smedes, who gave us the classic *Forgive and Forget*. Smedes recounts a play that illustrates the power of resentment. This play is the story of a German general and a French journalist. Herman Engel, the captured general, is sentenced to thirty years' imprisonment by the Nuremberg Court after the Second World War. Morrieaux, the journalist, is infuriated. His family was massacred by Engel's troops during the war, and he wants Engel to pay with his life, not with a prison sentence. For thirty long years he performs his own ritual death penalty in the execution chamber of his heart—again and again. He lives for nothing in the world other than the day when he can carry out the punishment in real life.

The old general, Engel, survives his long years of imprisonment and emerges, a tired and broken man. He wants only to be left alone and to be forgotten, so he and his wife build a cabin in the woods near Alsace. There they intend to live out their remaining years, quietly and inconspicuously. But they don't know that Morrieaux has followed the couple's movements. He's in the nearby village, trying to incite a mob of fanatics to rise up and take vengeance against the old Nazi. Their plan is to come by night, burn the cabin, and shoot Engel and his wife.

But there is one piece of unfinished business. Morrieaux, being a journalist, has always wanted to know more about what actually happened to his family's community. He decides to pay a visit to the Engels on the day before their death, just to ask a few questions.

Morrieaux visits the shaken Engel and begins to question him about every massacre, every atrocity. But he isn't prepared for the feeble old man he encounters, the one who struggles to recall old details. This man isn't a monster at all, merely a broken old man in the winter of life, waiting to die. Morrieaux isn't as angry as he thought, not after this face-to-face encounter. Suddenly he blurts out all the mob's plans for the next day; he offers to lead them out of the woods and save their lives. Engel listens and replies, "I'll go with you—on one condition. I'll go with you if you'll forgive me."

Morrieaux hesitates. This is a difficult question for a man who has built his entire life around the hope of destroying his adversary. He has killed the old German in his heart many times over three decades. Amazingly, Morrieaux discovers that he's perfectly capable of rescuing his old enemy; he's more than willing to call off the execution.

But *forgive* him? That he cannot do.

The Engels don't leave. And the next evening, they die at the hands of a rabid mob.[6]

We're left with this enigma: Why is it easier to forgive with our hands than with our hearts? Why is a man capable of rescuing another man but incapable of forgiving him? The answer is that bitterness is a cancer. It takes root so deeply that it can't be quickly extracted. Its teeth have sunk too deep. You can begin by nurturing a minor grudge, and if you feed it, the grudge grows into a powerful resentment. By then it has a life of its own, and you can't help continuing to feed it, to nurture it. Ultimately it's no longer something you own; it's something that owns *you*. Your entire life is defined and ordered around the principles of hatred.

None of us want to live that way. If we could see it in advance, we'd do almost anything to avoid falling under the demonic spell of resentment. What can we do? How can we resist?

FIVE STEPS TO RESISTING RESENTMENT

1. Think It Through

Why do most people harbor resentment against others? The answer may surprise you. Doctors believe that resentment affords people a sense of superiority over the people they resent. Hanging on to that person's misdeed makes them seem lower and the bitter person higher. It's clear that people who tend to think little of themselves are the ones who gravitate toward resentment, for it gives them a way—an *unhealthy* way—to place themselves a little higher in the pecking order.

Resentment places an angry individual in the judge's seat, pounding the gavel. It makes him the jury and the executioner, too. There's a sense of power in fantasizing the execution of what seems, in our imagination at least, to be justice. With every new episode of our inner fantasies, the story grows better, the antagonist grows more evil, the punishment becomes more dramatic. *That person gets what's coming to him!* Someone has said that our fantasies of bitterness bring about neurotic pleasure and religious pride. In our minds, at least, we're both high and mighty.

The first thing to do, then, is to simply think it through. Is this the kind of life you'd like to lead? Is this the direction in which you'd like to project your thoughts? Is this a fitting use of your emotional energy? A little rational thought will cure a great deal of misplaced resentment.

2. Write It Down

One of the most useful gifts God gave us is the talent to operate a pen on paper. We can use it in prayer; we can use it to preserve memories; we can use it to encourage others. We can also use it to organize our thoughts and feelings.

It's interesting to try getting to the bottom of a feud. Historians have long been fascinated by the famous feud between the Hatfield and McCoy clans. It was a bloody battle between two families set against a mountain backdrop, and it went on for generations and at the expense of many lives. Yet no one was ever very clear about what set the feud off. Everyone had a different story. There was nothing ambiguous, however, about the result of the feud. One of the two original patriarchs, "Ol' Randell" McCoy, lost five of his children—all of them gunned down. He was driven almost completely mad by grief and was known to walk the streets of Pikeville, West Virginia, telling and retelling the story of the feud to whoever would listen. His counterpart, "Devil Anse" Hatfield, struggled with guilt and remorse over the feud. Despite his name, "Devil Anse" finally turned to God, put away his bitterness, and was baptized in the waters of Island Creek.

Sometimes we're willing to fight to the death for a cause we can no longer articulate, if we ever could in the first place. There are families that perpetuate ill feelings long after the causes are forgotten and the original antagonists are dead. That's why the best thing for you to do is to *write it down*. Bring those feelings out, put them on paper before you, and get a good look at them in the light. You may be surprised by what you see. It could be that this thing, this person, this situation isn't at all worth the emotional energy you've expended. All too often the enemies of our emotional landscapes know not what they do.

Words have a way of bringing precision to vague and amorphous feelings. They crystallize our thoughts and show us what lies beneath. The situation is like the little boy who is afraid of the dark. There's something peeking out of the closet door at him, and it seems more and more terrible each night. But when his parents show it to him in the light, it turns out to be nothing but his old coat—the one with Big Bird on it! Who could get worked up over a Big Bird coat?

That's the way it is when you bring your bitterness out of the dark and into the light. The very best way for us to do that is to write it down, carefully, honestly. Charlie Shedd and his wife had a great altercation, and he left the house. When he returned, a note on the refrigerator said, "Dear Charlie, I hate you. Love, Martha." Be that honest. Begin your essay, "I am filled with resentment because . . ." Then add every detail and when you've finished, read your essay aloud. Return later and read it again. Are you still resentful?

3. Work It Out

A couple managed to stay married for fifty years. At the anniversary party, someone asked for their secret. The husband said, "We made a simple agreement when we were married. Whenever she was bothered about something, she should go ahead, tell me off, and get it out of her system. As for me, every time I got angry I should go out and take a walk." He concluded, "I guess you can attribute our marital success to the fact that I've largely led an outdoor life."

Actually, he does have a point. There's something to be said for good, physical exercise. There is no full physiological solution to what is a spiritual problem—let's be very clear on that—but a little perspiration is beneficial for strong emotions. It takes the edge off fresh anger. It provides an outlet. It becomes an escape valve so that we don't build up a backlog of bitterness.

Don't sit in a dark room and brood. Go out and take a vigorous walk. Sweat away some of your emotions.

4. Talk It Over

You can discuss your feelings with trusted friends. You can discuss them with your family. But please don't fail to talk your feelings over with the One who loves you most, and the One who has the power to make you, your mind, and your heart brand-new. Go to the Lord and tell it all. Bring that essay with you, no matter how many pages it took you to write. Even if it's the size of *War and Peace*, that's okay. The Lord never slumbers. He'll listen to every word.

Be just as honest with God as you were on paper. That's hard for some people who put on their emotional Sunday best before approaching God in prayer. It's good to acknowledge His holiness, but it's also important to be authentic in prayer. If you're furious, remorseful, frantic, sorrowful—whatever emotion you may have, bring it to God. Come as you are. It's not as if you can hide anything from Him, anyway. There's no hair on your head He doesn't know; no molecule within the marvel of your body that He didn't place there. Share it all with Him, and He'll begin to share certain things with you—things such as grace and forgiveness.

Hebrews 12:15, as we've seen, offers a compelling phrase: "Looking diligently [carefully] lest anyone fall short of the grace of God." What does that mean? Those with resentment in their hearts are coping with a grace deficiency. They need to approach God and recover what they've lost, for He is the only true source. To experience His grace and forgiveness is to find that we have plenty of it for others. Otherwise, we'll continue to play by the world's rules. We'll continue to keep our ledgers and tally up every little hurtful word and deed we perceive someone has aimed our way.

There is a story of two men who were traveling through the jungles in Burma, one a visitor and the other a resident missionary. Along their journey they came to a murky little pond, and the waters came up to their necks as they crossed it. When the two men emerged on the far side, the visitor was covered with leeches—all over his arms, his legs, and his torso. He began frantically plucking at the parasites, trying to pull them off. But the missionary said, "No—don't do that! If you pull one out suddenly, a part of the creature will remain under your skin, the wound will become infected, and you'll be in much worse condition."

The other man said, "Then what am I supposed to do?"

"We need to get you into a balsam bath, as quickly as possible," said the missionary. "Soaking yourself in the bath will cause those leeches to pull out their hooks, and you'll be free."[7]

Deep resentment is the leech that embeds itself in your heart. You can't pluck at it and discard it simply by making a resolution, reading a book, or any other simple action. You know from experience it's going to take more than that; those feelings have their hooks in you. But there is one thing you can do, and that's to bathe in the luxurious grace of God. When you do that, a lot of strongholds begin to loosen within your spirit. When you contemplate the forgiveness He has given you, your merciless grudges begin to fade into nothing. When you feel the wonders of His cleansing grace, you settle down into that bath until the waters rise up and overflow. They begin to soak all of those around you, your antagonists and rivals and enemies. Suddenly the thing you resented doesn't seem worthy of notice anymore.

It simply comes down to this: We can forgive because God has forgiven us. If you haven't accepted God's forgiveness for your sin, you'll struggle to forgive others. You'll know no way other than the strict rule of the ledger book. But if you've found the way of grace, you'll find how delightful and rewarding life can be when you stop keeping score.

Talk to God. Ask Him to help you see the depth of His love, His mercy, His grace and forgiveness. Ask Him to fill your cup with it. Then spend some time expressing your thanksgiving to Him for doing so. I have a feeling that, after doing so, the spell will be broken. You won't feel at the mercy of mercilessness any longer.

And yet there's one more thing you should do.

5. Give It Up

Always remember to forget. Two little boys had a quarrel as they were playing catch with ball and glove. Johnny slammed the kitchen door and told his mother he'd never have anything to do with Bobby again. And yet the next day, there he was on the way out the door with his ball and glove. "I'll be over at Bobby's," he said.

"I thought you were through with Bobby forever," said his mother.

Johnny said, "Oh, me and Bobby are good forgetters."

Be a generous, detailed forgetter. Maybe you've been an emotional "pack rat," but now it's time to get the jumbo-size garbage bag and clear everything out of your memory. A little selective amnesia never hurt anyone; it actually saves a lot of misery. If you're angry at your boss, it is as if you're carrying him on your back, everywhere you go. If you're angry at your mother-in-law, she's up there, too. How many people can you carry on that back? After a while, the burden becomes heavy. It's so much easier to walk if you simply let it all go.

There is only one portion of the Lord's Prayer that is repeated, and it's the part about forgiveness: "Forgive us our debts, as we forgive our debtors." Then, at the end of the prayer, we find this statement: "If you forgive men their trespasses, your heavenly Father will also forgive you. But if you do not forgive men their trespasses, neither will your Father forgive your trespasses" (Matthew 6:14–15). As you approach the Father, unburden yourself of those grudges. As you finish your prayer and go into the world, unburden yourself again. Travel light and you'll enjoy the journey for the first time. It's the only way to travel.

After all, that's the identifying mark of the children of God—people who bless their enemies, who return grace for evil, who never fight for the best position but look for the neediest recipient. Against all odds, God has turned the scales of justice upside down and found a way to forgive us. That allows beautiful fellowship between you and God, and between you and others. Wouldn't you like to live under that rule of grace and forgiveness? Don't you long to simply let go? "Be kind to one another, tenderhearted, forgiving one another, just as God in Christ also forgave you" (Ephesians 4:32).

I consider Corrie ten Boom one of the most remarkable Christians of the twentieth century. Her life has always fascinated and inspired me. It wasn't long ago that I had the privilege of traveling through her homeland and seeing where she grew up. You may remember that she and her family paid a high price for sheltering Jews in their home during the Nazi persecution. She and her sister were imprisoned at Ravensbruck, where her sister died; her father died in another concentration camp. When she was released, she had no family. She decided that the world would become her family. The atrocities of the Germans had been tragic enough—but in Corrie's estimation the sin of resentment on the part of the survivors would only perpetuate the tragedy through generations to come. Somewhere it all has to end; someone has to say, "No more." So she set out to travel everywhere she could and preach grace, forgiveness, and voluntary forgetfulness.

One Sunday morning Corrie ten Boom was speaking in Munich. She quickly recognized the man who was walking to the front of the auditorium to greet her. How could she forget such a man? He was the very guard who'd made the women shower as he watched, ogling and taunting them. He had also been savagely cruel to Corrie's sister, Betsy. He had played a part in her death.

Now that very man stood before her, but he clearly didn't recognize her. He said, "Fraulein, it is wonderful that Jesus forgives all our sins—it is just as you say. You mentioned Ravensbruck. I was a guard there, but I have become a Christian since those days. I know that God has forgiven me, but I would like to hear it from you as well. Fraulein, will you forgive me?"

Like the French journalist Morrieaux, Corrie stood there, paralyzed by that word *forgive*. In her mind, this man was a monster. Something within her said that she *couldn't* forgive. He had filled her with shame and misery every day; he was the instigator of a lengthy, unthinkable nightmare. Betsy, her precious sister, had died at his hands. Yet now she felt deep remorse about herself and her faith. How could she preach so fervently about something that, right here on the spot, she couldn't practice herself? She could think of only one thing to do. She looked up to heaven and prayed silently, "Forgive me, Father, for my inability to forgive."

Immediately things began to change. She began to feel the powerful sensation of God's forgiveness moving through her. She couldn't remember later how it happened, but she felt her hand surge forward to clasp the hand of the old guard, and she clutched it firmly and said, *"You are forgiven."* The man was set free. But even more, on that day, Corrie ten Boom herself was set free. She felt the burden of resentment fall away from her shoulders.[8]

Life is so much easier when we allow God to do this for us. The world is so much brighter, its colors so much more vivid, the world filled with so much more joy when we're not blinded by petty resentment. It's a lesson our world never learns. Resentment causes families to break apart, communities to be torn by violence, nations to remain at war for generations. It injects its teeth into countless souls of those who walk among us, so that lives that might have been productive, lives that might have been a blessing, become consumed by self-destructive hatred. It keeps us from knowing the goodness of God. It keeps us from being faithful parents, faithful children, good neighbors.

We need not live this way; we *must* not live this way. All we need to do is ask God to free us from the chains of the ledger book. We began by recalling a story by Charles Dickens. In another of that same author's tales, a man named Ebenezer Scrooge has become twisted by every manner of resentment—of his father, of his fiancée, of everyone and everything. Then the ghost of his old friend Jacob Marley comes for a visit on Christmas Eve. Do you remember the distinctive thing about Marley's apparel? His leg was chained to a long string of ledger books, *logizomai*, and he tells Scrooge that even now, an invisible ledger every bit as long is attached to Scrooge's own leg, and every day it's becoming longer and impeding his progress even more.

How many ledgers are you carrying around with you? Won't you allow Christ to cut them away for good? Throw away the books, walk free and lighthearted, and you'll live in an atmosphere of grace and joy you never thought possible.

Resist your resentment. Banish every trace of bitterness. Live by the liberating law of grace—and remember to forget.

9

DISARMING YOUR DOUBTS

YOU CAN WIN THE BATTLE AND
LIVE VICTORIOUSLY

*F*OUR CENTIMETERS. HOW COULD FOUR TINY centimeters make so much difference—cause so much suffering?

How could four marks on a metric tape so profoundly punish a family, strain a marriage, and call into question the very goodness of God?

"Your daughter has a condition called microcephaly," said the doctor. "Her head should have a circumference of thirty-five centimeters—but it measures only thirty-one."

For several days, Susan sat in the hospital pondering the ominous words. For now, nothing was sure. Mandy might lead a happy, normal life after all. But the uncertainty was cruel, almost intolerable. Marshall, her husband, was out of town. How could he be away at a time like this—a time when doctors were using words like *retardation* and *severe*?

For weeks the Shelleys prayed intensely, desperately, unceasingly. Countless friends joined them in prayer. Marshall was the editor of a successful Christian magazine, and he was known and loved by many. But God didn't seem to be offering special favors to Christian editors; the weeks only confirmed everyone's deepest fears. The Shelleys' third child, it seemed, would never walk or talk, sit up, or even recognize her caregivers. Her life would be defined by seizures, rounds of hospitalization, and an infinite array of medications.

At the age of three months, cataracts were detected in Mandy's eyes. There was corrective surgery, but did it really matter? Susan couldn't be certain her daughter ever saw her face—or heard her voice, for that matter.

Family life was totally dominated by the care of the suffering and unresponsive child; it was an open-ended emergency, a crisis never resolved. Eight hours were often required simply to feed Mandy. Late-night hospital trips were routine.

Meanwhile, the tensions only grew thicker between husband and wife. Where was God? *He's more than welcome to show up—any time now would be fine*, thought Marshall and Susan.

It was just then, in the midst of caring for Mandy, that the surprise came. Susan was pregnant again. Here, finally, was a ray of sunshine—a message that God approved of their strong faith in hard times. And the child would be their first boy.

In the fifth month, Susan went to see the doctor for an ultrasound. He brought this report: "The fetus has a malformed heart. The aorta is attached incorrectly. There are missing portions of the cerebellum. Clubfoot, cleft palate, and perhaps a cleft lip. Possibly a spina bifida . . . This is a condition incompatible with life." The little boy was likely to spontaneously miscarry, but in any case he wouldn't survive long outside the womb. The doctor suggested a "termination," but Susan, still honoring God as the giver and taker of life, carried the child to term. The only time she would have for getting to know her little boy, she reflected, might well be a few short weeks in the womb.

The Shelleys turned their prayers to survival and healing for the child. Again, the community of faith encircled them with intercession and support. The little boy was born, took a deep breath, and turned blue. Two minutes after he entered the world, he quietly departed it again. His name was Toby, from the biblical *Tobiah*, which means "God is good." It wasn't how the family felt, but it was still what they believed.

In a few months, Mandy followed her tiny brother into the next world, and she was buried beside her brother; two tiny coffins, two graves, two aching losses.

Susan grieved bitterly for her double loss; her prayers were angry and accusing. If God couldn't take any better care of His children here on earth, how could she know they were better off now? People offered all the usual pat answers about God's allowance of suffering; none of these lines were good enough now. Susan needed something for her *soul*. For three nights she lay awake, pleading for a simple thing: some assurance that Mandy and Toby were safe, whole, and cared for.

Just a simple answer would be enough; just a gesture from the hand that was supposed to offer love; then perhaps she could let go. Susan prayed. And even more, she listened—listened through the silence.

WHY?

Perhaps it's the defining question for our species: *Why?* Of all God's creatures, we are the only ones who seek to understand, to secure the reason and the rationale. Humanity will go to great lengths simply to find meaning. We challenge the atom; we push into space. But that meaning can be elusive. More essential questions haunt us: *Where is the child I've lost? Why am I here? What is the significance of my life? What would have happened if I'd chosen the other road—of marriage, of career, of faith?*

When the answers elude our grasp and the void ignores our questions, we suffer a kind of spiritual vertigo we call *doubt.* Suddenly all the assumptions on which we've built a life, large and small, are like a toothpick replica of the Eiffel Tower—pull out one support and, if it's close enough to the foundation, the whole structure topples. Every belief we have is threatened.

For most of us, it's in the aftermath of pain and shock that the questions come. *Why, Lord? Why?*

That word cruelly haunted the mother of Glenn Chambers. On February 15, 1947, the young man was waiting to board a DC-4 bound for Quito, Ecuador. Glenn was off to make his dreams come true; he was enlisting as a missionary through an organization called The Voice of the Andes. He had a few extra minutes before takeoff, so he looked for a scrap of paper on which to write a note to his mother. Then his plane disappeared into the clouds, never to emerge. It crashed into the peak of El Tablazo, near Bogotá. Consumed by flames, it hurtled from the skies into a ravine fourteen thousand feet below. The unthinkable news came to his mother— followed, a few days later, by his final note. He had scribbled it on the corner of an advertisement that happened to be dominated by one towering word: *Why?*

The word mocked and haunted the mother of Glenn Chambers. Here were his last known words, seemingly from beyond the grave. They were filled with cheer, ignoring those looming letters, black and blaring, that asked the unanswerable. The same letters stand poised in the backdrop of our own lives. We can't ignore them forever. Inevitably we must doubt.

The Greek words for doubt carry the idea of uncertainty. They have the connotation of being unsettled, of lacking a firm conviction. Doubt is not the opposite of faith, but the opportunity of faith, the growing pains of an eager, seeking spirit. The true enemy of faith is unbelief, which refuses to consider. But doubt is a necessary leg of the journey. It stands at the edge of past understandings and stretches painfully for new frontiers.

To doubt, then, is to be human. We read the Bible and find doubters at every turn, even among the greatest of men — David, Job, Solomon, Jeremiah. In the New Testament we quickly come to the man known as John the Baptist, who demanded faith. He proclaimed the answers in ringing oratories, but he also asked his share of questions. As he sat behind bars, under the arrest of King Herod, he found himself pondering deeply and darkly. He sent his men to Jesus with a question: "Are you the coming One, or do we look for another?"

John had been in the wilderness preaching his heart out, proclaiming the coming of the Deliverer. Jesus described him as the greatest "among those born of women" — quite an endorsement (Matthew 11:11). It had been a short time since John had baptized Jesus. It was a moment of supernatural power, and John heard the voice of God affirming Jesus as the Christ. But now, away from the crowds and the river baptisms, within the darkness of a prison cell, nothing seemed the same. John can't help but ask the question straight out: *Are You the real thing, or will all our hopes and dreams be shattered once again?*

If it could happen to the greatest man born of women, then none of us are exempt. Doubts are inevitable for the weak and the wise. I was raised in a wonderful home by believing parents, but I grappled with my share of doubts through my adolescent years. As a matter of fact, doubts are basically guaranteed in Christian homes. The essentials of the faith are so ingrained, so taken for granted, that we must test them before making them our own.

No, the questioning spirit is not sinful, but simply a rite of passage we must all pass through as we grow into a deeper faith. God understands. He's far more pleased when we ask the questions and challenge the assumptions than when we accept, secondhand and prefabricated, the faith of our parents. That's not a living, breathing faith at all, but an heirloom to display in some corner of the living room with the other antiques. Your Father wants you to work out your salvation with fear, trembling, confrontation, tears, and whatever else might be required to nurture an authentic personal friendship with the living God.

Most of us need to reinstate that word *doubt* as a friend, not an enemy. But there's another word we need to examine: *unbelief*. We might say that doubt asks questions; unbelief refuses to hear answers. The former is hard miles on a good journey; the latter is the dead end, a refusal to travel any farther.

DEALING WITH DOUBTS

John 20 brings us into the presence of history's most notorious doubter. His name was Thomas. The Bible often refers to him as Thomas *Didymus*. Many people assume the meaning is "Thomas the Doubter," but actually it means Thomas the Twin. *Didymus* travels down through the years and comes to us in the English language as *ditto*—double. We have no idea what happened to Thomas's twin, but we know he was often "in two minds," which is one definition of doubt.

He was the classic skeptic, adamantly unwilling to accept anything on simple hearsay—not without a razor-sharp question or two. Perhaps in our time he would be a lawyer. But there was a touch of melancholy about Thomas as well, a bit of the pessimist. You and I may not have placed him on the short list for Jesus' executive cabinet, but the Lord selected Thomas as one of His closest friends. Perhaps He needed a tough-minded disciple, as all our organizations do.

I wish we had time to review all the references to Thomas in the Gospels. One will have to suffice. It was that unforgettable evening when Jesus and His followers met in the Upper Room for their final meal, recorded in John 14:4–5. Jesus was gently preparing His disciples for the suffering and tragedy to come, and He said, in essence, "You know where I must go, and you know how it must happen."

Thomas was the first with a reply, which we might paraphrase as, "Lord, we have no idea where You're going. How would we know something like that?" Skeptics don't buy into subtlety and elliptical references. They're lovers of straight talk, clear words, and hard answers.

That's the Thomas of Scripture—practical, skeptical, taking nothing for granted—but *not* unbelieving. Thomas went everywhere the Twelve went. He saw and felt and heard all the miraculous events. He knew who could walk on water, who could raise a dead friend, who controlled the very winds of the storm. Surely the life of Thomas had been transformed along with the rest. But still he doubted. We can have faith, see miracles, and still have questions. As a matter of fact, the thinking believer will only have his questions increased when the miracles flow.

The defining moment in Thomas's life is found in John 20. For Peter, that moment came at a fish fry, when Jesus forgave him and sent him out to change the world. But for Thomas it happened here, in the room where the disciples had huddled together; the room entered in fear and departed in faith. This is the room where doubt was overcome and skepticism was left in awe.

Let's enter that room now and learn the timeless secrets of doubt and belief.

Doubt Develops in Isolation

John 20:24 gives us the key to the passage: Thomas has missed the fireworks. Jesus has appeared in the midst of His friends, shown His wounds, and pointed toward the future. Great joy and celebration have broken out in that room. Jesus *alive?* Can it be true? Yes, for He was right there in the flesh—but Thomas was not, and this is a significant point.

Ten men gathered together in the custom of the bereaved. When someone near to us dies, we rendezvous at someone's home; we bring food and gentle laughter and words of consolation. Solitude isn't recommended, for we need the encouragement available in the intermingling of our spirits. But Thomas, independent thinker that he was, had drawn apart and missed not only the consolation but also the miracle.

Doubt flourishes in the dark. It's a bit like those mushrooms that grow in damp cellars. It thrives on the cold, dank loneliness of the human spirit.

140

In solitude, the questions seem larger, more ominous, more hopeless. Where was John the Baptist when he began to question the very content of all of his own preaching? He was in a dark cell, away from the throng, there in the dungeon where the mushrooms grew. Darkness feeds doubt; daylight has a way of dispelling the worst of it.

That's why doubt is a wise occasion for examining our feelings. Sometimes our questions have less to do with theological enigmas than with a simple case of the blues. Our souls and our bodies live in such close company that they tend to catch each other's diseases. Physical illness dampens the soul, and emotional depression causes bodily fatigue. C. S. Lewis admitted to struggling with doubt when he was on the road in some inn or strange bed. He loved his home and his circle of friends, and absence often brought on a fit of soul vertigo for him.

Stay connected to people, and you're more likely to stay connected to your faith.

Doubt Demands Evidence

True doubt never turns away from the facts, wherever they may lead. It stubbornly pursues the truth. It's Galileo questioning that the world is flat; Chuck Yeager insisting the sound barrier is no barrier at all; Thomas requiring a handling of the evidence.

> But he said to them, "Unless I see in His hands the print of the nails, and put my finger into the print of the nails, and put my hand into His side, I will not believe." (John 20:25)

Consider the doubter's perspective. When Jesus had drawn up the group itinerary, Thomas had spoken against Jerusalem. As he saw things, it was simply too dangerous a place to visit—Jesus would die, and perhaps the disciples would die with Him. Sure enough, his direst predictions for Jesus have come true. If only they had listened to Thomas, master of the worst-case scenario. Skeptics draw a melancholy satisfaction from the words "I told you so."

Now, when the disciples are elbowing one another out of the way, shouting over one another to tell Thomas the incredible news (for we all love trumping the pessimist), how does Thomas respond? Just exactly as we'd expect—he recites the Skeptic's Creed. "I'll believe it when I see it," he says. "As a matter of fact, scratch that—I'll believe it when I *feel* it. You'll forgive me for not taking *your* word for it. I'll make my own evaluation, if it's all the same to you."

Just as we love chastising Peter for failing to walk on water—regardless of whether *we* would have stepped out of the boat—we're all too ready to condemn Thomas simply because he insisted on validation. At least he was honest; he called it as he saw it. He never called the disciples' claims impossible; he never ruled out miracles. He simply wanted to test the evidence *personally*.

As we'll see, Jesus met Thomas at the point of his questions. Ask God with an honest heart, and He'll always answer you.

Doubt Draws Us Back to Christ

Scene: the same room, but eight days later. For more than a week, the issue has separated Thomas and his friends. Have they witnessed the greatest event in history, or have they been cruelly deceived?

It's significant that Thomas, despite his reservation, has lingered among them. Here again is the difference between doubt and unbelief. Doubt says, "I'll stay and investigate." Unbelief stalks away and says, "Sure, you guys go on believing whatever you want. I'm out of here." Thomas stays to ask the questions—and therefore receives the answers.

> And after eight days His disciples were again inside, and Thomas with them. Jesus came, the doors being shut, and stood in the midst, and said, "Peace to you!" (John 20:26)

Christianity ultimately comes down to something more than theological questions. In the end it's all about a Person, not a proposition. The questions are the beginning of the journey, but the answer comes finally in experience, in reaching out to touch and to feel and in being ourselves touched by the power of the nail-scarred hands. This is the experience of Thomas, who asked the right questions and whose doubts kept him among the community of faith and guided him across the room to the presence of the Savior.

The questions remain, of course. I'm sure if we could talk to the disciples, they wouldn't be able to fully explain the mysteries of Jesus' resurrection body that day—one that could move through walls even while displaying the scars of physical execution. After a while, these questions are moot. In the radiance of a man fresh from conquering death, we're struck speechless and we forget to ask about the little things. Too often we become ensnared in some element of doctrinal minutiae, forgetting the miracles that transcend the details. I suspect that if Peter or John wandered by and caught a snatch of our arguments they might say, "What's the point? Jesus descended to hell, broke the chains, and destroyed the power of death. Why the trivial pursuit in the living presence of Jesus?"

Doubt Deepens Our Faith

Consider this: In the years to come, which disciple had the most definitive testimony of all? Who else plunged his hand into the jagged rift where the spear had been thrust? Who else ran a trembling finger along the slope of the wrists, where the nails had sliced through and splintered the wood? Who else would carry within his fingertips, for the rest of his life, the tactile memory of a resurrected body? Only the doubter. Only Thomas.

> Then He said to Thomas, "Reach your finger here, and look at My hands; and reach your hand *here,* and put *it* into My side. Do not be unbelieving, but believing." (John 20:27)

"But Peter," someone may have said, "your eyes played tricks on you."

"Don't you understand, John?" another might have offered. "We see what we long to see."

But Thomas *knew,* for his eyes and his hands offered consistent accounts. The Man before him was the friend he'd loved as a brother, the companion whose death was a matter of hard fact.

Assurance is the reward of the insistent seeker, and Jesus affirms it on a separate postresurrection appearance.

> And He said to them, "Why are you troubled? And why do doubts arise in your hearts? Behold My hands and My feet, that it is I Myself. Handle Me

and see, for a spirit does not have flesh and bones as you see I have." When He had said this, He showed them His hands and His feet. (Luke 24:38–40)

Read those words well, for Jesus looks beyond the page and into your eyes, and He makes you the same offer. "Are you unsure? Reach in and feel for yourself." And with that, He shows you His hands and His feet—if you'll only reach out and touch. Jacob was brash enough to wrestle an angel, and the angel wrestled back; God is big enough to handle the questions that trouble you. Just be *honest* about your doubts. The Bible doesn't affirm those doubts you keep in the box on the shelf, unused, unexamined, that you bring out whenever someone invites you to church. Doubts, useless in and of themselves, are useful when they lead us somewhere.

I commend whoever said that we should believe our beliefs and doubt our doubts. That may sound trite to you, but I find a certain amount of wisdom in that phrase. Repressed doubt, stuck away in the closet, can become a devil's wedge. It's like the letter from the IRS that you're afraid to open. After a while, the emotional weight exceeds whatever peril the envelope could possibly hold.

Don't block out your doubts, but examine them well; turn them around in your mind; discuss them with wise and patient friends. Have the courage of your (struggling) convictions. God has somehow outlasted thousands of years of champion doubters, lined up to ask their stumpers; He hasn't heard one yet that He can't answer, and yours probably won't knock Him from His heavenly throne either. But if you hide it under the rug or in the closet with that IRS letter, it will lurk at the back of your mind and breed a whole family of doubts. It will collect interest until it bankrupts your faith.

Don't let that happen. Bring it out into the light and "doubt it out."

Doubt Defines Our Faith

When you get a question mark all straightened out, what do you have? An exclamation point, of course! Honest questions lead to powerful declarations.

And Thomas answered and said to Him, "My Lord and my God!" (John 20:28)

It's very difficult for me to read this passage without feeling powerful emotion. It's one of the supreme turning points in all Scripture—perhaps the first ringing declaration of the Resurrection's transforming power upon an individual life. The most powerful courtroom testimony is that of a hostile witness. Thomas the skeptic replaces his questions with an exclamation: *my Lord and my God!*

I know we'd all like to have been there to see the wonder and worship shining from his eyes. I know we would join him in falling on our knees to worship the conquering King.

DISARMING YOUR DOUBTS

Confront your doubts head-on, as Thomas did. But you'll want to handle them carefully. Let's discover how you can disarm them.

Admit Your Doubts Personally

Has this ever happened to you? Sliding into a pew, late for church, you feel tired, edgy, and possibly coming down with a cold. Across the sanctuary, people are standing and testifying: "I won five more souls to the kingdom of God," somebody says. "And I bet some of you have won more souls than that! I don't know about you, but I feel God's sweet presence every moment of every day." Everyone around you is laughing, applauding, and saying, "Amen!"

Won five souls to the Lord? You can't even enter the church parking lot without honking your horn at someone who got your space. You'd like to stand up and give *your* testimony. "Hello, everybody. Let me tell you about *my* week. I haven't felt anything but a lousy sinus headache and a bushel of doubts. I haven't had the sense of God in my life for a long time. I'm barely getting by at work, my family life is in chaos, and to be absolutely honest with you, I haven't seen God doing much of anything." Then you would sit down, knowing not to expect many amens—just the kind of awed stares usually reserved for gorillas at the zoo; perhaps the same glances that Thomas got in that disciple-filled room.

But it would be far better for you to stand up and spill it in public than to smother your tangled emotions in sanitary smiles for months and years. If you're going to make it through the bad times and finally encounter the true goodness of God, you must begin with honesty. You must admit to yourself that it's *not* well with your soul.

Articulate Your Doubts Clearly

You can't get by with a simple, "Oh, I'm just a natural-born doubter, I guess." No, you're going to have to do better than that. You're going to have to crystallize your thinking and put your finger on precisely what it is that's causing your uncertainty. The nameless doubt is the one you can't harbor. Identify it, describe it clearly, and deal with it. Are you struggling with the historicity of the Resurrection? We have excellent source material to recommend. Are you grappling with the problem of evil? Great minds have grappled before you — and they're willing to share their thoughts. Are you wondering if one brand of faith is any different from another? Make a brand comparison.

Articulate *what* you doubt and *why* you doubt. What brought this on? Was it something someone said, perhaps some scholar or skeptic? Is there something amiss in the realm of your emotions? Clarify these issues; wipe the clouds away.

Acknowledge Your Doubts Prayerfully

Christian writer Mark Littleton found a little formula that I like. It goes this way:

Turn your doubts to questions.
Turn your questions to prayers.
Turn your prayers to God.[1]

You mean we can take our doubts directly to God? Won't He be offended? Not according to scriptural precedent.

• Consider the case of Gideon:

And the Angel of the LORD appeared to him, and said to him, "The LORD *is* with you, you mighty man of valor!" And Gideon said to Him, "O my lord, if the LORD is with us, why then has all this happened to us? And where *are* all His miracles which our fathers told us about, saying, 'Did not the LORD bring us up from Egypt?' But now the LORD has forsaken us and delivered us into the hands of the Midianites." (Judges 6:12–13)

Gideon's doubts surfaced in the very presence of an angel. The angel testified that God was present, but Gideon was bold enough to say, "You've got to be kidding me! If God is with us, why has our land been taken over by criminal gangs? If God is with us, where are all these miracles our grandparents were always going on about? From where *I'm* standing, it looks like God has gone over to the Midianite side."

It must have gotten God's attention, because the next voice we hear is not identified as the angel's—the text tells us that God replied *personally* to Gideon. He can handle our frustration and our questions.

- Sarah, the matriarch of the chosen people, had a bit of the same abrasive edge. God promised a child, then seemed to forget all about it for *decades*. Who could blame Sarah for becoming a little on the testy side? She was pushing one hundred anyway. At any rate, she had not only her doubts, but also a good laugh in the bargain. In the face of God's promises, she laughed, not realizing that God was present—as, of course, He always is.

- If Sarah could laugh, Jeremiah could cry. You may not have read Lamentations for a while, but the "weeping prophet" came head-on at God with tough questions. And God answered them every time.

- David, in the psalms, often pointed an angry finger at God and accused Him of desertion.

- Job was a man of the widest faith, but he sometimes flirted with the deepest doubts.

The Bible's best and brightest weren't heroes for their lack of doubts; they were heroes for confronting and conquering them.

Analyze the Evidence Diligently

Why won't we confront our doubts? Because deep down, we're afraid the doubts will win. We think Christianity is somehow weaker than its accusers.

Young people buy into the notion that evolution must be a proven commodity, just because the mainstream academic community proclaims it so. But I've watched as creationists and evolutionists debated the issues—and I've never seen the evolutionists win. Few people stop to realize that the theory of evolution is, as theories go, "the new kid on the block"—it has only a century of acceptance under its belt. The idea of a world created by God has always been with us. Our fundamental doctrines provide a strong foundation, built to last not simply through time but for eternity.

The biblical propositions will be here when all the trendy theories of the day have passed away. In the nineteenth century, Friedrich Nietzsche proclaimed, "God is dead." Two hundred years later, God proclaims that Friedrich Nietzsche is dead. That's the way it goes. You don't find flaws in the Word of God; it finds flaws in you.

A lawyer by the name of Frank Morison set out to debunk the crazy idea of Jesus' resurrection once and for all. He examined the historical evidence with all his legal logic and evidential expertise. Morison sifted through every possibility that might account for the disappearance of Jesus' body—and was left with the biblical explanation. In the end, he wrote a book called *Who Moved the Stone?* The only thing it debunked was his skepticism. His book has become the classic apologetic text for the historical resurrection of Jesus Christ. Like Thomas the doubter, Morison brought honest questions and a willingness to investigate. And God moved the stone that was in Morison's heart.

Accept the Limitations Humbly

There's one other thing we must account for—the limitations of dealing with doubt. In the end, some mysteries linger. If it weren't so, we'd be left with no holiness, no God of transcendence. Faith must ultimately encompass its own degree of mystery.

1. Accept your own limitations. I blush to admit this, but the older I get and the more I learn, the more I become aware of my own ignorance. Just when I think I'm pretty smart, I look a little closer and discover the limitations of my knowledge. All I have to do is tune in to the Discovery Channel, read the latest on the world of science, or listen to some of the sharp, cyber-slick young people in our church—and I'm quickly and hopelessly left in the dust. That's when I discover I'm an old-fashioned abacus in a computerized world—and if you don't know what an abacus is, I'm probably just showing my age all the more.

In the face of my limitless limitations, all I can do is bow in humility before our awesome God and say, "Lord, You know my deficiency. You know the limited capacity of the hard drive You wired within me. Help me understand that I'll never have all the answers."

2. Accept the Bible's limitations. I may be venturing where angels fear to tread here. This is a sensitive topic, and I hope you'll read this section carefully before firing off an angry letter.

I accept the Bible as the inspired Word of God, and I regard every word as true, from the opening of one cover to the closing of the other. You can put me down with the crowd that holds out for plenary verbal inspiration, and I'm proud to take my stand among them. The Bible is my full and total authority.

God's Word has every shred of truth we need for our lives in this world, but it doesn't take on every question. There are many issues that God didn't see fit to cover in His Word. What we *were* given is our spiritual meat and living water, the daily minimum requirements for the children of God. Side issues must wait for another day.

Sometimes we face difficult questions. People come to me and ask, "What does the Bible say about this?" We need to accept the fact that, occasionally, the Bible opts for silence. God has an answer, but we must trust the Spirit and our own sound mind as we make our decisions.

3. Adjust to the complexity of the universe. The more we learn about this world, the more complexity we discover. Our great-grandparents knew nothing of molecules, of atoms, of whirling electrons. Our children will delve even deeper into wonders as yet unfound. And on the other end, we knew space was infinite—but somehow it seems to keep growing as we learn more. Today it's possible for astronomers to look through a telescope and see incredible distances across the galaxy—and we're told that their range is only the equivalent of a wet thimble at the edge of an ocean, so vast is our universe. Realizing the rich detail of the microscopic world, and the infinity of the telescopic world, we come to a deeper appreciation of the majesty of God. Finally, in humility, we're content to know that our minds are too small to encompass the wonder of it all.

Therefore we'll have those moments when we look into the stars with our questions and realize the simple answer is that there *is* no simple answer. We are finite, physical beings with spirits prone to stretch toward the infinite. We seek to know Him. We seek to understand His universe. We seek the answers to all that we see and touch, within and without. But for now we must rest in the sufficiency of what is given. Someday, in a better place, all questions will be accounted for, all tears will be dried, and all doubts will be finally laid to rest.

But for now, we can join hands with Paul to embrace the infinite:

> Oh, the depth of the riches both of the wisdom and knowledge of God! How unsearchable *are* His judgments and His ways past finding out! *"For who has known the mind of the* LORD? *Or who has become His counselor? Or who has first given to Him and it shall be repaid to him?"* For of Him and through Him and to Him *are* all things, to whom *be* glory forever. (Romans 11:33–36)

Or we can stand with Isaiah and hear God's gentle disclaimer:

> "For My thoughts *are* not your thoughts, nor *are* your ways My ways," says the LORD. "For *as* the heavens are higher than the earth, so are My ways higher than your ways, and My thoughts than your thoughts." (Isaiah 55:8–9)

We'll never have a handle on the nature of God. We'll never find the box that will confine Him. Be thankful we have room for worship, to stretch toward something so much greater than ourselves. What a terrifying world this would be if we human beings, with all our violence and foolishness, represented the highest authority and the wisest counsel this universe had to offer. Instead we're free to be children, happily deferring to a Father who will take care of everything. If need be, we can bring Him our questions and be certain of receiving, if not precisely the answers we expected, then certainly the answers we truly needed all along.

Susan Shelley, who watched two of her children slip away, kept pounding on the doors of heaven, demanding some reply. For three consecutive nights she asked God for some assurance that her little ones had found comfort and caring. On the third night, as she was asking God again, she heard the sound of little footsteps in the hallway. Her two daughters, seven and four, often came and crawled into bed with their parents. But this time the footsteps came to the doorway and stopped—then receded back down the hall.

The next morning, Palm Sunday, Susan found it difficult to awaken Stacey, the older of the two. Stacey was too sleepy. Her mother asked, "You wouldn't happen to know anything about a midnight wanderer who came to the door of our bedroom last night, would you?"

"Oh, yes," said Stacey, perking up. "That was me. I came to your room to tell you that God spoke to me, but you were asleep. So I went back to bed."

Susan wanted to know what God had said.

"He said that Mandy and Toby are very busy, that they are preparing our house, and that they are guarding His throne."

A little chill ran down Susan's spine. "How did God say these things?"

"He spoke to my mind," said Stacey simply. "Then when I thought you were asleep I came back to my bed and repeated the words over and over so I could remember to tell you. It seemed like an important message."

Susan Shelley didn't know what to think. Was this the answer to her prayer? Could God really have spoken through a seven-year-old? That, of course, is yet *another* question; we never come to the end of them. All that matters is that Susan, from then on, felt no more worries for her two lost little ones. From the mouth of a babe had come words of reassurance and blessing, consistent with all the Bible tells us of the next world. *Her children were busy! They were guarding the throne!* And they were preparing that place where the family would one day be reunited in wholeness and joy.

The grief wasn't dissipated, of course, and the "why" questions endured. But what God supplied was enough—more than enough. With the strength that proceeds from such wisdom, Marshall and Susan dared to keep enlarging their family. A year after Mandy's death they welcomed a little boy into the world. They named the little one Bayly, after a wise Christian well acquainted with grief. He is well; the whole family is well and happy.

Pain lingers in this life, for the Shelleys as for all of us; questions never end. But God is good. We tell Him what we want, and He gives us what we need. And in the end, we can only stand with Thomas, reaching out to handle for ourselves the impenetrable mystery, and whisper,

"My Lord and my God!"

10

POSTPONING YOUR PROCRASTINATION

YOU CAN WIN THE BATTLE AND LIVE VICTORIOUSLY

IT'S MEL'S FIRST DAY OF WORKING OUT OF HIS HOME. Boy, has he waited a long time for this!

Mel is giving this whole "work at home" thing a try after two years of pleading with his boss. The one-hour commute was robbing him of productive energy, and he insisted that he could increase productivity by at least 15 percent simply by using a home office. "Let me try it for three months," he said, "and if my numbers don't increase, I'll come back to my desk and drop the subject."

The boss finally gave in. Now he has the home office all set up, the software installed, and the phone line ready for action. At 8:30 A.M., Mel is ready for work—in his T-shirt! *Isn't this great?* He takes a deep breath, cracks his knuckles, and prepares to dig in.

At 8:35, Mel decides to make a trip to the pencil sharpener. To be efficient, he takes a full box of pencils with him.

At 8:45, Mel returns to his desk and prepares to resume his work. But he has a thought—that pencil sharpener needs to be emptied, doesn't it?

At 8:46, Mel begins performing routine maintenance work on the pencil sharpener. He empties the shavings, wipes the base with a paper towel, and then cleans the rollers. Some of the shavings missed the wastebasket, so he goes for a broom and sweeps the area. Then he takes the wastebasket outside to empty it in the trash. Then he carries the trash cans out to the street and has a nice chat with Mrs. Murgatroyd across the street. It's good public relations for the company.

At 9:32, Mel returns to his desk and prepares to resume his work.

At 9:33, Mel decides a quick computer game of Minesweeper will stimulate his creative juices a little better.

At 11:14, Mel achieves his all-time best record in Minesweeper. His creative juices are flowing now.

At 11:15, Mel makes a sales call. The line is busy. Mel decides it's time for a break.

At 11:32, Mel returns from the kitchen with a fresh cup of coffee. For extra efficiency, he reads e-mail while sipping his coffee. He forwards the cute e-mail with the penguin joke to forty-three of his friends. While he's on-line, Mel feels this would be the smartest time to check prices on new pencil sharpeners for home offices.

At 12:31, Mel has a list of prices on pencil sharpeners. He stops for lunch. For extra efficiency, he reads e-mail while chewing his tuna fish sandwich. Twenty-two of his friends have replied to the cute e-mail with the penguin joke, many of them offering cute jokes of their own. Mel takes time to reply to each one, which is good public relations for the company.

At 1:53, Mel takes a deep breath and prepares to resume his work.

At 1:54, Mel calls that number again. Still busy.

At 1:55, Mel drives to the office supply store to shop for pencil sharpeners. While he's out, he stops at the park and plays baseball with two nice kids who have never been taught how to choke up on the bat and swing from the back foot. This is good public relations for the company. On the way home, he stops for a car wash after buying new glass to replace the window knocked out by the baseball.

At 4:43, Mel arrives home and calls it a day. This home office routine is even more tiring than he expected!

A scholar once surveyed the Scriptures to discover the most significant words in all the Bible. He wanted to find the saddest word, the happiest word, the most emotional word and so on. When he came around to the Bible's most dangerous word, he identified it as *tomorrow*. The word is a thief, he said, that robs dreamers of their dreams and the talented of their greatest achievements. It keeps men and women from coming to Christ and discovering the kind of life God longs for them to have. The prince of preachers, Charles H. Spurgeon, agreed. "Tomorrow, tomorrow, tomorrow!" he wrote. "Alas, tomorrow never comes! It is in no calendar except the almanac of fools."[1]

THE THIEF OF TIME

Larry, a friend of our radio ministry, wanted to work independently just as Mel did. But Larry went all the way: He formed his own tree service and logging business. And unlike Mel, he had no problem getting his work done. He put in long, physically exhausting days for his career and his family. But deep down, he knew there was one thing missing—he wasn't working for Christ. He'd prayed for God to bless the new company; he went to church every Sunday. But being a believer made no significant difference in his life; he knew in his heart that Christ wanted more from him.

Larry, however, was raised to be self-reliant. What was it his parents loved to say? *Do for yourself.* So he focused totally on his work and his business flourished, all the way up to the day when Larry felled his final tree.

It was a routine maneuver; he didn't do anything differently. Larry had a great pine ready to fall, and he stood clear. But as it slid, the pine collided violently with another tree at the edge of the clearing. Suddenly it was coming down in a different direction—the direction Larry had chosen to run for safety.

Before he knew it, Larry was pinned to the ground, in a world of pain. He rasped out the words, "God, help me." He was certain that death was near. He felt no fear, but what was that other thing that seemed to be filling his spirit? *Regret.* His thoughts began to move toward what must lie ahead: a face-to-face meeting with Jesus. And that would bring no joy at all to Larry. How could he ever explain to Jesus an entire life of ignoring His voice? He knew God had special things planned for him, but he had consistently gone his own way. There was always later—after he had his business running smoothly, after he raised his family, after his youth was gone. *Later.*

But now he was fresh out of later. Now he would stand and give an account before the throne of grace. Now he wished he had a second chance.

After Larry's crushed body was found, he spent three days in critical condition, hovering between life and death, fighting for that second chance. On his behalf, a prayer chain began in his family and rippled out to friends and associates. Larry's vital signs began to rally. The doctors repaired both his legs, narrowly avoiding amputation. Amazingly, there was no damage at all to the spinal cord. He was home for his thirty-seventh birthday with a big cake and a heart filled with gratitude to God. Larry is determined to walk again—with his family and, above all, with his Lord. He had started a business to work for himself. But from now on, he's reporting to a much higher authority.

Procrastination is the thief of time. You may never confront it as dramatically as Larry did, but there's no doubt you'll confront it in some form time and time again. What would be the value of a human life for a person who could use it without ever procrastinating? That life would be incredibly successful. Before we discover some ways we can move toward that level of lifestyle stewardship, let's explore a few reasons why procrastination is such a deadly vice.

Procrastination Robs You of Opportunities for Service

How strict was Jesus on the issue of time-wasting? Take this example under consideration:

> Then He said to another, "Follow Me." But he said, "Lord, let me first go and bury my father." Jesus said to him, "Let the dead bury their own dead, but you go and preach the kingdom of God." And another also said, "Lord, I will follow You, but let me first go *and* bid them farewell who are at my house." But Jesus said to him, "No one, having put his hand to the plow, and looking back, is fit for the kingdom of God." (Luke 9:59–62)

It seems like a stringent approach to young recruits, doesn't it? Shouldn't we take time out for funerals? Shouldn't we show our families the courtesy of checking in to tell them we're checking out?

Of course we should. Jesus' point is that we must keep in check our own tendency to put the big things aside for the little ones. It's what Charles Hummel called the "tyranny of the urgent"—putting the more important thing behind the more immediate thing. At any given moment we need to be aware of the wisest possible way to invest the moment we so briefly hold in our grasp. Too easily a lifetime has passed and we've done little or nothing of eternal value. Stop to attend that funeral and you'll find five different reasons to change your mind about following Jesus; check in with your family and you're liable to be talked out of your new resolution. Jesus is simply making the point that a commitment to Him means a radical reprioritization of life's values—effective immediately.

It was an issue Jesus confronted at every turn. How could He help people understand the magnitude of following Him? If you find the finest pearl, He would say, you'll sell everything you have just to possess it. If you stumble across buried treasure, it will take precedence over everything else. You'll completely reorder the way you live (Matthew 13:44–46). Time is the ballot that records your vote on what matters in life.

Even Jesus' inner circle struggled to understand these teachings. In Matthew 26, Jesus brought Peter, James, and John with Him into the Garden of Gethsemane. He left the other eight behind. Jesus told His friends that He had a sorrow unto death itself. He implored them to stay with Him and pray. Then He went a few steps farther and entered a deep, passionate time of prayer.

When Jesus checked on His disciples, they weren't supporting His supplication with their own; they had drifted off to sleep. So He admonished them to watch and pray, and to fend off temptation. The spirit is willing, He told them, but the flesh is weak. How true—we really *do* desire to serve God the right way, but our humanity keeps getting in the way.

Twice Jesus rejoined His spiritual battle, agonizing over the crisis of human fate. He was dealing with our sin, our punishment, His submission to the will of the Father. The devil must have battered Him with every weapon from the demonic arsenal. Jesus faced it alone. He yearned for the circle of His most intimate friends, locking arms and upholding Him in prayer. But each time He checked, they were asleep. They napped away their final—and most meaningful—moments with Jesus before the Crucifixion. In this very garden, the destiny of the human race was in the balance. The three friends couldn't have known; they couldn't have comprehended the spiritual implications of the moment. All the same, they gave in to weakness. They slept on their watch.

In time, each of them would write books about Jesus and the meaning of His incarnation. Each of them would perform miracles and fully devote himself to the spread of the gospel. Two of the three would give their lives in martyrdom for their Master. Surely they atoned for their moment of weakness. But as long as they lived, they must have had regrets—sad memories of the lost twilight in the garden, the squandered opportunity to support Jesus when He needed it the most, the chance to make the last moments before His arrest a bit less painful, and to be a part of a singular moment where time blended into eternity. Spilled water never returns to the cup.

Pinned beneath a tree, Larry understood the power of this truth. He knew the time will come when we must stand and give an account for every moment of our time, what we've done with it as well as what we haven't done. It's written across the parables of Jesus again and again: Your time is your treasure; spend it carefully. What can you do for God? How can you invest this hour?

I believe that sometimes God gives us explicit instructions for the moment before us. I know He does for me. I don't hear voices, but in the midst of all my busyness and distractions the still, small voice breaks through: *Why don't you call this particular friend? Why don't you go to that particular place?* I think it's common in the life of ministers. Sometimes I obey what I know to be the voice of God. Other times, to my shame, I let the moment get by; I tell God, in essence, "Let me go bury the dead first." And I know deep down that I've missed a divine appointment. It's an empty feeling to comprehend, much later, that you've missed something special God had for you to do.

We need to learn to hear His voice, particularly as it pertains to the immediate use of our time. If we could do that, even moderately well, the fruit of our lives would be orchards ample enough to feed the world. But we grow busy, don't we? We become taken with the urgent rather than the essential.

Charles Hanson Towne wrote a poem that burns my soul with conviction every time I read it:

AROUND THE CORNER

Around the corner I have a friend,
In this great city that has no end;
Yet days go by, and weeks rush on,
And before I know it, a year is gone,
And I never see my old friend's face,

For Life is a swift and terrible race.
He knows I like him just as well
As in the days when I rang his bell
And he rang mine.
We were younger then,
And now we are busy and tired men:
Tired with playing a foolish game,
Tired with trying to make a name.
"Tomorrow," I say, "I will call on Jim,"
Just to show that I'm thinking of him,
But tomorrow comes—and tomorrow goes,
And the distance between us grows and grows.
Around the corner yet miles away . . .
"Here's a telegram, sir," Jim died today.
And that's what we get, and deserve in the end:
Around the corner, a vanished friend.[2]

A lot of people and opportunities and perhaps miracles vanish when the thief of time breaks into the house. We might enjoy the goodness of simple friendship. We might bless one another's lives. We might enrich our own lives—but procrastination holds us back. Right at this moment you could list fifty worthy uses for your time over the next two or three hours. Without even thinking hard, you could name fifty ways of serving God without driving five minutes from your home. Some of them would involve your family; others your good friends. Some would involve people you don't know who need the touch of Christ in their lives. Some would involve direct biblical ministry. Others would involve simple cups of cold water.

What if you made that list? What if you took this paragraph literally, wrote down your action points, and began crossing them off over the next two months, every day getting a new one accomplished? Do you think your life would change? Now, think about the lives you touch—in your home, at work, in your church—people who aren't reading this book but would take note of your movements. Do you think their lives would change? Who knows? You might start a revival.

Isn't it a shame that we read paragraphs like the one you've just read, we think about them for a moment—then we turn the page. Why don't we act? Because we procrastinate. And because we procrastinate, we rob ourselves— and others, too—of blessings we'll never realize.

Procrastination robs you of opportunities for service.

Procrastination Robs You of Opportunities to Be Successful

You don't need to be a Christian to understand this point. You need to be a Christian to enter heaven, and to live the abundant life, and to escape punishment—but this particular point holds true for every human being, saved or unsaved. There is no successful person who is a procrastinator.

I hope you've taken that in. For if you describe yourself as a chronic procrastinator, that's another way of saying, "I'm planning on avoiding a successful life." James Gordon Gilkey has pointed out the popular misconception that we're each standing in the middle of a great circle filled with tasks, burdens, problems, annoyances, and responsibilities that are rushing upon us all at once. There are too many things to do simultaneously, so we're overburdened, overtaxed, and exhausted. According to Gilkey, it's all a myth. He substitutes a much more accurate metaphor.

What is the true picture of your life? Imagine that there is an hourglass on your desk. Connecting the bowl at the top with the bowl at the bottom is a tube so thin that only one grain of sand can pass through it at a time.

That is the true picture of your life, even on a super-busy day. The crowded hours come to you always one moment at a time. That is the only way they can come. The day may bring many tasks, many problems, strains, but invariably they come in single file.[3]

One of the great secrets of success is simply taking each moment as it comes and investing it the best way possible. John Keeble, a fine Christian and a primary founder of the financial planning industry, built a successful career on a simple plan to cut off any possibility of his procrastination. First, he decided he needed to talk to four or five potential customers per sales day. It had been proved that anyone who does that consistently would have a high likelihood of success. Then, Keeble completely dedicated Fridays to the goal of setting up those appointments. He had to make himself a strict promise that he'd use Fridays for no other purpose than to work the phones and set the dates.

What was so great about this? Keeble knew that once he had locked himself in to twenty personal appointments for the following week, he would have no option, no "wiggle room," for time-wasting. He locked himself in to time management, and he threw away the key. On that foundation, Keeble became a millionaire, an industry founder, and a beloved Christian philanthropist.[4]

Read the stories of men and women who have found success, and you'll inevitably discover they were men and women who took time seriously. There was a management consultant some years ago named Ivy Lee. Charles Schwab, chairman of Bethlehem Steel, hired him to come in and help him become more productive. Lee smiled and gave him a plan of underwhelming simplicity. He said, "Each evening, write down the six most important things you should do on the following day. List them in order of importance. The following morning, come into work and do whatever tops the list. When you've finished with that one, move to the next one down."

Schwab asked Lee how much he was going to charge for such advice. Lee replied, "Use the plan strictly for several months. Then you decide on the value of my plan and send me a check." Eventually Lee received a check for $25,000 from Schwab, for that simple piece of advice—a good bit of money at the beginning of the twentieth century.

You might not be impressed by that story, but have you tried the plan? If someone made a "to-do" list that recorded, after the fact, the *actual* use of your time—would you be pleased with the list? Would it show the enjoyable things at the top, and the important but dreaded activities always at the bottom, always being shoved back down whenever they threaten to climb the chart? I keep my "to-do" list on a yellow legal pad, and I don't know what I'd do without it. If I can show discipline in deciding the most important task, and keeping it at the top of the list, then my day will be a success.

It's all about time, isn't it? Arnold Bennett said, "Time is the inexplicable raw material of everything." It's the spiritual molecular structure of our world. Your career is composed of time. Your marriage and family success are measured in time. Your relationship with God is measured in time. Will the time chart of your life please you when you give an account of it?

Procrastination Robs You of the Opportunity for Salvation

Here, of course, is the most dangerous possibility of all. Every year, every day, every moment, procrastination cuts people off from the gates of heaven. And perhaps the greatest biblical account of it is found in Acts 24. This passage lays out for us a classic model of time tragically squandered—beginning with our cast of characters.

The identity of the procrastinator. The first portion of Acts 24:24 sets the scene:

> And after some days, when Felix came with his wife Drusilla, who was Jewish . . .

Who are these people? Let's stop and discover a bit more about them.

- *Felix,* whose real name was Antonius Felix, was Greek by birth. He had some strong ties in the Roman Empire and was appointed procurator of Judea by his brother. Because of that appointment, Felix was the man to hear Paul's case when the apostle was wrongfully accused of sedition. As we'll see, Paul used the opportunity to share the gospel with him.

- *Drusilla, the wife of Felix.* You might be surprised to learn something about Drusilla's family. She was one of three daughters of Herod Agrippa I, and Felix had stolen her from her husband to be his third wife. Her sister was married to the king. Her father murdered James, brother of John, and tried to kill Peter. Her great-uncle Herod Antipas beheaded John the Baptist. And her great-grandfather Herod the Great instituted the mass murder of babies in Bethlehem in an effort to weed out the newborn Messiah. This was the family of Drusilla—a distinguished and diabolical line.

Now, as we enter the story, Paul is appearing before Felix. It has been suggested that this was only the initial arrangement; it ended up with Felix appearing before Paul. Certainly it had to be a livelier hearing than the usual legal proceedings, for Paul wasted little time defending himself.

Instead, he launched into a defense of Jesus Christ, the Son of God and the salvation of men.

It didn't much matter to Paul where he was, what he was facing, or what the prospects might be. Everywhere he went, he shared the gospel. The world was his pulpit. I see a bit of this in my good friend Franklin Graham. Wherever he goes, he keeps talking about Jesus. Whomever he faces, the gospel quickly becomes the subject matter. And his message is simple and direct, so that it can get through to anybody, anywhere, at any time. This is Paul's style—an urgency to share Christ, for there's not a single moment fit for procrastination.

The instruction of the procrastinator. I'm delighted that Luke, the author of Acts, gives us Paul's sermon outline.

> He sent for Paul and heard him concerning the faith in Christ. Now as he reasoned about righteousness, self-control, and the judgment to come . . . (Acts 24:24b–25a)

As a preacher I can tell you it's an inspired three-point sermon plan. Consider its procession:

1. *Righteousness*
2. *Self-control*
3. *Judgment to come*

If you'll think for a moment about Paul's audience, you'll agree that this was a strategically chosen outline. Felix and Drusilla were *unrighteous;* they had no *self-control;* they were facing the *judgment to come.*

The royal couple, of course, could not have been expecting to hear this kind of thing. It was very seldom that a prisoner came in with an organized evangelistic sermon. They were expecting to hear a dissertation comparing and contrasting Christian and Judaic thought systems. Instead, the prisoner came in with his gospel guns blazing.

Point one, *righteousness,* passed without much incident. The listeners must have breathed a sigh of relief. Who would argue that righteousness is nice?

Then point two got under way: *self-control.* These two were leading lives of serial matrimony and unbridled consumption, and they must have had a few raw nerves jangled at this point. The Holy Spirit was surely at work, convicting mightily. By the end of that second point, we can imagine Felix and Drusilla gritting their teeth, visibly fidgeting.

Point number three, of course, wasn't exactly a soft landing: *judgment to come, payday someday.* Point one raised the spiritual issue. Point two zoomed in on the target and took aim. Point three fired! The procurator and his wife were sitting behind the judge's bench when this meeting began; now it felt more as if they were sitting at the defendant's table—a table that had been turned by Paul.

The impact on the procrastinator. In the early days of America, books tell us that the great preachers—men like Jonathan Edwards—would preach with such power, create such conviction, that their listeners would clutch the pews. Edwards had a sermon called "Sinners in the Hands of an Angry God," and he described sinful men as tiny spiders dangling over the flame. The story is that people felt such deep emotion, such utter conviction, that they would drive their fingernails into the hard wood of the pews, trying to keep their bodies from slipping into the great abyss of hellfire! That's the power of conviction when the Holy Spirit gets into the room, and we don't see enough of it anymore. You can still go into some of those old frame church-houses in New England and see the "clutch-marks" pressed into the pine.

This was the kind of reaction Paul's sermon brought from Felix. One translation says Felix was *terrified.* Another translation says he *trembled.* The voice of God came through, loud and clear, to Felix's heart and reduced him to his bare spiritual essentials. And there was the procurator of Judea—trembling in the face of his own sin and guilt.

The intention of the procrastinator. Now we come to the moment of truth—and sadly, it's true for most moments.

> Felix was afraid and answered, "Go away for now; when I have a convenient time I will call for you." (Acts 24:25b)

Look at those familiar lines! "Could you call back later, Paul? This isn't a good time. Don't call me; I'll call you." The words of Felix are hauntingly contemporary. You've used them; I've used them. They're the favorite words of procrastinators everywhere.

You'll find two words very close together in your dictionary: *inter* and *intend*. The first means "to bury." The second often means exactly the same thing. To merely *intend* is to bury any chance of getting something done, to *inter* it in the graveyard of Might-Have-Been. The road to hell, after all, is paved with good *intentions*. And Felix lays the first brick in his hell-bound highway in this verse. It's important to point out that Paul appeared before Felix at least one more time. But it wasn't the same; the moment of truth had passed. The man who had trembled had now grown cold in his heart toward the gospel.

When the voice of God calls to you, never make the mistake of counting on tomorrow. As we'll see, that can be a fatal blunder.

TWO MAJOR PROBLEMS WITH PROCRASTINATION

Procrastination cuts off our service, our success, and possibly even our salvation. Let's discover the two greatest mistakes made by those who would misuse time.

1. Procrastination Does Not Take into Account the Uncertainty of Life

Spurgeon was once preaching on eternal life, and he caught the eye of a godly woman sitting near the front. She had been in his church many years, and Spurgeon knew her faith was strong. There was some special gleam in her eye today; Spurgeon couldn't be certain what it meant, but preachers draw power and encouragement from attentive faces. He caught her eye repeatedly as he preached on paradise—until a certain possibility occurred to him. Spurgeon paused in his preaching and asked the man beside this woman to check her wrist for a pulse. She had none. The woman had gone on to the next life with the gleam of heaven already present in her eye.

In her case, everyone was able to praise God for the assurance of her salvation and the peaceful and appropriate manner of her death. But what about you? What unfinished business do you have? Are you counting on the next day, the next month, the next year without really being certain if such things will be available?

Tomorrow is an uncertain proposition. "Do not boast about tomorrow, for you do not know what a day may bring forth" (Proverbs 27:1). The Bible makes this point on several occasions. Only today has been placed in your hands; God set you in time. He locked you into the present to cut you off from the past and the future. The Bible employs eighteen different metaphors to remind us of the brevity and uncertainty of life. It's like a vapor, for example, appearing for a moment before dissolving forever. You planned a picnic for *tomorrow*, and it rained. You expected to pay your bills *tomorrow*, and your child became ill. Tomorrow you'll start that diet; tomorrow you'll spend time with God; tomorrow you'll call your grandparents. Let's pause with that one.

Have you ever wished you had just a piece of yesterday back—*just a tiny piece*—to speak one more time to someone who passed away? Are there things you wish you had said to your departed parents? A brother or sister you've lost? An affectionate grandmother you never thanked? A question you'd like to ask?

If you pile up enough tomorrows, you end up with a lot of empty yesterdays.

James was one of the three men who slept in the garden while Jesus agonized on the night of His passion. After Jesus' ascension, James knew what it meant to lose the most important person in the world—to long to say, in the flesh, the things that went unsaid. He lived to write a letter about the Christian life. Perhaps the most *urgent* of all the epistles, it efficiently contains one command for every two verses. Included in James's wise counsel is this:

> Come now, you who say, "Today or tomorrow we will go to such and such
> a city, spend a year there, buy and sell, and make a profit"; whereas you do
> not know what *will happen* tomorrow. For what *is* your life? It is even a vapor
> that appears for a little time and then vanishes away." (James 4:13–14)

Tomorrow, James is telling us, is the most deadly word in the Bible. It is lazy. It is presumptuous. It is reckless. The word God prefers is *today*. Hebrews 3:13 warns us that we'd better exhort one another "while it is called 'Today,'" before sin hardens the heart. It happened to Felix. It can happen to you.

But even so, even if we did have control of tomorrow, there would still be a problem with procrastination.

2. Procrastination Does Not Take into Account the Uniqueness of Conviction

Life holds its defining moments for each of us—times when God reaches into time and space and deals with us, directly and personally. You and I have known these times. Perhaps on the day you met Christ, there was a sense of God's almost tangible presence. You heard His voice, loud and clear. He spoke into your mind. As we grow wiser in the faith, these moments become more frequent. We move toward a time when His voice is nearly always clear and discernible.

Maybe there is a tomorrow. We can't be certain of anything, but every yesterday has been followed by one so far. Even so, you may never again hear Christ's voice as clearly as today; you may never have the same strong mandate to obey Him. We may never pass this way again—in all probability, we won't. When God speaks, the moment is *now*. His timetable and planning are perfect and not for our personal convenience.

God is persistent, but your life is less predictable. Your mind may be filled with other thoughts. You may not be as sensitive tomorrow. The ministry need may have evaporated by that time, and your window of opportunity may snap shut.

Tomorrow changes everything. *Today* is the day God chose to get your attention, and with God there are no coincidences. So the Bible makes this point again and again: Don't delay! Don't push it back. Don't lose the moment. Augustine said, "God has promised forgiveness to your repentance, but He has not promised tomorrow to your procrastination." Isaiah 55:6 says:

Seek the LORD while He may be found, call upon Him while He is near.

God never ceases speaking; it is we who cease hearing. There are defining moments when His lips and our ears are in sync, just for a moment of clarity, just for a moment of urgency. And that is the time to act. As Psalm 119:60 puts it,

I made haste, and did not delay to keep Your commandments.

And Solomon, who was gifted with godly wisdom but drifted spiritually as time went on, gave us this insight:

> Remember *now* your Creator in the days of your youth, before the difficult days come, and the years draw near when you say, "I have no pleasure in them." (Ecclesiastes 12:1)

We know that God calls each of us. He calls us to salvation. He calls us to service. What is lost when we hear without heeding? Salvation may be lost forever, as we suspect may have been the case with Felix—as we suspect may have been the case with the rich young man who met Jesus, encountered his defining moment, and sadly turned away. We have no record of a change of heart from the rich young man.

Billy Graham was at a hotel in Seattle, fast asleep, when he suddenly woke with a powerful burden to pray for Marilyn Monroe, the actress and sex symbol. Graham understood something of the urgency of the Spirit's prompting. He began to pray, and the next day the burden was just as strong. He had his assistants try to contact Monroe over the phone, but her agent made it difficult. She was too busy, the man said, but she would meet with the Reverend Graham—*sometime*. "Not now," said the agent. "Maybe two weeks from now."

Two weeks were too little too late. Two weeks later the headlines of America shouted out the news that Marilyn Monroe had committed suicide. She would never have that opportunity to find peace for her soul.[5]

D. L. Moody, the famous evangelist, was preaching on October 8, 1871, in Chicago. It was one of the largest crowds he ever addressed, and his topic was "What will you do with Jesus?" He focused on the decision that faced Pilate, and Moody concluded by saying, "I wish you would seriously consider this subject, for next Sunday we'll speak about the cross. Then I'll ask you, 'What will *you* do with Jesus?'" The service was closed with a hymn, but the hymn was never completed—the roar of fire engines filled the auditorium. The streets erupted in panic. The famous Chicago fire of 1871 broke out that very night and almost singed Chicago off the map.

That sermon on the cross never came. Moody often said afterward, "I have never since dared to give an audience a week to think of their salvation."

The question haunted him: How many were ready? How many were hearing the voice of God, and would have laid their souls before Christ that evening? How many windows of opportunity closed at the first shrill whine of the fire engine?[6]

As you finish reading this chapter, there is one question that confronts you: *What are you waiting for?*

- Is it time to surrender to Christ, who loves you and died for you? Is it time to turn from the old sin-life that can lead only to misery and destruction?

- Is it time to say *yes* to something the Spirit of God has tugged at your heart to do—some mission, some ministry, some calling God has set aside with your name engraved upon it? How long will He continue to tug? How long before the embers of your heart are reduced to ashes?

- Is it time to get your house in order? Time to mend fences with your husband, your wife, your children? Time to guide your family back to the arms of a loving Christ and to rebuild the loving home He wants you to have?

- Is it time to begin pleasing God with the work of your hands? To honor Him better in the workplace, and to eliminate the practices that bring Him grief?

Jonathan Edwards led a remarkable life. He entered Yale University at the age of thirteen. As an adult, his preaching launched the first two revivals ever to sweep America, including the Great Awakening. Edwards ultimately became the first president of Princeton University. He was regarded as one of the greatest intellectuals our country has ever produced. Before the twentieth century, it was often said that only two Americans had a world impact through their philosophies: Benjamin Franklin and Jonathan Edwards. His books are still in print and influential after 250 years.

Edwards had made the following covenant with himself:

I resolve to live with all my might while I do live. I resolve never to lose one moment of time and to improve my use of time in the most profitable way

I possibly can. I resolve never to do anything I wouldn't do if it were the last hour of my life.[7]

This spiritual giant has had many admirers over the years, and one of them decided to study Edwards's family tree. He traced 1,394 descendants, and among them he found:

- 13 college presidents
- 65 college professors
- 3 United States senators
- 30 judges
- 100 attorneys
- 60 physicians
- 75 army and navy officers
- 100 preachers and missionaries
- 60 prominent authors
- 1 vice president of the United States
- 295 college graduates, including state governors and ambassadors

Some of the greatest names in American history are included in that one family tree.[8] A closer look at the great business leaders of America in the twentieth century, it has been said, would show the fingerprints of Jonathan Edwards everywhere. His life embodied the final truth in our study of procrastination, which is this:

If you treat time well, it will return the favor.

Handle the present with honor, and you'll be honored by the future. We call it *legacy*. Like the lineage of Abraham, whose children would be as many as the sands on the beach and the stars in the sky; rich will be the legacy of a man who honors God through his investment of the precious moments God gave him. Such a person will arrive in heaven to see, with fresh and un-restricted eyes, his rich impact in history, his ministry expanding across the earth, and he will hear a voice saying, "Well done, good and faithful servant."

What kind of legacy are you leaving to the future—this week, this day, this moment? Everything is made of time, and this very moment rests in your hands.

What are you waiting for?

11

FACING YOUR FAILURE

YOU CAN WIN THE BATTLE AND
LIVE VICTORIOUSLY

JERRY WAS A HARD WORKER. He had the only job he'd ever really wanted, and he hustled constantly to keep up with its demands. He was content with life. Then came the great power shift.

Almost overnight, everything changed in his company. Griffin, the CEO, had been forced out of the organization. Jerry was shocked and disappointed. Griffin was a man he loved and trusted. The older man had given Jerry his break, promoting him to middle management. Out of deep gratitude, Jerry had served him faithfully. He had focused on his work and avoided the antiboss gossip.

Now Jerry was paying the price for that loyalty. He could see the whole scenario unfolding around him. He wasn't invited to key meetings that involved his department. Certain others seemed to bypass him. They were now the favorites of the management. Memos to Jerry were carefully worded, almost methodically. These memos carefully documented any little failure of Jerry's division. Someone was building a careful paper trail.

Jerry knew he was being targeted for an ouster. What really hurt was the new realization that his job security had depended mostly on one man—the departed CEO. It began to dawn on Jerry that he wasn't irreplaceable. He'd been struggling with aspects of his job for a long time. As he looked at himself through the merciless eyes of the new management group, he could see that he'd become expendable.

The new group was clearly hoping to provoke a resignation, but Jerry wasn't a quitter. He'd been hired to do a job, and he intended to keep doing it. He decided to simply ignore all the political machinations and dedicate himself to honorable work. He went at it harder than ever. Maybe if he proved himself, they'd change their minds and keep him on. Jerry prayed hard to that end.

But powerful people don't change their minds too often, and God didn't intervene. It was only a matter of time until the word got back to Jerry: He would be given two months, until December 31, to find new work.

Jerry couldn't help losing a bit of his composure when he heard these things. He stormed into the office of the vice-president, the man who had orchestrated his dismissal. Jerry demanded to know why, after all these years, he was no longer good enough for this company. The vice-president picked up a thick file and began reading out carefully compiled notes about problems in Jerry's division. "And since you've barged in and brought this matter to a head," said the vice-president, "you can clean out your desk today."

Jerry will never forget the feeling he had as he collected his personal belongings. Everyone stopped to watch; you could have heard a pin drop in that office. These were his friends, his work family. He had socialized with these people, confided in them, spent the best hours of his day with them. Now they had all become rubber-neckers at the scene of a highway collision, gaping at the twisted metal of his career.

That's what Jerry felt like, of course, a complete wreck. He had crashed and burned, and the top of his résumé read: *Failure.*

The lanky, quiet boy never had much of a chance. He had to work from the age of seven, when his family joined the homeless. His mother died two years after that.

As he grew to adulthood, the young man held a series of small jobs until his twenties, when he was fired as a store clerk. But the idea of operating a store appealed to him. At age twenty-three he took out a loan that would enable him to buy into a small business. But the run of bad luck continued; his partner died three years later. Now the young man's debt was more than doubled, and it looked as if he'd spend years just repaying it.

He fared no better at relationships. Approaching his thirties, he was still a bachelor. He proposed to one young lady after four years of dating, but she turned him down. It was just another failure; he was used to that.

Twice he ran for Congress, and twice, unsurprisingly, he lost. To put it kindly, his credentials were unimpressive. But at the age of thirty-seven, with more than half his life over, he was finally elected to an office—only to be subsequently voted out! He failed in two separate runs for the Senate. He failed in a vice-presidential try. No one was more conscious of his legacy of failures. "I am now the most miserable man living," he said. "Whether I shall ever be better, I cannot tell."

Some would say he didn't know when to quit—and most of us are glad he didn't. For at the age of fifty-one, Abraham Lincoln became perhaps the greatest of all American presidents.

If there's anything that fascinates us more than a success story, perhaps it's the opposite: a portrait of failure. The most beloved of all cartoonists, Charles Schulz, captured the hearts of America with the unforgettable creation of Charlie Brown, who never quite got his toe into that football held before him. He never earned the love of the little red-haired girl. In baseball, he never made it off the pitcher's mound without getting his socks, shoes, cap, and shirt stripped from him by a line drive. Even Snoopy, his own dog, could never remember his name, and his best friends called him "Blockhead."

Charlie Brown once said, "I'm learning to dread one day at a time," and you and I know exactly how he feels. We know what it's like to walk back to the bench, dragging a baseball bat after the strikeout that loses the game.

We also sympathize with the poor fellow at Coca-Cola—the one who convinced one of the world's proudest corporations to switch over to "New Coke," a humiliating misfire. And we're quick to forgive the architect in charge of towers in Pisa, and the committee at Decca Records who rejected the Beatles, and whoever designed the Edsel. You remember the Edsel—in the 1950s they called it the Car of the Decade, and sure enough, it stood out from the fleet. It had a door that wouldn't close, a hood that wouldn't open, and a horn that wouldn't honk. Someone observed that there was no record of anyone ever stealing an Edsel.[1]

We laugh, but we forgive. We even forgive that fellow named Stephen Pile, who ridiculed history's most monumental foul-ups in a book called *The Incomplete Book of Failures*—then published the book with two missing pages and a little note apologizing for the error. It's impossible to miss the message: We're *all* failures, every one. If you've ever messed up—and we all have—we're laughing *with* you, not *at* you.

Then, after a good laugh, we wrap an arm around your shoulders and open our Bible to find out how to stand up to a giant called Failure.

FACING THE GIANT OF FAILURE

When opening day rolls around in baseball, everyone smiles—even Charlie Brown—for every pitcher has a 0.00 ERA. Every batter has an average of 1.000. All teams have perfect records, are tied for first, and feel as if they're headed for World Series immortality.

But it takes no more than a day before half those teams have faced the sting of failure; many of those batters have gone 0-for-5, and many a pitcher has taken an early shower. The best batters in the league will fail two of every three at-bats. Babe Ruth set home run records, but he made the record books in strikeouts, too.

Facing the Reality of Failure

Failure is guaranteed: mark it down; expect it early and often. This isn't an outbreak of pessimism but a healthy dose of reality. Writing to the Corinthians, Paul approached the problem of failure and managed to describe it in poetic terms:

> But we have this treasure in earthen vessels, that the excellence of the power may be of God and not of us. (2 Corinthians 4:7)

What is the treasure? The gospel, of course. God has given us the most precious gift imaginable, and He entrusted it to the frailty and failure of humanity. Ancient copies of God's Word have been found in real earthen vessels: jars of clay set in a cave. The vessel will crumble, even the cave will be worn away, but the Word of God stands forever. Everything on this earth is doomed to failure, for even the seas and the mountains will one day be gone. But God trusts us by pouring into us His Spirit and the truths of His Word. And why? Because the light—the "excellence of the power . . . of

God"—shines all the more brightly from its cracked earthen container. We may be capable of Edsels, but we're also capable of producing an occasional Mother Teresa, a Billy Graham, an army of missions organizations filled with countless people pouring their lives sacrificially into service. Given the depth of our depravity as human beings, the light can have only one source. God's light shines brightly through our darkness, and His strength appears even more powerful beside our weakness.

Paul continues,

> We *are* hard pressed on every side, yet not crushed; *we are* perplexed, but not in despair; persecuted, but not forsaken; struck down, but not destroyed—always carrying about in the body the dying of the Lord Jesus. (2 Corinthians 4:8–10)

Yes, we're hard-pressed on every side. We're beset by failure, by being "struck down." And that's what it means to be human. As James put it, "We all stumble in many things" (James 3:2). And you've seen the lists of famous failures. Stephen Pile listed them in his chronicle of failures: the teacher of Edison, who said he was too stupid to learn; the teacher of Einstein, who described the boy as "mentally slow, unsociable and adrift forever in his foolish dreams"; the Hollywood talent scout who said Fred Astaire was balding, couldn't sing, and could dance "a little"; the newspaper editor who fired Walt Disney because he lacked ideas—and, in turn, the Disney executives years later who rejected *Star Wars*, claiming it would flop at the box office.

As we tell all those stories, we laugh scornfully at the teachers and agents and executives who rejected the geniuses. We have the benefit of hindsight. But at the time, in the heat of the rejection, don't you think the Beatles, Fred Astaire, Thomas Edison, and Walt Disney all felt that *they* were the failures? The best and the brightest, throughout history, have this in common: They've all stumbled. The Scottish preacher Alexander Whyte offered this description of the saints: They fall down; they get up. They fall down; they get up . . . all the way to heaven.

God, after all, is not surprised by our failure. Psalm 103:13–14 offers us this striking insight:

As a father pities *his* children,
So the LORD pities those who fear Him.
For He knows our frame;
He remembers that we *are* dust.

He knows our frame; He anticipates our failure. Nothing surprises God, and on those occasions when we stumble, He doesn't shake His head in disdain. The Bible assures us He has compassion for His children. He reaches down in power to lift us up again. Even Jesus knew, as His disciples failed to support Him in the garden, that the spirit is willing but the flesh is weak.

And we're told that we don't have a High Priest who fails to understand our weaknesses—He understands (Hebrews 4:15–16). He knows how this world works, and how these people fall again and again.

When you experience failure, the first thing to remember is this: *God understands.* Never does He condone failure, of course—especially when sin is at the root of it—but He has compassion that has no limit.

Facing the Reason for Our Failure

Paul not only affirms the reality of our failure. He offers a reason for it:

For our light affliction, which is but for a moment, is working for us a far more exceeding *and* eternal weight of glory, while we do not look at the things which are seen, but at the things which are not seen. For the things which are seen are temporary, but the things which are not seen *are* eternal. (2 Corinthians 4:17–18)

This is an extremely interesting passage. In it, Paul brings together several key contrasts: light affliction and weight of glory; things seen and unseen; fleeting impressions and eternal realities. And as he stretches our minds with these opposites, he sets up four crucial paradoxes:

1. *We fail now to succeed later.* Present affliction means future glory. Jesus said it so many times through His many enigmatic statements about the first and the last, the poor and the rich, the master and the servant. Christ brings about great reversals, and He promises that if we'll suffer with Him in

176

this world, we'll reign with Him in the next one. Every tear is an investment to reap diamond returns.

2. *We fail in the incidental to succeed in the important.* Paul refers to these as "light affliction" and "weight of glory." Yes, we suffer. Yes, we feel humiliation and hurts. But we step back and take a second view of life, one from the perspective of God's kingdom. Given the gravity of the King's business, the weight of present issues begins to seem negligible. Paul, of course, had his share of troubles. But he viewed them not from the bars of a prison window, but from the stars of an infinite heaven.

3. *We fail in the temporary to succeed in the eternal.* These things, Paul tells us, last only a moment. Your present preoccupations will be ancient history even by next year. But eternal truths are timeless; they never fade. If we give ourselves to them, we're connected to eternity and freed from the passing and petty.

4. *We fail outwardly to succeed inwardly.* This is a truth I come to see with more clarity each passing year. We worry so much about appearances; God worries so little about them. This is another subject Jesus returned to constantly: the superficiality of the surface; the seriousness of the heart. We're all wrapped up in public perception, but God's steady gaze never wavers from the heart. God loves us most deeply when we drop the pretenses, forget our all-important facades, and come to Him not like the proud Pharisee but like the trembling tax collector: "Lord, have mercy on me, a sinner!"

These, then, are reasons for failure, and they're very encouraging ones. If we're wise, we'll come to understand that failure isn't isolated and meaningless; it's part of the process of sainthood. We fall down, we get up. And each time we rise, we're a little stronger. We grasp a bit more of the eternal truths.

Facing the Result of Failure

"Therefore," says Paul, "we do not lose heart." Life is a miserable thing for those who lose heart. But as believers, we keep hold of the truth that "even though our outward man is perishing, yet the inward *man* is being renewed day by day" (2 Corinthians 4:16).

Failure makes philosophers of us all. The view from the top can blind us, but the view from the bottom often brings wisdom. We learn to stop evaluating people and things from the outside in; the real stuff is found when we observe what comes from the inside out. That "outward man," Paul says, is like a suit of clothing; it may look shiny and new at one point, but soon it will be threadbare and discarded. Clothes don't make the man after all, for the "inward man" is shiny and new every single day. The inner man is woven with eternal thread, so take care how you dress your soul.

FIGHTING THE GIANT OF FAILURE

We've established that failure is a real-world inevitability, and that we have reasons for failures—reasons that actually look to our long-term benefit. But we need a little bit more than these reassurances when we're standing in the rubble of shattered dreams—when the marriage has been destroyed, the dream job has been torn away, or the children have broken our hearts. We need a few smooth stones, at least, to hold in our hand as we face the giant.

What ammunition is available to us in God's Word?

Acknowledge Your Failure

First, we might as well stand up and admit it. It's no good to call it something else—call it by its name, *failure*. You didn't "select an alternate strategy path" in that big work assignment; you fouled up! You and your spouse didn't have "irreconcilable differences." Your God has already bridged the greatest estrangement there could ever be: the one between humanity and Himself. Do you really think that your "differences" were irreconcilable in His power? No, and for that matter, marriage never fails. God created it perfectly. It is *people* who fail. It sounds harsh, it feels uncomfortable, and yet the truth doesn't care much for comfort; it promises only to set us free.

Before all else, we need to call a failure by its true name, and we need to borrow that sign from President Truman that says, "The buck stops here." Going easy on yourself or passing on the blame shows a disrespect for your spiritual identity and godly potential. Own up to your failure. Step up to take responsibility. Then you can move forward. Living a lie doesn't work, so wise believers deal with their past honestly before walking away from it.

President Truman, by the way, was once asked if he'd been popular in school. He replied, "No, I was never popular. The popular boys were good at games and had big fists. I was never like that. Without my glasses, I was blind as a bat, and to tell the truth, I was kind of a sissy. If there was any chance of getting into a fight, I took off. I guess that's why I'm here today."

The buck stopped with him, didn't it? He owned up to the truth, embarrassing as it might have been. He was more right than he probably realized when he smiled and said, "I guess that's why I'm here today." Oddly enough, it is only those who honestly connect with their past who successfully walk away from it. Those who run away from the past are bound to it forever.

As you face up to your misfires, keep in mind that not every failure is sinful. Some things are out of our hands. They're simply the product of living in a broken world. Job lost his family, his home, and all his holdings, but he committed no offense against God to bring any of it about. Jesus was seized, convicted, and executed, yet He lived a sinless life. Perhaps you've failed in the past despite the purest motives and godliest actions. Failure doesn't always point to sin—at least not always your own.

On the other hand, of course, if you have disobeyed God in some way, the Spirit will make you aware of it. There will be no peace in your heart until you confess it and repent—which, of course, is the Bible's way of saying that you acknowledge your failure.

Admit. Confess. Then you can look to the perfect forgiveness of God.

Accept God's Forgiveness

Psalm 103:10 assures us that "He has not dealt with us according to our sins, nor punished us according to our iniquities." The implications of that idea are profound for you and me. He doesn't deal with you on the basis of your failures, but in the light of His grace.

People come to me all the time, troubled by some terrible event in their lives. Many of them walk the aisles of our church as we give the invitation. I find great joy in telling them they can look beyond any failure God is willing to look beyond. If there's anything we can know for sure about our Father, anything that is crystal-clear, it is that forgiveness is His specialty. I'm able to tell them that no matter what they might have done, no matter how terrible it seems, it can never outweigh the infinite grace and forgiveness of God.

You need only put out a hand to accept the gift. You need only come, confess, and repent. Acknowledge your failure; accept His forgiveness. What a radical change God has made available for our lives.

Apply the Lessons of Failure Toward Success

Failure is difficult enough, but failure without new wisdom is empty indeed. The one great redeeming factor of failure is this: We have a chance to learn something we could never learn otherwise. It can be a doorway to new insight and new opportunities. As a matter of fact, deep failure is a necessary ingredient toward sainthood. A. W. Tozer, a very wise man, wrote, "It is highly doubtful that God can use a man until he has hurt deeply."

My son Daniel played quarterback in college football. He went through a period of time when he couldn't seem to get any velocity on his passes. He was throwing the football accurately, but there was simply no "zip" on the ball. He tried everything but came up empty. None of the coaches had the answer. This, of course, is always the cue for dads to trot into the huddle.

So I gathered all my son's videotapes and edited all his passing plays together. I sat before the screen and watched those plays over and over again, studying every little mannerism in his throwing arc. And since I knew how competitive Daniel was, how much he was agonizing over this problem, I began to pray for him. I kept a large action photo of him in my office suite, and I said a little prayer whenever I looked at it.

One day as I glanced at the photo and offered a short prayer, something jumped out of the picture—something I'd never noticed. His arm was in a different place than it was in the videos. Daniel was dropping his arm and losing velocity on his passes, for the *zip* comes from the top of the throwing arc.

I ran to the phone—boy, was I excited! Coach Jeremiah had done the research and solved the problem. My heart was pumping as Daniel picked up the phone. "I figured it out," I told him. "I found your zip!" And I told him he was dropping his arm.

"Oh, really?" said Daniel noncommittally. "Thanks, Dad, but I don't think that's it."

About a month later, one of Daniel's coaches told me Daniel had the zip back in his passes. Then he added, almost as an afterthought, "Oh, yeah—I hear you had something to do with that."

I said, "Sure, I found out from failure how to get back to success."

Sometimes, when the zip goes out of our lives, we need to watch the mental videos and see where we've gone wrong. Don't put those failures completely out of your mind, because they can have a productive use. Jonas Salk failed two hundred times in his efforts to find a vaccine for polio. But he didn't look at it that way; he said he'd simply found two hundred ways how *not* to make a vaccine for polio. Fall down enough times and you'll eventually learn to walk just by process of elimination.

Then there's an important distinction for us to keep in mind.

Accept Failure As a Fact of Life, Not a Way of Life

Keep this concept at the front of your mind: Failure is an *event*, not a *person*. It's something you do, not something you become. Don't ever let anyone call you a failure or a loser. You are not your résumé.

If you see yourself as a failure, you'll doom yourself to endless repetitions of what you've done. You'll pile failure upon failure. And it will all be based on a tragic misperception of yourself, because God doesn't see you as a failure. He sees you as His child—even when the zip goes out of your delivery.

Peter knew all about failure. Jesus warned him about his failure when they were in the Upper Room. Jesus told Peter he'd have three chances, and he'd fail every one of them. Peter wasn't about to buy that prediction for a minute—until it came true. Three times Peter denied his greatest Friend, his Master, his Savior. The Bible says that when the truth came down upon him, he stole away and wept bitterly. Some people would never recover from such a negatively defining event.

But that's only the first act of Peter's story. Later, we find him again in the book of Acts, preaching on the Day of Pentecost. There he delivers one of the greatest sermons in the history of Christianity. Christ has chosen Peter—Peter the denier, Peter the *failure*—to deliver that message. On this day, thousands come to Christ under his mighty preaching.

Obviously something has happened between the failed service and the fiery sermon. Peter has faced his Master again, at a beach breakfast recorded in John 21, and discovered that failure can be transcended by forgiveness.

From that day on, he is a new man. He becomes the powerful apostle Jesus always knew he would become.

Failure isn't final. It's a fact of life, but not a way of life.

Arise from Failure and Start Again

We have no record of wallowing in self-pity as a helpful strategy for anyone. You can spend years reliving the failure of a business, of a marriage, of a dream. But the only wise move is to bring it before God, to acknowledge it, then to rise up and walk on, a stronger and wiser human being.

I've always been transfixed by the story of Jonah, and not because of the great fish. What I love about the story is found in the first two verses of the third chapter:

> Now the word of the LORD came to Jonah the second time, saying, "Arise, go to Nineveh, that great city, and preach to it the message that I tell you." (Jonah 3:1–2)

You might pass over those verses quickly, as a simple transitional sentence toward the next part of the story—again, the curtain between acts. But I find those verses incredible, enlightening, and encouraging. Jonah has just failed miserably. As a matter of fact, he has failed in the issue of obedience to God. He was sent to Nineveh, and he headed in the opposite direction.

Jonah has failed in obedience. He has failed in compassion. He has failed in good old-fashioned common sense, thinking for a second he could find some hiding place beyond the searching eyes of God.

And what does God say to all this? "Arise, go." *Here's that map again, Jonah; be sure to bring your compass this time.*

I imagine a lot of good, focused contemplation can occur inside the belly of a fish. Jonah is now the very picture of obedience—and something else, too: *success.* A total of 120,000 Ninevites repent under his preaching. That makes it one of the greatest revivals in the history of humanity. Do you see a pattern in the lives of Jonah and Peter? *Get up. Keep going. You're just that close to a breakthrough!*

As long as we listen to the voice of God, and not the voices of the crowd, the best is yet to come. The crowd may call you a failure, but it is those voices, ironically, who are the ones that represent failure—failure to encourage, failure to understand the simple principle of how wisdom is procured and how successes are launched. I remember one of my all-time favorite television commercials featuring basketball icon Michael Jordan. The camera follows Jordan as he walks down a long hallway in a sort of slow-motion, awe-inspiring gait. You then hear Jordan saying, "I've missed over 9,000 shots in my career. I've lost almost 300 games; 26 times, I've been trusted to take the game-winning shot, and missed. I've failed over and over again in my life . . . and that is why . . . I succeed." Michael Jordan has found success in the sports realm, not because he never fails, but because he arises from each failure and starts again.

Anyone in the world of sports will tell you where the best coaches are found: They're found on the benches, among the players who were beaten out by better athletes. A third-stringer can sit on the bench and dwell on his failure, or he can keep trying, keep hustling, and learn everything there is to know about that sport. That's why the best coaches have often been obscure athletes in their youth.

They fell down, and they got up.

Avoid Judging Failure in Others

Finally, we need to be careful how we see others when it comes to this subject. Perhaps you've been reading this chapter and thinking, *I know someone else who needs to read this.*

I hope your friend does read this book, but I also hope you'll be careful before applying any label of failure to another person. The Bible has three particularly instructive stories to help you remember that lesson. You'll recognize them all, and hopefully you'll take them to heart. They hold much truth to apply to the way we think.

The rich man and the beggar. Two men enter your church sanctuary, walking down the left aisle and the right. One is dressed in a suit that cost one thousand dollars. The other is clad in rags. It's clear to you who the successful one is.

And according to Jesus, you're wrong.

In Luke 16:25, Jesus explains His point of view. In the next world, the rich man will discover that he's already enjoyed his reward; the poor man will just now be coming into his legacy, and it's an eternal one composed of the riches of God's kingdom.

The man in the fine suit looks successful to the world, but in the case Jesus describes, the inner men aren't reflected by the outer apparel.

Be careful before you count your friend a failure.

The Pharisee and the tax collector. Your eye captures a contrast in the sanctuary of your church. On your right sits a fine, respected deacon. And on your left is a cut-throat businessman. You know you're sitting next to one man who is close to God's heart, and you're quite certain which man it is— and again, you're wrong!

Jesus turns your evaluation on its head in Luke 18. The deacon might have been, in Jesus' time, a Pharisee. His prayer is particularly enthusiastic on this Sabbath morning. You hear him pray, "Thanks for letting me be a major financial contributor here at church, and for my prayer and fasting program. But most of all, I thank you that I'm not an unethical businessman like that guy sitting two seats over, Lord!"

You turn to your left, where the businessman in question is sitting. The Gospels would identify him, of course, as a tax collector. He isn't as animated in his prayer. He doesn't lift the holy hands and gaze toward the ceiling like the deacon, but he does seem to be praying; you can hear little bits of it, and he's pleading for the mercy of God because of his sins. A tear is running down his cheek, and he's trembling. "Have mercy on me, a sinner," he whispers.

Jesus closes this vignette by telling us that one of those two men leaves your church forgiven, and it's not the one we might expect. "For everyone who exalts himself will be abased, and he who humbles himself will be exalted" (Luke 18:14).

Perception doesn't always reflect reality.

A Pharisee and a prostitute. This one is found in Luke 7:44–47, and now we're really pushing the envelope. Jesus asks you to compare and contrast Simon, a Pharisee, a respected religious leader, with a common prostitute.

Who would you rather talk to at a party? Which will you look up first in heaven? And yet Jesus says to Simon, "I visited your home, My friend, and you took Me for granted. You even forgot to give Me a pan of water for My dusty feet. But this woman—this prostitute—didn't forget. She washed My feet not with a pan of water but with tears from her face. She wiped the dust away not with a towel but the hair from her head. You forgot to kiss My cheek, but this woman has kissed My feet repeatedly. She has many sins, but every one is forgiven, because her love for God is so overpowering."

Who was the failure, and who was the success? As Jesus evaluated things, the successful one was that person who loved God the most sincerely. And it wasn't the Pharisee who knew all the right answers. It was a woman whose life was filthy but whose love was pure.

We must take very great care before tending to the little filing cabinets in our minds, the place where our people observations are stored. We can never forget that we see the outer reality; God looks within, to the heart. That can make all the difference in the world.

There was a time when appearances might have fooled you profoundly. You might have been standing at the foot of a hill, watching as guards drag a prisoner to his execution. This is the punishment they've reserved for the foulest of criminals, so the prisoner must be getting what's coming to him, or at least that's how it would seem to you. The guards are roughing him up, spitting on him, ridiculing him. There seems to be a great deal of attention directed at this seemingly unremarkable convict. So you ask a few questions.

The forthcoming facts would make it appear to you that this man was a failure—a teacher who claimed to have great supernatural powers, who claimed to be the triumphant Messiah, no less. Now he seems to have very few friends in the world. As the nails are driven home, no one steps forward to comfort him. The man supposedly has twelve followers, but they're nowhere to be found. It's only his mother and a smattering of others—women, mostly—who openly weep.

You might shake your head as you walk away from the scene. This man was clearly a failure, judging from appearances. As he gasps out those three words, "It is finished," you'd never guess the scope of what exactly was finished. It certainly wasn't the man himself.

You'd have no way of knowing that death was destroyed that day, that the "failure" on the crude wooden cross-posts would soon sit on a throne in heaven, and someday on a judgment seat. On that day, you won't be judging Him at all; the tables will be turned.

And now, in the modern world, you might be unimpressed by the group of men and women who stand before you as a sad visual testimony of the life of the disabled. Infirmities of every kind are here; perhaps you would shake your head in pity.

But the sound of a gun would startle you from your reverie, and the motley group would be off, moving around a track in the unlikeliest of activities: a race. A race of the slow and struggling. This, of course, is the Special Olympics, and it spotlights competition among the developmentally and physically disabled. Here, in the 100-meter dash, the runners struggle around the track, shoulder to shoulder. Suddenly a young woman staggers. She topples gracelessly to the dusty track. Perhaps, being compassionate, you avert your eyes from her humiliation.

But then something unexpected happens. It's a sight you may never forget. Ten or fifteen meters up the track, the contestants—*all* the contestants—stop moving and turn around. Without speaking, without anyone suggesting it, they move back toward their fallen competitor. The contestants pull her up, offer words of comfort and encouragement, and carry her with them toward the finish line. Each of them would rather finish the race together than win it individually.[2]

And perhaps then you would understand a deep truth—that beauty can spring from failure, and victory from defeat. A fallen, misshapen human body is not discarded, not forgotten, when we discover the beauty of God's truth. After all, don't we all find ourselves in this race, struggling forward with the scars and frailties of the fallen? The course is treacherous, and we're all bound to stumble. But we find an overcoming power, a transcending victory, when we extend a hand of support, a word of consolation, and finish the race shoulder to shoulder.

Jerry had plenty of time to think after the new management dismissed him from his company. Perhaps the turning point came during a conversation with an old friend over the phone. "Remember Joseph in the book of Genesis?" asked the friend. "He told his brothers, 'You meant it for evil, but God meant it for good.' Forget the managers, Jerry. I don't want to ever hear you bring them up again other than in the context of your forgiveness. It's totally irrelevant why they fired you or whether they were justified in doing so. The only thing that matters is that God has something better for you around the next bend. Men may intend things for evil, but God always has the last word. That's the only thing you need to care about right now."

The words rang true. From that moment on, Jerry knew he wasn't a failure in God's eyes. That kept him from being bitter. In heaven, no meticulous files were kept to document his shortcomings—only a file labeled, "Future blessings for my precious child." He couldn't wait to see what was in that folder.

Several days later Jerry received two phone calls. Each one offered him a freelance assignment in the area of his most expertise. Both projects would take about a year. When Jerry added them up, they came to one year's salary at his old job—almost to the penny! Jerry recognized God's unmistakable calling card. He had stumbled, but God had helped him up. Now he was more excited than ever about the future.

Jerry was running the race with a second wind now. The winners, he knew, aren't those who never stumble. They're the ones capable of rising up one more time than they go down. Then, having overcome failure, they run with new strength. Or maybe they're no longer running. Isaiah would say that they mount up with wings like eagles and soar above the turmoil and confusion.

12

Journeying Beyond Jealousy

YOU CAN WIN THE BATTLE AND
LIVE VICTORIOUSLY

Please, Lord," she prayed, "give this man a woman—and let that woman be me!"

It was a bold prayer, but it was the desire of her heart. Eliza had been deeply in love with Mark almost from the moment she met him. But she was also a committed Christian. Her greatest ambition was to stay in the center of God's will through the big decisions of her life.

Eliza found herself praying frequently and fervently about her relationship with Mark. "If You don't want me to have these feelings, please change them," she whispered to her Lord. But it all seemed so right, so perfect. Mark was exactly what she'd been looking for in a man. He was handsome, considerate, funny, and best of all he loved the Lord just as Eliza did. And if he didn't seem responsive to her, that was all right. Eliza was willing to give it time; the important things in life were worth a little patience. *Persistence*—that was the word for now. Good things come to those who wait.

For well over a year, Eliza waited. She hoped and prayed that Mark would start to return her little attentions. She spent money on clothes she couldn't afford. She invited Mark over to share gourmet dinners she planned and cooked for countless hours. She wanted him to be impressed with her style. She wanted him to see her attention to the little things. Sooner or later, there had to be sparks. And still she prayed to God: "Make him notice me, Lord. Give him feelings to match the ones I have—or if that isn't Your will, then change *my* feelings."

Eliza was in the midst of her Thanksgiving plans when Dana, her room-mate, asked her to sit down and have a talk with her. Then she dropped the bomb: It was Dana that Mark loved; *Dana*—her own roommate. Dana and Mark had been together for some time, but they'd kept it secret. They had been worried about Eliza's feelings.

And well they should have been. Eliza couldn't believe what she was hearing. It was a joke in poor taste—or it was a mistake, something that could be undone. Surely Mark wouldn't do this to her; surely he wouldn't reject her for her own roommate.

But as the truth set in, Eliza began to tremble. Anger seeped through every part of her until it took firm hold, and she knew it had come to stay a while. She was angry with Dana. She was angry with Mark. She was angry with God, who let her carry on with feelings that could lead only to terrible emotional pain. Maybe He loved Dana more. Maybe He was punishing Eliza for some unknown sin. What else could it be?

When she saw the hopelessness of her situation, Eliza asked God to take away the romantic love she felt for Mark. But a heart has no on/off switch. Her feelings couldn't be conveniently discarded—particularly when she had to live with the woman who had ended up with *her* prize. Watching them together and carrying on as their friend, all the while pretending she had no more of those feelings, was more than she could bear. The bitterness was there; the anger was there. Most of all, the jealousy was deep and wide.

The ancient Greeks told the story of a swift athlete who came in second. He stood at the finish line, huffing and puffing as the crowd cheered—not for him, but for the winner.

The second-place finisher had to stand there as they brought the victor's crown and the other prizes. He had to stand with the other also-rans as con-gratulatory speeches were made in the victor's honor. And he had to walk through town to reach home, hearing nothing but the name of the winner on the lips of everyone he saw.

The victor had a great statue erected in his honor, right in the center of town. The second-place finisher had to see it every day of his life, and he came to think of himself as a loser. The envy and jealousy began to take charge of his soul until he could accomplish almost nothing from day to day.

Why hadn't *he* been the winner? Why hadn't *he* been able to find within himself those two or three strides that separated the champion from the chump? Every night, as sleep eluded him, he crept out into the darkness and made his way to the victor's statue. There he chiseled away a few more bits of stone from the foundation. Each night the great marble figure was weaker.

But one night he got more than he bargained for. He chiseled away one more bit of stone, and the massive athletic figure cracked loudly and slid forward. The great marble champion crashed down on the little man with the chisel, and death came instantly. The athlete had been crushed by the very image of the man he'd despised.[1]

Some would say the man with the chisel didn't die in that one crashing instant, but by tiny increments. It was the weight of jealousy that ultimately destroyed him, day by day, thought by thought. It transformed the soul of a proud champion to a cheap chiseler, someone who would scrape away at the good fortune of someone else.

That's the deadly poison we know as jealousy.

IT'S NOT EASY BEING GREEN

Color this giant green—the color of envy. When you buy a new car, your friend is likely to smile and say, "I'm green with envy." But there are no smiles in the Greek concept of the word. The literal meaning is *to boil within*. And we can all vouch for the truth of that. Even if we smile on the outside, true envy heats up a cauldron inside us. Anger, jealousy, and covetousness seethe and boil within our hearts.

Paul addressed the problem among the immature Christians at Corinth:

> For you are still carnal. For where *there are* envy, strife, and divisions among you, are you not carnal and behaving like *mere* men? (1 Corinthians 3:3)

The church had split into little cliques—the Paul supporters versus the Apollos supporters—and they directed all their energy into being jealous of each other. Finally the church could do nothing productive, and Paul had to step in and scold them.

The words *jealousy* and *envy* are often used interchangeably, even in the

Scriptures. But there's a significant difference between the two. Let's examine it.

Envy appears benign and subtle. It's the stock in trade of the have-not, the person who resents everyone else who does have. It's quiet and sinister, ready to rejoice over someone else's misfortune.

Jealousy, however, tends to refer to having something and living in fear of losing it. It is always on the lookout for some new rival. Far from benign and subtle, jealousy is coarse and cruel. Shakespeare calls it "the green sickness," and Sir Francis Bacon said that it takes no holidays.

The Bible tells us to rejoice with those who rejoice and to weep with those who weep. But the person consumed with envy does just the opposite: he rejoices in the mourning of others, and mourns when others dance with joy. In that way, envy is the loneliest of vices; it isolates us because everyone becomes a potential enemy.

Proverbs 14:30 tells us that "a sound heart *is* life to the body, but envy *is* rottenness to the bones." We might paraphrase that to say, "rotten to the core." Envy is indeed a form of rot. It works its way inward, spoiling all innocence and trust and virtue. The sound heart, on the other hand, "is life to the body." With a life free of envy, you'll be healthy; you'll be happy; you'll be going somewhere in life. But when you give in to jealousy, as we'll see, you move in never-ending circles of hopelessness.

JEALOUSY TRAVELS IN CIRCLES

What exactly are these "circles" of jealousy? We can find active jealousy in several prominent circles around us. Let's investigate them.

Jealousy Travels in Proprietary Circles

The first place to look for jealousy is among the circles of those steeped in materialism. Those who have built their world in the realm of materialism are easy targets for envy and jealousy.

Note, for example, this reference to Isaac, the son of Abraham:

The man began to prosper, and continued prospering until he became very prosperous; for he had possessions of flocks and possessions of herds and a great number of servants. So the Philistines envied him. (Genesis 26:13–14)

It's difficult to miss the idea of prosperity in that passage, isn't it? The writer uses it three times, then uses the word *possessions* twice. Isaac had *stuff*, and plenty of it. The Philistines couldn't handle the amount of stuff he had, and they began to covet it. Even when covetous people have all they need, they can never be satisfied. Their eye is not on the treasure they possess, but on the one that someone else possesses. Nathan told David the story of the man with the largest flock in the land, who coveted the one sheep someone else had. That's how it works.

We need to be careful not to condemn wealth on its own. Many families are both wealthy and godly. We all know believers who have enjoyed great abundance of worldly goods, and who have kept every penny in spiritual perspective. But in a general sense, we can't help but observe how often the affluent materialist talks about what someone else has. Someone else has a larger house. Someone else has a faster car or a more spacious vacation home.

Jealousy Travels in Power Circles

Read through the Old Testament and you'll find it. There's the story of the man named Korah, who envied Moses' position of power among the Israelites. He led a rebellious faction that once said to Moses and Aaron, "You take too much upon yourselves" (Numbers 16:3)—another way of saying, "We'd like some of that power for ourselves." Psalm 106:16 tells us they "envied Moses in the camp."

Then, as you move through the history of the kings of Israel, you'll see the twin themes of jealousy and envy over and over again. Kings seize the throne through traitorous acts, only to suffer the same fate. It's a self-perpetuating circle of envy, and we'll find it always in the halls of power.

When you come to the New Testament, look closely at the Sanhedrin. In the book of Acts, the Hebrew ruling council was upset with the new Christian believers, who were bringing in a new code for living. We're told that the high priest and the Sadducees became so resentful they began throwing Christians in prison. But why? Because the apostles were becoming more popular every day. The balance of power was shifting, and the Sanhedrin couldn't stand the thought of it. There were factions in all the early churches, as we've seen—Peter and Paul spent valuable time handling controversies—and even among the disciples, there had been disputes about who would sit at the right hand of Jesus in heaven.

Look at the business where you work. You'll find that if you follow the power, you'll find a little trail of envy and resentment—office politics, power struggles, power-grabs. This division envies that division, and this vice president covets the power of that one. As soon as a gifted worker becomes consumed, the envy spreads into those around him, and in time an entire company can be poisoned. It's a vicious circle of jealousy.

Jealousy Travels in Performance Circles

Here is one of the most dangerous of all the circles of envy. Take a look at it closely, then search your soul to see if it applies to you.

Study the saga of Saul and David for a glimpse at how the performance circle works. It all began with young David, a shepherd boy who came to the battle lines and volunteered to stand against the giant, Goliath. From the moment he brought down that giant, a far more powerful one began to stalk through the palace of the king—the not-so-jolly green giant of jealousy. Saul could sit at his window and hear the women singing, "Saul has slain his thousands, but David his ten thousands." He could sense the arrival of a new hero, and the resentment spread rapidly through his heart. And after it had spread, the effect was so pervasive, so powerful that Saul devoted the rest of his lifetime to hunting down David for the purpose of murder. No late-night chiseling for this second-place hero—he came after the new champion with armies, arrows, and arrogance. After David slew the first giant, the second giant slew Saul; never would he live up to the promise of his early, anointed reign. Jealousy took up so much room in his heart that the Spirit of God, we're told, had to leave. That's the power of jealousy.

But all of that was thousands of years ago, and it was a matter between kings and contenders. How does it affect us today? Look at the average church—perhaps your own. In the choir, Jane got the solo that Audrey wanted. Fred is teaching the Sunday school class on which Jack had set his heart. The pastor broods over the superior popularity of an elder or a deacon. When the devil goes to church, he knows just what buttons to push. He knows how to get control of your mind as you sit in your pew in the house of God; he manipulates your envy.

Elva McAllaster captured this disquieting thought in her little bit of free verse entitled, "Envy Went to Church":

> Envy went to church this morning.
> Being legion, he sat in every other pew.
> Envy fingered wool and silk fabrics,
> Hung price tags on suits and neckties.
> Envy paced through the parking lot
> Scrutinizing chrome and paint.
> Envy marched through to the chancel with the choir
> During the processional . . .
> Envy prodded plain-jane wives,
> And bright wives married to milquetoast dullards,
> And kind men married to knife-tongued shrews.
> Envy thumped at widows and widowers,
> Jabbed and kicked college girls without escorts,
> Lighted invisible fires inside khaki jackets.
> Envy conferred also this morning
> With all of his brothers.
> He liked his Sunday scores today
> But not enough;
> Some of his intended clients
> Had sipped an antidote marked Grace
> And wore a holy flower named Love.[2]

It slithers through the halls and pews of the godliest of congregations. It tears at the body of Christ. And the only antidotes are heaping helpings of love and grace.

Jealousy Travels in Professional Circles

I've always been intrigued by a certain line in the first chapter of Paul's letter to the Philippians. He writes from the dark cell of a Roman prison, and he's introducing the epistle to follow. But he offers a preliminary warning:

Some indeed preach Christ even from envy and strife, and some also from good will: The former preach Christ from selfish ambition, not sincerely, supposing to add affliction to my chains. (Philippians 1:15–16)

Paul is saying, "Take a look at what these people are doing. They know I'm behind bars, and they've quickly set up their own pulpits not to spread the gospel, but to damage my ministry to you." Paul tells us he experienced envy in professional circles.

What about that coworker two offices down from you? Is there envy or jealousy between you, over salary or position or even over having an office with a window? It's amazing how petty we can all become when we give in to the green giant.

Jealousy Travels in Personal Circles

We've saved the most common circle for last. This is the one the Bible deals with most frequently.

Jealousy begins at home, and before any other institution, it seeks to destroy the family. It all begins at the dawn of history with Cain's envy and murder of Abel. We see the terrible jealousy between Jacob and Esau—a perfect case study of how to destroy a family. And in the New Testament, there's always the older brother in the story of the prodigal son. We usually focus, of course, on the son who ran away and came home. It's easy to overlook Big Brother, who watched the party preparations and smoldered inside. His question is, "Why shouldn't the fatted calf be killed for me? Why shouldn't I have a party? Why shouldn't I have the robe and the ring and the revelry?" You can see it in Luke 15:29. We see from the story that jealousy is ugly, and yet we also see ourselves. It's probably true in retelling this parable that more of us identify with the older, envious brother than with the younger, rebellious one.

Perhaps the most dramatic jealousy of all was among the sons of Jacob, who inherited his birthright—envy. Jacob played favorites, and he lavished gifts on the younger Joseph. But instead of one older brother, we have *eleven* this time—and they didn't throw a party, but they threw him into a pit. So rabid was their envy that many of them were ready to murder him. Jealousy comes through the family's front door and sends love out the back. It leaves no room for any other emotion.

Jealousy, then, runs in circles. Whether it's your family circle, your fellowship circle, or your Fortune 500 business circle, you're bound to run into it. It pervades every walk of life. We need to be vigilant and watch out for it in every circle we inhabit.

An old legend about the devil tells us he was crossing the Libyan desert when he came upon one of his own circles—a circle of demons. This little group was working together to tempt a holy man, and they had pulled out every weapon in their arsenal. They had tried the seductions of the flesh first, but the holy man had held out. They came at his mind with doubts and fears, telling him he was wasting his life in aspiring toward holiness. That didn't work either. They tried everything they could think of, but the holy man was strong in the faith.

Satan listened carefully to their account, then asked them to step aside and watch the master at work. Then he whispered only two sentences into the ear of the man: "Have you heard the news? Your brother was just promoted to bishop of Alexandria."

Just like that, the holy man's mouth sank into a little frown. A crease formed a small canyon in his brow, and the devil knew he had won. It works every time.

THE CHARACTERISTICS OF JEALOUSY

How does jealousy work? We'll look at two key characteristics.

Jealousy Destroys Others

We've already seen examples of this, beginning with the murder of Abel. People lose their lives because of someone else's resentment. Others lose their jobs or their reputations. Lives are destroyed by jealousy and envy, which are so poisonous they can drive us to do the unthinkable and irrational. Study the resentment of Adolf Hitler that took him from obscure soldier to German dictator, and you'll see just how irrational and demonic a force we're dealing with.

Why did the cheerleader's mother in Texas go over the edge? You may remember that story from the headlines a few years ago. Two teenagers were competing for a spot on the cheerleading squad, and the mother of one of them murdered her daughter's rival. We wonder how such a thing can happen, but the green monster makes no claims to advanced logic—just single-minded domination.

Jealousy Destroys Us

Here is the deeper victim of envy—the person who envies. Cain destroyed Abel, but he destroyed himself in the process. Jacob's jealousy sentenced him to years of wandering and hardship. Joseph landed on his feet in Egypt, but his brothers suffered under the terrible burden of guilt for years. Saul hunted David, but the only life he destroyed was his own. And yes, the crowd that was so jealous of Daniel had him thrown in the lions' den—but when he came out unscathed, they were thrown in themselves and devoured instantly. Jealousy ultimately devours anyone who gives in to it.

It has been said that Envy shoots at others and wounds herself. Jealousy runs in circles, and it always seems to come back around to *us*.

FACING THE GIANT OF JEALOUSY

There comes a time when we have to stand up and face the giant, and the strategy may be a painful one: We must renounce our jealousy as *sin*.

Please don't deal with jealousy as a personality disorder. Avoid thinking of it as a genetic trait you never chose. Don't ascribe it to social environment or upbringing. The Bible never points to any of those factors to discuss jealousy. The Scriptures do, however, deal with it as sinful disobedience. Galatians 5:20 includes it in a group including "hatred, contentions, *jealousies*, outbursts of wrath, selfish ambitions." That's a deadly gang, and jealousy can cause each of the other four sins listed there. Paul included envy as a sign of "the debased mind," describing those who are "full of *envy*, murder, strife, deceit, evil-mindedness" (Romans 1:29). Again, an unpleasant roll call of personality traits.

It's clear from God's Word, then, that we need to face the sin of jealousy with deadly seriousness. Peter says we are to lay it aside and leave it—to walk away briskly (1 Peter 2:1). James says we will find envy and self-seeking in the places where confusion and every evil thing lurk (James 3:16). Paul wrote to the Romans about jealousy, and he said, "Let us walk properly, as in the day, not in revelry and drunkenness, not in licentiousness [lust] and lewdness, not in strife and *envy*" (Romans 13:13). According to Matthew, it was envy that delivered Jesus Christ to the cross: "For he knew that because of *envy*, they had delivered Him" (Matthew 27:18). It's the ace up the devil's sleeve, the weapon that never fails.

Jealousy and envy, according to the verses we've seen, are right up there with lust, lewdness, drunkenness, murder, and evil-mindedness. We can't afford to dismiss these as personality disorders. Instead, we need to do four things:

Renounce Jealousy As Sin

Above we have only a sampling of the many scriptural denunciations of this terrible sin. But it's enough to make us search our hearts, root out any weed of jealousy, and see it for the gross sin that it is. If this is something you struggle with, I recommend that you copy down some of these verses and keep them on note cards beside your bed, on your desk, in your Bible, and everywhere they may remind you of the sin you need to confess and eliminate.

At the very least, envy and jealousy will cause deep pain in your soul and damage to your relationships. At worst, it will consume you and those around you. Begin by calling it *sin*. Then you can look to the second step.

Remember Your Rival in Prayer

Now it gets interesting. Do you have the discipline to pull this one off? Jesus commanded us more than once to pray for our enemies, for He knew that if we could sincerely do that, the battle would be won. The very second we grab the arm of a rival and walk before the throne of God together, the petty, shameful things quickly dissolve in the radiant light of His grace. You can't hold on to a jealous grudge with the eyes of heaven upon you.

At the end of the nineteenth century, there were giants on the earth—not the kind we've discussed in this book, but giants of the faith and of the pulpit. The city of London had both F. B. Meyer and Charles Haddon Spurgeon, two living legends. London was barely big enough for the two of them. But then in 1904 the great preacher G. Campbell Morgan came to town. Morgan was a world-class Bible expositor, and all of London was buzzing with his arrival.

"It was easy," said Meyer, "to pray for the success of G. Campbell Morgan when he was in America. But when he came back to England and took a church near to mine, it was something different. The old Adam in me was inclined to jealousy, but I got my heel upon his head, and whether I felt right toward my friend, I determined to act right." Meyer began to pray for his pulpit rival, day and night, even as he worried about losing members to the hot new preacher in town.

F. B. Meyer later explained, "My church gave a reception for [Morgan], and I acknowledged that if it was not necessary for me to preach Sunday evenings I would dearly love to go and hear him myself. Well, that made me feel right toward him. But just see how the dear Lord helped me out of my difficulty. There was Charles Spurgeon preaching wonderfully on the other side of me. He and Mr. Morgan were so popular, and drew such crowds, that our church caught the overflow, and we had all we could accommodate."[3]

God not only rewards us when we pray for our enemies and (as Meyer did) act upon the feelings we *intend* to have, He often brings miracles about in our lives. The weed of jealousy is deep and firmly entrenched, but if you want to drive it out quickly, simply do this: Pray for the person you envy. Pray for him daily. Pray for him even if your teeth and fists are clenched. See if God doesn't honor your faith and change your heart.

Reaffirm God's Goodness to You

I think I've learned an important truth about envy and jealousy. Our resentment implies an assumption that God hasn't given us everything we need. If we went about our lives in the assurance that He had, how could we be jealous? Whom or what could we envy?

When you detect feelings of jealousy, those feelings call for a blessing inventory. When was the last time you took one? Count them; name them one by one. What do you truly lack that God hasn't given you? Conversely, what abundant blessings has He showered upon you that you actually don't deserve? If you'll examine the ledger very carefully and very frankly, I believe you'll discover it tilts well in your favor. God has blessed you far beyond any realistic claim you could ever exert. It has been said that if we truly understood what justice would require, we wouldn't be so eager to have it. If we could only see the extent to which we're the beneficiaries of His wonderful and rich blessings, and the grace of God's patience with our countless imperfections, we wouldn't have the *nerve* to come up with a shred of envy!

A season of thanksgiving—*any* time of year—is a wonderful antidote to the poison of jealousy. You can find out exactly how it works in the center of your Bible. So many psalms begin with the writer consumed with self-pity, anger, and resentfulness toward his enemies. But as he reviews God's past blessings, His goodness today, and His promises for tomorrow, the psalmist closes his song on a totally different note; what began as a dirge ends as a dance.

Why don't you try it? Write a psalm of your own, based on your envy and resentment. Tell it like you feel it! But here's the hook: After pouring out your honest feelings, you are hereby commanded to review the goodness of God in your life—past, present, and promises. After a few pages, I think you'll find your heart changing, and the first section of your psalm will end up in the wastebasket along with the unworthy emotions that inspired it.

Gratitude transforms attitude.

Rekindle God's Love in Your Heart

Love does not envy. That's what Paul tells us in 1 Corinthians 13:4. This is worth thinking about. Paul is telling us that envy and love can't stand to be in the presence of each other, for they're very close to opposites and they function like magnetic poles. The magnetic charge of envy repels the force of love—though it attracts many other unworthy emotions such as the ones in Galatians 5. Love, on the other hand, pushes envy away just as surely. Love and envy are both fires that must be tended. One crackles pleasantly; the other smolders and seethes.

So love is the answer, but what if it has been reduced to ashes? How do we rekindle it? The answer is very simple: through prayer and Scripture. Only by experiencing the transforming presence of God can your heart be changed. His Spirit will give you His mind, His perspective, His loving servant attitude toward the people you would otherwise envy. Perfect love casts out fear, but it casts out so many other things as well. It casts out jealousy. It casts out anger and resentment and discouragement. Love is the force that causes even giants to turn and flee.

I do know of one instance in which love and envy occupied the same room. Let's visit that room and discover how it came about.

The Hospital of the Mind

The scene is a small room in a large hospital. The four walls are just spacious enough for two patients and two lockers. A door opens on the hall, and a window opens on the world.

Both men need, above all things, peace and quiet for their healing; neither is allowed to read, listen to the radio, watch television, or accept visitors. But one of them is propped up daily for one hour, and he sits and gazes out the window as the fluids slowly drain from his lungs. The other lies flat on his back, every hour of every day, staring at the ceiling. He knows its every dimple, every ridge.

Generally speaking, the two men are not encouraged to speak—no excitement, that's the rule. But when the halls are quiet and the nurses are ignoring them, the men softly converse. They speak of wives and children, homes and occupations. They speak of wars and travel and aspirations. But both of them are waiting for that hour—that particular hour when the one by the window will be lifted into position to gaze out the window. Finally, when that moment arrives, all of the words are his. The man by the window paints a portrait in words of the world beyond the curtains. He tells of a park with flowers, a lovely lake with swans gliding upon its glassy surface. He tells of the children who come every day about this time, throwing bread, floating their newspaper boats, and sailing into the sky on their swings. Young lovers walk hand in hand. The man by the window elegantly describes the changes of season, as reflected in the trees. He gives the progress of touch football games, of hide-and-seek and of the boyfriend pushed into the lake. He renders in vibrant colors the setting sun in its final glory, painting the contours of a chrome skyline.

His friend lies on his back, staring at the ceiling but with a mind's eye filled with the world conjured daily by his friend's elegance. He can see the football players and the beautiful girls in their summer dresses. He can see the boy and his new puppy frolicking by the park bench. He sees and cherishes every image layered upon the one before it, for there's nothing else in his world. Nothing but four walls and a gray ceiling.

One day is particularly remarkable—a parade passes through the park. And then, for the first time, an alien thought passes through the mind of the bedridden man: Why can't *he* have the place by the window? Why can't *he* be the one to see—to really see, with real eyes instead of imagination? Why should it always be the other man?

He knows the notion is unworthy, but there it is. Once it finds its way into his mind, it can't be so easily expelled. So the thought lingers, and it gains power. *Why not me? Why shouldn't I be the one by the window?*

Soon he can't sleep, and his blood races. The charts show a sudden downturn in his medical status. The doctors and nurses are puzzled by this unexpected downturn. And one night, as the man lies awake entangled in resentfulness, his companion suddenly wakes up coughing violently. The man by the window is choking, struggling to catch a breath. His hands frantically reach for the button to summon the nurse, but he can't get to it.

His friend lies very still, regarding the situation. He only waits. The coughing sounds go on for perhaps a few minutes, then the other bed is completely still. Still the bedridden man lies on his back, quietly staring at the ceiling.

Morning comes, and the staff finds the man by the window, dead. Efficiently, professionally, they remove the body and clean the area.

As soon as the interval seems decent, the surviving man asks if he can move to the place by the window. It's a reasonable request, one quickly granted. The nurses get him all situated, move his locker, and finally they leave him alone. Wasting not an instant, the survivor struggles to prop himself on one elbow. It's painful and difficult, but he is spurred on by the thought that he will finally see the park, the wind rippling the lake, the elm tree with the kite stuck in its branches, the lazy swans. He'll see all the things his friend rendered for him in exquisite detail. But when his face hovers above the sill and he glances out, he finds himself regarding . . . an ugly yellow brick wall. Nothing more.

In an instant the truth floods terribly across him. There never was a park. There never was a lake or swans or swing sets; nobody ever played touch football. The parade and the puppies and the girls of summer were all the work of one man's loving craft of fiction—a craft that was practiced completely on *his* behalf.

It was all for him. And in the end, he snuffed it out.

In that hospital, the poison of envy claimed two more victims. One, a champion of love, lay dead and buried; the other lay in bitter self-loathing, staring at the ceiling but no longer seeing much of anything.[4]

Eliza wondered if her feelings would ever pass. It was painful loving the man who loved your best friend. For months upon months, *persistence* had been the word; now she wanted more than anything for those feelings to stop persisting and fade away forever.

Often she turned to the psalms, and stayed her mind on the foolishness of trusting in men's affections rather than the God whose love never failed and was always sufficient. She and her roommate spent time together in prayer, and Eliza confessed her bitterness, her envy, and her stubborn emotions. And day by day, prayer by prayer, those emotions began to loosen their grip.

Then a turning point finally seemed to come, a doorway to something new. She and her roommate prayed together one night, and she felt revitalized as they concluded. On the way to work and home again the next day, there were three different Christian radio programs dealing with God's purposes in adversity. One of them was about Joseph, who went through so much wrongful persecution, and yet God meant it for good. Joseph never gave in to bitterness but honored God—and in time, God rewarded his faith.

Now Eliza could see her feelings of envy and jealousy for what they were: *lies*. It was only for her to trust God. He had His seasons and timetables; He had His plans—even for Eliza. If Mark wasn't for her, then someone better was; even if there wasn't any man at all, there was a hope and a purpose with her name on them, and nothing could be better. She trusted Him on that.

It was indeed a doorway to something new. Eliza felt the last of the turbulent emotions fall loose and scatter with the four winds, like so much clinging dust. She was free! She didn't have to live as a slave to her feelings, or to anything at all short of the loving lordship of Christ, the only Master who can make us whole. No human partner can do that. No dream job can do that, and there's no amount of money in the world that will ever buy it.

The best things in life are free. What's there to be jealous about?

NOTES

CHAPTER 1

1. Jerry Adler et al., "The Fight to Conquer Fear," *Newsweek*, 23 April 1984, vol. 103, no. 17, 69.
2. Craig Massey, "When Fear Threatens," *Moody Monthly*, September 1970, 22–23, 69–70.
3. Joe B. Brown, "Caught in the Grip of Fear," *Moody Monthly*, September/October 1996, vol. 97, no. 1, 11.

CHAPTER 2

1. John Maxwell, *Failing Forward*, 153–54, quoting "Luck Rivals Worst of Sick Joke: 'There's Hope' New Yorker Says," *Los Angeles Times*, 19 March 1995, © Reuters Ltd., 1995.
2. Andy Andrews, ed., "Erma Bombeck," in *Storms of Perfection 2* (Nashville: Lightning Crown Publishers, 1994), 51. Cited in John Maxwell's *Failing Forward: Turning Mistakes into Stepping Stones for Success* (Nashville: Thomas Nelson, 2000), 24–25.
3. Leith Anderson, *Leadership That Works: Hope and Direction for Church and Parachurch Leaders in Today's Complex World* (Minneapolis: Bethany Publishing House, 1999), 166–67.
4. Ibid.
5. Fred Smith, "The Gift of Greeting," in *Christianity Today*, 13 December 1985, vol. 29, no. 18, 70.

CHAPTER 3

1. Philip Zimbardo, "The Age of Indifference," *Psychology Today*, 30 August 1980.
2. Max Lucado, *Six Hours One Friday* (Portland, Oreg.: Multnomah, 1989), 36–38.
3. Morris L. West, *The Devil's Advocate* (New York: Dell, 1959), 334–35.
4. Ann Kiemel, *I Love the Word Impossible* (Wheaton, Ill.: Tyndale House, 1976), 136–38.
5. James L. Johnson, *Loneliness Is Not Forever* (Chicago: Moody, 1979), 151.
6. A. W. Tozer, "Of Loneliness and Saintliness," *Moody Monthly*, September 1979, vol. 80, no. 1, 52–54.
7. Otto H. Frank and Mirjam Pressler, eds., *The Diary of a Young Girl*, transl. Susan Massotty (New York: Bantam Books, 1997), 194–195.

NOTES

CHAPTER 4

1. *Daily Bread*, 11 December 1999.
2. Thomas Tewell, "The Weight of the World [1995]," *Preaching Today*, tape no. 147.
3. Daniel R. Mitchum, "The Needless Burden of Worry," *Discipleship Journal*, 1 March 1987, 44–46.

CHAPTER 5

1. Cornelius Plantinga, "Natural Born Sinners," *Christianity Today*, 14 November 1994, vol. 38, no. 13, 26.
2. Lynnell Mickelsen, "Robert's Deadly Secret," *HIS*, April/May 1986, 24–27.

CHAPTER 6

1. Tom Eisenman, "Fighting to Win," *Discipleship Journal*, November/December 1992, 36–38.
2. Mark Littleton, "Looking for the Escape from Sin," *Charisma*, October 1991, 82.
3. *The Amplified Bible* (Grand Rapids: Zondervan, 1965), 309.

CHAPTER 7

1. Eugene Peterson, *The Message* (Colorado Springs: NavPress, 1993), 17.
2. Mark Porter, "Just How Righteous Is Our Anger," *Moody Monthly*, December 1983, vol. 84 No. 4, 79–80. First published in Carol Travis, *Anger: The Misunderstood Emotion* (New York: Simon and Schuster, 1982).
3. James S. Hirsch, *Hurricane: The Miraculous Journey of Rubin Carter* (Boston/New York: Houghton Mifflin, 2000), 310.

CHAPTER 8

1. Adapted from Charles R. Swindoll, *Killing Giants, Pulling Thorns* (Portland, Oreg.: Multnomah, 1978), 34.
2. Lewis B. Smedes, *Forgive and Forget* (New York: Pocket Books, 1984), 40–41.
3. Gary Inrig, *The Parables* (Grand Rapids: Discovery House, 1991), 63.
4. Helen Grace Lesheid, "Breaking Free from Bitterness," *Discipleship Journal*, vol. 14, no. 6, November/December 1994, 29.
5. Dick Innes, *Forgiveness: The Power That Heals* (Clairmont, Calif.: ACTS Communications), 3.
6. Smedes, *Forgive and Forget*, 42–44.
7. Gary Preston, "Resisting the Urge to Hit Back," *Leadership*, vol. 19, no. 2, 64.
8. Inrig, *The Parables*, 78.

CHAPTER 9

1. Mark Littleton, "Doubt Can Be Good," *HIS*, March 1979, 9.

CHAPTER 10

1. Tom Carter, ed., *2,200 Quotations from the Writings of Charles H. Spurgeon* (Grand Rapids: Baker Books, 1988), 167.

NOTES

2. From Charles Swindoll, *The Tale of the Tardy Oxcart and 1,501 Other Stories* (Nashville: Word, 1998), 470.
3. Quoted in Glenn Van Ekeren, ed., *Speaker's Sourcebook II* (Englewood Cliffs, N.J.: Prentice-Hall, Inc., 1994), 359.
4. Personal interviews by Rob Suggs.
5. Adapted from Paul Lee Tan, *Encyclopedia of 7,700 Illustrations* (Garland, Tex.: Bible Communications, Inc., 1996).
6. Ibid.
7. Van Ekeren, *Speaker's Sourcebook II*, 358.
8. The study was published by A. E. Winship as *Jukes-Edwards, A Study in Education and Heredity* (R. L. Myers & Co., 1900). The basis of the study is a comparison of the prolific and productive Edwards descendants to those of one "Max Jukes," the fictionalized name of a real person. Jukes was a non-Christian contemporary who married an unbelieving wife, and their progeny included 130 convicted criminals, 7 murderers, 100 alcoholics, and 100 public prostitutes. It was estimated that the shoddy and sordid legacy of Jukes cost the state $1.5 million without any positive contribution to society. At the time of the study, descendants of Jukes were discovered in multiple New York prison facilities, and it was observed that one of Jonathan Edwards's descendants presided, at that time, over the New York State Prison Commission. It was a rich irony.

CHAPTER 11

1. Charles Swindoll, *Come Before Winter* (Portland, Oreg.: Multnomah Press, 1985). 251–252.
2. Jim Dethmer, "The Gift of Mercy," *Preaching Today* audiotape series, Christianity Today, Inc., tape no. 112.

CHAPTER 12

1. Lloyd Ogilvie, "Life on the Fast Track," *Moody Monthly*, November 1985, 19–20.
2. Elva McAllaster, "Envy Went to Church," *Christian Life*, January 1970.
3. Tan, *Encyclopedia of 7,700 Illustrations*.
4. Adapted from G. W. Target, "The Window," in *The Window and Other Essays* (Nampa: Pacific Press Publishing Association, Inc.).

SUBJECT INDEX

INDEX

Scripture Index

ACKNOWLEDGMENTS

With every year that passes, I become more aware of my total dependence upon the Lord. For what He has determined to do through me I am so thankful.

As this book is being released, Donna and I are celebrating our thirty-eighth wedding anniversary. From the beginning we have been a team and we have battled more than a few giants together. In everything I do, she is my number-one fan, and her encouragement is one of the reasons I keep writing books.

Carrie Mann worked directly with the publisher in the finalizing of this project. Helen Barnhart, Dianne Stark and Leeana Miller read and reread the manuscript and their suggestions were invaluable. Helen also worked with all the Turning Point listeners who submitted stories for this book.

Paul Joiner teamed up with W Publishing Group in the conception and design of the cover. Sealy Yates is my literary agent, and he wonderfully represents me to our publishers and faithfully represents them to me as well. Thank you, Sealy!

Rob Suggs worked tirelessly to make sure the final product represented my heart. I am so blessed to have Rob as a writer, editor, and friend. The projects that we work on together bring both of us great joy.

Finally, I would like to acknowledge all of the people who hear me preach at Shadow Mountain and through Turning Point network. You bless me with your words of affirmation and encouragement. It is my prayer that this book will in some small measure help you to face the giants in your life.

About the Author

DAVID JEREMIAH is Senior Pastor of Shadow Mountain Community Church in El Cajon, California, and President of Christian Heritage College. His radio program, "Turning Point," is broadcast on more than 950 stations nationwide. Dr. Jeremiah is the author of *A Bend in the Road* as well as *Escape The Coming Night* and *The Handwriting on the Wall*, co-written with C.C. Carlson. Dr. Jeremiah and his wife, Donna, live in El Cajon, California.

A Bend in the Road

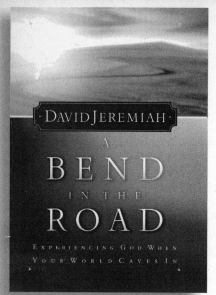

Drawing on his insightful sermon series, renowned pastor/teacher David Jeremiah shares the comfort and hope of the Psalms and how these truths can guide believers through life's greatest challenges.
By interweaving his own journal entries, his fight with cancer, and other real-life stories, *A Bend in the Road* becomes an invaluable source of help and encouragement for people facing major obstacles in life.

Escape the Coming Night

David Jeremiah's dramatic narrative and perceptive analysis addresses the challenging issues in the perplexing book of Revelation. Through the mysteries posed in the book, Jeremiah guides the reader on an electrifying tour of the future.

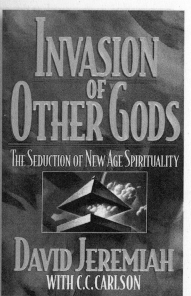

Invasion of Other Gods

New Age philosophy is really ancient paganism repackaged for modern consumption.
David Jeremiah shows how this new spirituality is flooding our culture with teachings, techniques and terminology that clearly contradict the Christian gospel.

W PUBLISHING GROUP

The Handwriting on the Wall

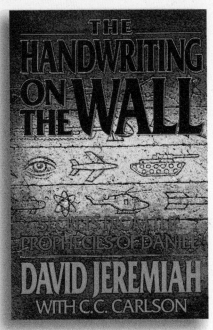

In *The Handwriting on the Wall,* prophecy expert David Jeremiah shows how an understanding of prophecy in the Book of Daniel opens a pathway to dynamic, faithful living today—with confidence and hope for the future.

Jesus' Final Warning

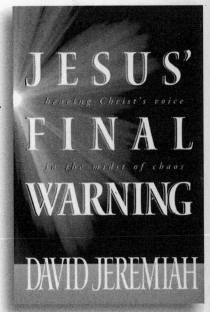

In the confusion of voices at the turn of the millennium, Christians need to hear one voice above all others: the voice of Jesus Christ. Based on the Olivet Discourse in the book of Matthew, *Jesus' Final Warning* offers perspective and timely insights from the Lord Jesus to comfort, encourage, and challenge His church in these climactic times.

PUBLISHING GROUP